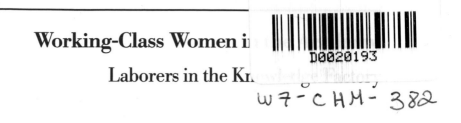

Working-Class Women in

Laborers in the Knowledge Factory

W7-CHM-382

Edited by **Michelle M. Tokarczyk**

and **Elizabeth A. Fay**

The University of Massachusetts Press

Amherst

This book is published with the support and cooperation of the University of Massachusetts at Boston.

LC 92–34935
ISBN 0–87023–834–5 (cloth); 835–3 (pbk.)

Designed by Susan Bishop
Set in Berthold Bodoni Antiqua by Keystone Typesetting, Inc.
Printed and bound by Thomson-Shore, Inc.

Library of Congress Cataloging-in-Publication Data
Working-class women in the academy : laborers in the knowledge factory
   / edited by Michelle M. Tokarczyk, Elizabeth A. Fay.
      p.   cm.
   Includes bibliographical references (p.   ) and index.
   ISBN 0–87023–834–5 (alk. paper). – ISBN 0–87023–835–3 (pbk. :
alk. paper)
      1. Women college teachers–United States–Social conditions.
   2. Social classes–United States.   I. Tokarczyk, Michelle M., 1953–   .
   II. Fay, Elizabeth A., 1957–   .
   LB2332.3.W68   1993
   378.1'2'082–dc20   92–34935
                                                                CIP

British Library Cataloguing in Publication data are available.

Acknowledgment is made to South End Press, Boston, for permission to reprint "Keeping Close to Home: Class and Education," from bell hooks, *Talking Back: thinking feminist–thinking black* (Boston: South End Press, 1989). An earlier version of Elizabeth Fay, "Dissent in the Field," appeared as "Mothers, Fathers, and Dissent" in *NWSA Journal* 1, no. 1 (1988); an earlier version of Pat Belanoff, "Language: Closings and Openings" appeared first as "The Generalized Other and Me: Workingclass Women and the Academy," *Pre/Text* 2, nos. 1-2 (1990). "Writing and Teaching with Class," copyright 1991 by Valerie Miner.

Contents

Preface

IN SOLICITING pieces for this volume, we wanted to represent a variety of viewpoints on the intersection of gender, class, and the academy. We realized that a book on class and gender would be marked immediately as Marxist feminist, cutting us off from a broad range of orientations and affiliations. Our intent was not, in fact, to define ourselves or the volume as Marxist, but to engage useful ways of conceptualizing class to understand more fully the emerging issues of contemporary academia. The anthology's diversity may perplex some readers accustomed to a more unified approach within a collection. But by selecting multidisciplinary essays written from different feminist ideological perspectives, we seek to represent more accurately the variety of voices that make up our pluralized academic community. What does unify the collection is a repeated attempt to conceptualize class position in relation to other factors such as gender, race, ethnicity, and sexual orientation.

These essays develop ways of thinking about class privilege, lack of role models, academic hierarchy, the desire to nurture students, and the renegotiation of one's background as resource rather than as detriment. The contributors devote much thought to defining the place of class in a university setting. As working-class women, they are in a position to recognize the institution as class stratified and approach it personally, pedagogically, and theoretically to produce challenging critiques and possibilities for change. We see this volume as interventionist.

We would like to acknowledge the many people who helped in the conception and realization of this book, including Pat Belanoff, Jane Bennett, Bruce Robbins, and Hephzibah Roskelly.

Our support staff, Maya Fitzpatrick, Allan Forsythe, Sue Walsh, Mary Vancura, Madeline Kotowski, and Linda Fowble, are greatly appreciated, as is the generosity of Goucher College and the University of Massachusetts, Boston. We would especially like to thank our emotional supporters, Paul, Eleanor, and Chuck.

Working-Class Women in the Academy

Introduction

WE BEGIN ethnographically.[1] That is, not with a theory but with a question that pokes into disciplinary corners and pockets: What are the issues—pedagogical, theoretical, and personal—that affect academic women from working-class backgrounds?

Our project began in 1987 at the Modern Languages Association Convention with Michelle Tokarczyk's proposed session on "Working-Class Women in Academia." We hoped for an engaged audience, but neither of us expected that the room would be filled to capacity, that questions would be nonstop, or that people would have to be ushered out at the end. What surprised us most was the passion.

Our work grew from the strong sense that there were a number of concerns in that room that had never been addressed. To Marxist scholars, the most obvious questions might be: How does class manifest itself in American society, and how is the class hierarchy played out in academia? The question we, as feminists, kept asking ourselves was what difference does gender make in the intersections of class in the academy? We found that women academics from the working class clearly felt torn; they wanted to maintain their ties to their families, but wanted to fit into the academy as well. Often, they feared they fit into neither world. They were frequently uncomfortable with the language they used, afraid their voices would slip into dialect or working-class patterns. And they were angry at being ignored or at being expected to be middle-class professionals, socially and economically. These issues should be confronted not only by working-class women within the academy, but also by the academy itself. Like any other institution, the academy is affected if a number of its members feel alienated. Ironically, many are drawn to the academy because of its reputation as a place where nonconformists are welcomed, where diversity is respected. Indeed, diversity among faculty members is said to stimulate intellectual endeavors.

3

II

One of the first problems in addressing the concerns of working-class women academics is definition. To discuss the working class at all in contemporary North American culture presents grave difficulties: precise analysis of a social structure is impeded by the unwieldy size of that group. We instead have had to pinpoint pockets of experience and move outward. There is some truth to the supposition that not only is the current language about class inadequate, but that the term "working class" itself may also no longer be viable. If we choose to define class in larger economic terms, then paychecks belie the blue-collar/white-collar distinction, and even the difference between salaries versus hourly wages loses significance when skilled workers earn more than professionals. We cannot distinguish class at a glance any more, as Sharon O'Dair points out in her discussions of "vestments," included in this book. When in *Sartor Resartus*, Carlyle discussed his tailor re-tailored as a way of talking about the social fabric, he depended for his complex metaphor on a visible clothing difference in nineteenth-century Britain, a difference based on discernible luxury and waste of fabric for the middle and upper classes, uniforms for the servant class, and literally threadbare clothing for the working classes. Today, when jeans torn at both knees may denote a well-to-do student and not an impoverished one, it is nearly impossible to perform a similar cultural semiotics, although a cult of "taste" is still pervasive.[2]

Several contributors noted that, because of the privileges associated with faculty status, becoming an academic can mean passing out of the working class. Perhaps more important, academia barely acknowledges working-class existence. In American society, class is, as Paul Fussell says, "America's dirty little secret"; because it is not as readily visible as gender and race, it can seem invisible. Surveys have repeatedly shown that the vast majority of Americans describe themselves as middle class, whether they are employed as sanitation workers or lawyers. Such a monolithic conception of what is "middle class" is as inaccurate as stereotypes of what is "working class." Without a clarification of the diverse components of class stratification, academics from working-class backgrounds often feel in conflict about their identifications. Hence, an underlying cause for working-class women academics' anxiety and confusion is that their combined class and gender status has rarely been

4

recognized nor adequately named. (Indeed, we must acknowledge the awkwardness of the term "working-class women academics" and our frustration at the inadequacy of our language to convey power relationships.) Many contributors to this anthology recount that they never identified themselves as working class until they reached a level of higher education; others never realized their working-class status contributed to conflicts they experienced as undergraduate and/or graduate students. We hope to escape societal vagary in our definitions of the working-class academic woman by assuming the need for, if not multiple definitions, at least a fluid one. We prepare the ground for a defining structure by noting that a number of factors characterize working-class status. The working class often does work that is physically demanding, repetitive, or dangerous. Women are waitresses and cleaning women; men are lumberjacks, janitors, and police officers. Salary is often an important determinant (although some blue-collar workers are paid well, none have the earning potential of lawyers or doctors), but working-class positions are largely differentiated by their lack of autonomy. Clerical workers, factory employees, and other "workers" are all closely supervised; management and professionals do the supervising or work within a peer system. We are using the term "working-class women academics," then, to denominate women whose parents had jobs such as these and who themselves were the first generation in their family to attend college.

Some people believe that the fact that women from the working class have achieved careers indicates that there is mobility in American society; and, hence, class is nonrestrictive. We maintain that there is a definitional problem with this, that people do not pass out of one class into another, although their tastes, expectations, and habits may change as class identity shifts. Moreover, people raised in working-class families that have been subtly and consistently demeaned through America's class structure retain the scars of that experience. Academia, too, has a class structure: its hierarchy of professors, assistant professors, and part-timers is not solely a ladder based on merit, but a track based on a number of gender, racial/ethnic, and socioeconomic factors. The degradation many working-class women experience in academia replicates that of the larger classed society. Despite the claims of some recent, highly publicized spokespersons for higher education,[3] we do not believe that professors can easily function in the classroom without ac-

5

knowledging, at some level, the impact of their combined class and gender position in the academy and in the society as a whole.

Women from the working class who have achieved tenured positions often emphatically insist that they have severed all connection with their working-class backgrounds, and they have the titles and salaries to prove it. These women often display a middle-, even upper-middle-class aesthetic; we would ask, is the display equivalent to the "natural ease" of these born to the middle-class aesthetic?[4] And what of those who have not "made it"? Do we retain the characteristic taste of our class background, or does the initiation process of the doctorate dissatisfy us with our backgrounds, instilling in us a desire for elite values and prejudices?

And what of those who feel themselves to be resituated by class? What of the conflict resulting from the repression such a process of transformation necessitates? Several of the essays that follow acknowledge an anger at the way academia construes its communal identity on a class basis, and a coexisting realization of the privileges gained from acceptance (however tentative) into this community.

Many of the voices in this anthology speak from departments of literature. This is not only because our project emerged from discussions in literature departments, but also because literature departments, we suspect, have been both particularly beset by class structures and particularly concerned with the issue of voice. Mikhail Bakhtin, a literary theorist who thinks about voice and class conflict, speculates that the register of social voices is made up of different discourses deriving from class, ethnic backgrounds, and vocational vocabularies. Further, when we speak, our voices are composites of all the voices we have internalized from domestic and public environments. Yet Bakhtin notes that poetry—that most literary of literary forms—is necessarily single or monologic because of its reduction of all competing languages to the one poetic voice that speaks to and for us all.[5] The difference between the social reality and the literary fiction is a difference we come up against repeatedly in our writing, in our classrooms, and in conversations with colleagues and students. Is the single voice we confront here male? Academic? Elitist? White? And what does our voice responsively turn to as we teach the literature of our system?

The question of language is hotly debated, in particular among working-class academics. Is language a transparent vehicle for meaning-making or is it a difficult tool, which defeats us even as it enables our ability to communicate our ideas? Should academics use a specialized language that reflects this conceptual complexity? Is such a discourse elitist? This anthology represents different kinds of language orientation; some of the writers—Pat Belanoff, Joanna Kadi, and Elizabeth Fay—draw on poststructuralist theories, whereas Rose Zimbardo and Elisabeth Johnson embrace an American plain style. Sociological discourse and humanistic discourse also represent competing language orientations. We have chosen essays from different disciplines and theories of language to provide an array of voices that collectively negotiate the prevailing voice of the institution.

Many of the following essays treat the silencing and appropriation of working-class women's voices by the singular voice of the institution. We have learned, inducted, entered into that voice, and we have taught it to others, certain that its *poetry* offers a truth—discourse worth paying tuition for. That discourse, characterized by our vocational vocabulary (although we seem to disagree just as much on which words belong in the lexicon as on which do not), constitutes us, reformulates our class orientation and status, reconditions us in society. In the end, we often no longer speak as our families do. Rather than retaining multiple inflections, we try to discard others' voices from our internal space.

What becomes increasingly apparent is a political imperative to open the discussion up to our students, our colleagues, and our families, as well as to resist the one authoritative master-voice that speaks to us. As the following essays reveal, pain and anger often come from this opening up. But something else comes out as well, something we hope leads to a better understanding of who and what we are and of what our experience allows us to offer others.

III

Institutional prejudices against women have been extensively commented upon. True, in recent years departments have made efforts to hire women—to the extent that many men now complain of discrimination. However, women are still concentrated in part-time and temporary positions and are still granted tenure at rates far lower than men. According to the 1989–90 *A Fact Book on Higher Education*, in the 1985–86 academic year there were 283,828 male full-time faculty members and 112,029 women. Women were concentrated at the lower ranks. Data on the women who were instructional faculty indicate that in 1985–86, 11.9 percent were full professors, whereas 38 percent were assistant professors. Similarly, a study by the Modern Languages Association published in *Profession 90* indicates that, despite some apparent improvements in the status of women, in 1987 approximately 1 in 5 women served in a non-tenure-track position compared with less than 1 in 14 for men.[6] Granted, one might interpret these numbers as indicating that women have begun only relatively recently to enter the profession; assistant professors do usually have the hope of getting tenure and moving up the ladder. Many women, however, are concentrated in ranks that afford little hope of mobility; 52 percent of faculty at the instructor level, and 48.8 percent at the lecturer level were women.[7] It is also well known that women are turned down for tenure at far greater rates than men, and that being denied tenure—or, more basically, a tenure-track appointment—has more consequences than depriving one of job security. For example, full-time tenure-track appointments often present the possibility of release time for research, money for conference travel, and access to grants. Without these benefits faculty cannot do the crucial research and publishing that will indeed keep them from perishing. Faculty in temporary and part-time positions then find themselves in a "Catch-22" situation: they cannot get tenure-track appointments because they have not published enough and they cannot publish enough because they do not have tenure-track appointments.

Some institutional prejudice against women may still be attributed to sexual stereotyping. At a time when women are becoming increasingly accepted in business and the professions, however, it seems we must look beyond this explanation to understand women's lower status in academia. The problem is not only in the existence of the "old boys'" networking system, but also in the values represented by this system. Communal, collaborative, and nurturing ways of thinking and interacting—often associated with women—are antithetical to the old network, but if widely practiced among academics they could help heal the rifts between class, gender, and power. Although academia accepts the idea of women faculty, it does not accept women's ways of thinking and/or women's values. Laura Weaver and other contributors discuss how they conceived of their work as labor that would benefit the community, not merely themselves. In many of the positions for which women were

8

traditionally socialized (nursing, secondary and primary school education, social work) this orientation was crucial. In academia, however, a much more individual orientation is required. Although teaching and committee work are often important criteria in tenure decisions, publications are increasingly weighed at four-year institutions and universities. Furthermore, in most cases single-author books are rated more highly than those written collaboratively. Hence, women who value communal identification and collaborative work are at a disadvantage in the publish-or-perish scenario.

Often this conflict comes to a head in the areas of teaching and mentoring. A recent survey by the American Studies Association revealed its women faculty members felt that, because of their relatively small numbers, they were overwhelmed by female students who sought them out for advice.[8] At a 1988 National Women's Studies Association Convention panel, one participant similarly stated that when many of the working-class women students from her school learned she had a background similar to theirs, there was a line outside her door during most of her office hours all the time; students needed to share their problems with someone who would understand. It is common for women in general, and for women from working-class backgrounds in particular, to put high value on advising and teaching. They often devote what some might judge to be disproportionate time to these activities, believing they are doing their jobs. When these faculty come up for tenure or reappointment, they learn that their colleagues do not judge the labor of pedagogy as highly as they have.

Some women, of course, do learn what is necessary to succeed in academia. Those who come from middle-class families, who have seen fathers and brothers adapt to professional demands and espouse individualistic values, at least have some childhood role models. Women from the working class, in contrast, often have no academic role models in their backgrounds. To have to invent an idea of one's self as an academic is a difficult task that can prove insurmountable for both men and women.

Yet as our anthology indicates, many women do surmount these obstacles and build academic careers. How they feel about their status in academia, we hypothesize, partially depends upon what point they have reached in their careers. What we found was that many of the contributors who had achieved tenure—Rose Zimbardo, Patricia Smith, and Laura Weaver among them—were able to assess how their working-class backgrounds had benefited them. They acknowledged the struggle, but perceived less loss to their self-worth. Younger nontenured faculty, in contrast, often wrote with more bitterness toward the academic hierarchy and with a greater sense of loss at having been torn from their roots. It is not just that younger faculty are closer to their working-class experience, but also that as junior faculty or graduate students they experience the treatment typical of that given to working-class laborers.

The intersection of gender and class in pedagogy demands that we compare women's ways of knowing with traditional, male-oriented ways, that we examine group versus individual orientation, and that we consider goals that place process above product, nurturance and valuing of growth above standardized achievement. When we look at ourselves not only as teachers but also as scholars, then we add to this list discussions of how women's research is evaluated and rewarded. The now-familiar works of Carol Gilligan, Nancy Chodorow, and Belenky, Clinchy, Goldberger, and Tarule argue that women have distinct ways of interacting, reasoning, and evaluating. These theorists have been criticized for their generalizing tendencies, but the various critiques raised need to be addressed, and throughout this anthology we have found ourselves thinking about women's ways of knowing, teaching, understanding, relating, and evaluating.[9] Carol Gilligan's work in particular has come under attack, and critics charge that her research involved class-privileged subjects, whereas her resulting model of female moral growth essentializes all women regardless of class, sexual, race, or ethnic difference.[10] It is interesting that what has evolved from the articles that follow are expressions of concerns nearly identical with those that Gilligan found prevalent, despite class difference between her middle-class subjects and ourselves. Indeed, some of our contributors, in writing or in conversations, commented on the individualistic orientation of some women who had become tenured professors. These women might be better characterized as male-identified women, to use Adrienne Rich's distinction: in other words, their career goals outweigh their sense of responsibility to their community of colleagues and of students. This is not to declare that class difference means one group works to provide an "ethic of care," and that the other does not, but to say that such models might be useful for understanding the class ideology that manipulates women's behavior. That is, class difference within the academy might be more profoundly drawn along the lines of who is willing to give up which identity for economic gain and class privilege.

Yet theoretic models do need to be questioned. Hephzibah Roskelly's article, for instance, draws on group process, image making, and storytelling for a narratology of social behavior in the rural South. In revealing the reality behind the "redneck" stereotype,[11] her essay describes a communitarian oral practice, which might in any other study be denoted as a feminine mode. After all, the stories are group narrated and process oriented so that they vary with each telling: all truth depends on strong associative images in this mode of communication. Yet the tale tellers are both men and women, relating within the group. Similarly, what Laura Weaver describes as the Mennonite "work ethic" is echoed in many of the other essays, with contributors remarking, "I know how to work hard." Thus what Weaver defines as her mark of difference might equally be seen as a working-class ethic, or a feminine relation to ethical responsibility to the group. Other qualities are equally bidirectional: it seems the world is not as well defined as we would like, and we cannot group men and women either as completely the same, or as completely different. Rather, what we have are social constructs into which we fit as best we can, given the choices (or lack of choices) at hand. We are reminded of Maxine Hong Kingston's attempts to understand her own personality in *The Woman Warrior:* "Chinese-Americans, when you try to understand what things in you are Chinese, how do you separate what is peculiar to childhood, to poverty, insanities, one family, your mother who marked your growing with stories, from what is Chinese?"[12] As we theorize about the intersections of class and gender and are aware of purely individual dynamics, we come back to the realization that each of these factors constantly impacts upon the other, and that it is sometimes difficult to attribute specific successes or failures exclusively to class, gender, or individual personality.

Indeed, the more we have worked on this book, the more wary we have become of generalizations. As the articles in this volume indicate, there is tremendous variety in how easily women from the working class are accepted into academia. Valerie Miner worked as an adjunct for years; Rose Zimbardo became a full professor at a research institution. There are a number of factors that, interacting with class, influence the status a woman will achieve in the academy. Such factors as race, ethnicity, age, and sexual orientation affect how well any woman from the working class will combat a number of economic and institutional barriers to upward mobility within the academy.

First, consider the economic barriers. There is a well-known bias in favor of Ivy League schools. During job searches at some highly rated research institutions, the first screening of candidates looks for Ivy League degrees. Few would question that the academic reputation these schools enjoy is well deserved, but many state and other private schools also have fine reputations. Many students from the working class do not decide upon a graduate school solely, or even primarily, on the basis of its reputation. In order to attend an Ivy League graduate school, if one is not fortunate enough to be granted a generous fellowship, one must have a source of money.[13] The real value of these prestigious degrees may be surprising even to many academics: *Strangers in Paradise: Academics from the Working Class* reported that 83 percent of the faculty at the top twelve graduate schools had their highest degrees from the same institutions.[14] In addition to the value of a prestigious degree, graduates of Ivy League doctoral programs make many contacts with people who will also be in demand in the profession; indeed, part of their education is apprenticing to the "old boy" network, which will ensure their successful careers. Women from working-class backgrounds come from families with few financial resources, and what resources there are, are often devoted to sons rather than daughters. True, there was a period during the 1970s when the academic job market was so dismal that even those from prestigious schools were lucky to get adjunct positions. Any academic job was a good job. But the people who were more likely to be able to afford to move from one adjunct job to another during those lean years were not working-class women.

The cost of an Ivy League education is but one part of the cost of an academic career. As with any profession, there are numerous associated costs: one must buy current books the libraries have not yet acquired, subscribe to at least a few journals, make research trips to special library collections, and attend conferences around the country. The first job search itself is formidable to many students as they begin to experience the rounds of uncompensated professional expenses. The numerous economic career demands coupled with the notoriously low salaries academics in the humanities receive have led us to think of an academic as practicing a "gentleman's profession," one associated with the genteelness of a man of letters. As some of our contributors indicate, there is often an expectation that family will subsidize the fledgling academic. For those who are doubly not gentlemen—women from the working class—these expectations represent difficult barriers.

In addition to suffering double marginality on financial grounds, working-class women do so in terms of their values. Paul Lauter has pointed out that the working class stresses group affiliation rather than the individual; cries of "solidarity" are not just rallying cries, but represent deep-seated values.[15] For the working class, work has often involved manual labor or other efforts that produce concrete results.[16] In an academic's life, teaching and committee work often seem like more concrete activities than research and writing (particularly when it can take a year to get an article into print after it has been accepted for publication). As the essay by Valerie Miner suggests, many working-class women academics have to remind themselves that sitting in a library or at a computer all day is working. And the situation is further complicated for women who were trained to perform manual tasks. In conversation, one successful woman related how much easier it was to work in her office—even though this was a substantial commute from where she lived—because at home she always felt she should be cleaning or performing other household chores.

All women have to contend with the effects of their gender socialization, but working-class women find their struggle is complicated further by the frequent disparagement of the working class in academia. It is only recently that scholars have begun to challenge the prevailing social stereotypes that see the working class as unambitious, racist, and sexist.[17] In the classroom, the working-class experience is rarely discussed or even acknowledged. Many faculty members are men from the middle or upper-middle classes, who are doubly uncomfortable working with female colleagues of a different class. Contributors Suzanne Sowinska and Michelle Tokarczyk refer to the insensitivity of faculty and administration to the needs of working-class graduate students and faculty. Moreover, while other oppressed groups have had courses developed especially to address specific issues of gender, ethnicity, and race, class studies does not exist as a field. In her provocative article, Sharon O'Dair argues that there is a fundamental conflict between the interests of academics and the working class, a conflict that accounts for the academy's failure to address class issues.

13

The working-class experience as a subject has been devalued in the study of literature as well. In this respect, literature departments' biases have reflected those of the larger society. As Valerie Miner points out, many contemporary novels about the everyday problems of the middle classes are published; yet there is the assumption that the lives of people who do less interesting work are somehow less interesting. And the pursuit of working-class literature, unless it includes studying a few big-name authors, is likely to be discouraged in graduate school. There are some indications this is changing as a response to a call for departments to be politically correct. Still, the fashionableness of the term "politically correct," now bandied in magazines such as *New York*, highlights the deep-seated resistance to acknowledging diversity in literature and academic departments.

Henry Giroux remarks in *Theory and Resistance in Education* that although schools, "like most social sites, are marked by contradictions and struggles which, while primarily serving the logic of domination, also contain the possibilities for emancipatory practice," these sites must "be understood within the broader historical, social, and economic conditions that characterize the wider society."[18] This is no longer in itself a radical statement, yet behind the walls of academe a prominently displayed purity of motive continues to resonate, as if sociohistorical and political contexts do not exist. A holdover from Arnoldian perceptions of the cultural value of education, this purity is resoundingly displayed in Allan Bloom's and E. D. Hirsch's best-selling morality plays. Such purity is reducible to the Great (ivy-covered) American Dream, and as the liberal humanist needs to be reminded now and again, the Great American Dream—a leftover of 1950s expansionist economics—cannot be expected to succeed in the uncertain economy of the 1990s. Therefore, the Bloomian pessimistic view that poor academic skills in this country reflect a loss of esteem for things cultural and intellectual, which compares unfavorably to the values of other superpower nations, is a statement about class and about the anxiety of class. The Great American Dream, after all, is the achievement of a middle-class life-style; it assumes that one holds the power to make life choices, and it ignores the inescapable, disempowering economics of working-class lives.

However, Bloom has forgotten his history. It was not until after the eighteenth century that state college and university systems began to be conceived of as a public responsibility. Even then, the eight state universities founded to serve a broader range of the population were divided between an elite faculty of letters and a service-oriented faculty of technical and vocational education. Because of this divide, humanities faculty remained entrenched in the thinking of private institutions.[19] After two hundred years, the situation has not changed; although economically disadvantaged students are sometimes able to win scholarships at private universities, the majority of those who seek higher education attend state schools. But who teaches at these schools? A look at faculty rosters at the state university level shows that tenured and tenure-track professors are for the most part graduated from the Ivy or near-Ivy leagues, while lecturers and adjuncts are typically from less-privileged schools. No wonder our classrooms and faculty meetings resound with middle-class ideologies that work to cover up, even as they produce, the tensions that undermine our vocational efficacy.

For despite our unabashedly Arnoldian, elitist profession in the humanities, upholding the truth statements of art in order to continue to let the lamp of high culture shine, ours is also a service-oriented profession. English departments, at least at state universities, are often quite large in comparison to other departments; it is not for love of literature that deans recruit new English faculty, but rather because of the disproportionate number of service courses English departments are expected to provide. In his 1988 talk for the MLA Presidential Forum, Dominick La Capra described universities as large patriarchal families, with "the administrator [as] the father, the natural scientist . . . the potential—or at least the surrogate—fathers, the humanists [as] the mother and the students as the kids." La Capra's model makes clear the status of the humanist in academe: "The role of the humanists is to stay at home and take care of the kids, usually in and through a teaching schedule that is significantly heavier than that of the natural, or even the social scientists, and one that is further embellished by all sorts of devices for independent majors, courses, programs, and so forth."[20] But this analysis leaves out hierarchy within departments themselves, a hierarchy that is predicated upon, and imposes its own, class distinctions. The distinctions in this hierarchy, as many of our contributors are quick to point out, determines who teaches the service courses and who teaches the courses geared to specializations and current research interests.

We wondered if one reason our contributors often leave the problem of gender out of their meditations on class and the classroom is

15

fundamentally the same reason why British Marxist theorists so often relegate women to the sidelines in their discussions, a fact Marxist feminist critics have pondered. The notion that class supersedes gender, like the hierarchy of race and ethnicity over gender that feminist theorists of color have had to both embrace and question, is a difficult argument to contest. Yes, all working-class women are working class, whereas not all those of the working class are women. The argument, however, that working-class women should proceed via a male model does not hold true; nor does the assumption that gender is so irrelevant that it adds little to the discussion.[21]

To understand further the crossroads of class and gender in our elitist, yet service-oriented profession, we must cast an oblique glance sideways at working-class men in the profession and ask what is different for them. Their economic and family backgrounds are necessarily the same. The difference must then come from societal pressures to provide the larger paycheck for their own family, from their career expectations, and from their attitudes toward service. Another glance sideways reveals that the majority of adjuncts, lecturers, and composition faculty are women; tenured and tenure-track faculty are men. We come back, necessarily to the question of gender privilege, as well as women's socially constructed attitudes toward nurturance and care. It is not uncommon to encounter women who have been in the profession ten or twenty years who still feel anxiety in the classroom about the worth of their material: Are they giving the students enough? Are they including enough texts, enough analysis, enough writing, enough context, enough space in which to speak? It is the voice of the mother asking if she has done a good enough job. Conversely, women students often feel this tension differently, allowing their own voices and questions to be swallowed in the presence of fellow students. It is not until the class breaks into small groups, where the men sit silent, that the women speak up. Group work, after all, does not earn any one individual "points" and allows space for anxiety and differing perspectives to surface. Most important though, it is communal activity, the students' version of "service."

Working-class women academics, perhaps, are more likely to accept heavy teaching loads and committee work because of the psychological toll of crossing gender and class barriers. The chances that a woman from the working class will become an academic are slim, and those women who do are highly aware of their new privileged status. Many feel a need to "pay back." Rose Zimbardo, a full professor, volunteers in a program for working adults in gratitude for the free undergraduate education she received at the City University of New York. Some of our contributors are or have been political activists, volunteering time and energy so that others will not have to face the class and gender inequities they did. Patricia Belanoff and Pam Annas, to name two, are examining pedagogies in their disciplines in order to make them more inclusive.

Such paybacks are noble, and fortunately some women are able to achieve them without damaging their academic careers. However, many others face a constant pull between the need to devote themselves to research and the need to devote extraordinary amounts of time and energy to mentoring students, especially young women from the working class who are at a loss in college. Again, the toll of coming from a working-class background and having "survived," in the words of Suzanne Sowinska, is compounded by having been socialized as women to parent.

Working-class women academics' struggle to do "their own work" while mentoring or being politically active is exacerbated by the rigorous demands they often place upon their own work. As outsiders in academia, many have an impostor complex; they fear they've scammed others into giving them doctorates and academic positions and constantly have to prove to themselves and others that they are worthy. Often they are perfectionists about their work, sometimes endangering their careers by refusing to part with manuscripts until they believe the writing is impeccable or refusing to take part in projects to which they are not completely committed.[22]

Considering the previously discussed prejudices against the working class in academia, it is not surprising that many women do not readily admit—or even recognize—their working-class roots. The "call for papers" for this anthology gave such women the chance to face their pasts. One of the more curious responses is the number of "confessional" letters we received: many women queried or proposed articles, and in the course of sometimes theoretical discussions strongly recounted their working-class backgrounds, life stories, and the way they had been marked by their backgrounds. Some women queried the call for articles but never sent a proposal; instead, they sent a few confessional pages or spent a half hour on the phone expressing the conflicts their backgrounds had caused them.

Undoubtedly, some women did not ever intend to write an article; they simply needed to tell someone how they felt. Others, however, were likely dissuaded by the emotional difficulty of writing about their experience: several of the contributors to this book remarked that the article appearing here was one of the hardest they had ever written. Part of this difficulty stems from unearthing suppressed memories, from trying to write about conflicts that no one else has adequately described. Some women, trained as they were to analyze and theorize, were unable to write; they simply could not use these skills on their own lives. Their predicament reminds us of a comment a working-class undergraduate made in a City University of New York classroom about fifteen years ago: "We know where the rich can go to learn to understand their lives and their place in society. They can go to Harvard. Where can the poor go?" What have our most educated, most literate women from the working class learned if they have been disempowered from understanding the forces and institutions that have shaped their lives? The question is frightening, but there is comfort in the fact that most women are not totally or constantly disempowered. This volume is a testimony to their power to understand themselves and the forces around them.

And although there are many psychological reasons why women may have been impeded from telling about or analyzing their lives, there are also very practical ones. Many women were apprehensive about criticizing the academy, fearful of reprisals. Others worried about spending too much time on an article outside their literary specialization. Michelle Tokarczyk, while in the midst of a job search, showed her vita to a senior colleague at a research institution. He cautioned her that her work on the intersection of gender and class was on the periphery of literary study: the only young academics who could afford to do such work were those who had degrees from Ivy League schools. Others should devote themselves to more traditional literary criticism.

This advice prescribes a typical double-bind situation. On the one hand, women of working-class backgrounds are told, as Michelle Tokarczyk was, to mainstream; on the other hand, the realities of the academic ranking system, personal conflicts, and economic difficulty have in fact relegated working-class women academics to the margins. Although this is a condition we all share, it is important for us to recognize that some of us are more marginalized than others. Some groups of women are triply marginalized. Black women have unique concerns articulated in different ways by bell hooks, Elisabeth Johnson, and Jacqueline Burnside. Joanna Kadi, an Arab-Canadian lesbian, strives to understand the "conquered self," as a self that takes part in its own oppression.

These contributors' works are provocative and insightful, but we fear they are not enough. We worry about unrepresented voices. Articles by women of color were particularly hard to find. Numerous queries from us were unanswered. In part, this is due to the small number of minority faculty on college campuses, and the even smaller number who come from lower-class families. In trying to solicit an article by an Asian American, we contacted a woman who responded that most of the Asian-American women scholars she knew were from middle-class backgrounds. And regardless of their class background, minority faculty are often overcommitted exactly because they are relatively rare. Also, we suspect, many women of color were uncertain of their affiliation, particularly, perhaps, Native American women, who may find the Anglo concept of class alien.

Lesbian women face additional barriers, partially because, lacking relationships with men, they lack access to the financial privilege and security men typically enjoy. Indeed, several of our contributors in letters or in their articles have acknowledged that their careers were helped by the income and security that accompanied marriage to relatively successful men. Finally, there are other kinds of marginality that are less obvious, less talked about, but equally important for all of us in the academy to confront. Hephzibah Roskelly writes of dominant northeastern bias against southerners, particularly rural "rednecks." Just as the middle class has often tried to deflect its own bigotry on the working class, northeasterners have often used southerners as scapegoats for their racism and sexism.[23] The northeast gentry associate urban living with culture, and thus feel justified in mocking southern rural "rednecks"; similarly, universities and colleges west of the Mississippi face the charge of being too removed from northeastern "centers" of intellectualism.

Those who are multiply marginalized have had to overcome additional barriers, and although they decry the injustice of the situation, many have derived strength from their battles. Indeed, one of the traits that most of the contributors share (but do not all discuss), is a sense of pride in their background. While we are all aware of the underprivileged position a woman from the working class has, we are also aware that our original status taught us valuable lessons. We learned to work hard and thus were able to get our advanced degrees under sometimes very difficult circumstances. We learned to empathize with outsiders, and many of us found this helped us in dealing with multicultural, disabled, or otherwise marginalized students. Furthermore, as this anthology's existence suggests, we learned to maintain a healthy skepticism toward social institutions and, even when we were devoted to them, to critique them in the hope of making them fairer.

IV

When we begin to think of the hierarchy within the educational institution, we must think in terms of the cultural, intellectual, and economic power structures that Antonio Gramsci has defined as hegemony. Hegemony is the power structure kept in place by the consent of the dominant groups within a society; it is informed by an ethics and perspective representative of those dominant groups. We are integrated into the hegemony our society or vocational establishment adopts or manifests through the daily experiences of living in that society. Robert Babcock explains that living in capitalism forms us in the capitalist mold because "workers, and others, hold the values and political ideas that they do as a consequence both of trying to survive, and of attempting to enjoy themselves, within capitalism. These activities require money; the cash nexus remains, therefore, a major means of social, economic and political control."[24] It should be no surprise to us that this remains the motivating force even within the high moral and intellectual aspirations of academic hegemony.

Pierre Bourdieu explains social and institutional power structures as a three-dimensional "field," rather than as a state and power ladder. In *Homo Academicvs*, Bourdieu works out the academic field in terms of the oppositions at play and the rules of the game that allow one to pass along the routes of social and intellectual dominance:

The characteristic of the arts and social science faculties lies in the fact that . . . on the one hand these faculties participate in the scientific field, and therefore in the logic of research, and the intellectual field—with the consequence that intellectual renown constitutes the kind of capital and profit which is specifically their own; on the other hand, as institutions entrusted with the transmission of legitimate culture [they are] invested because of this with a social function . . . of specifically social powers. . . .[25]

Both Gramsci and Bourdieu offer models for understanding the complexities of the social matrix, and whether we discuss intellectual hegemony or gameboard strategies—both accurate descriptions of institutional structures—it is easy to see the sources of rage, disjuncture, and alienated voices we have been discussing. Several of the writers that follow strive to understand the institution by going one step beyond Gramsci and Bourdieu—like top-down models—in order to view the institution from their particular ethnographic pocket of experience.

It was particularly difficult to grapple with definitions of class, both within society and within academe. One colleague suggested we use the term "working class" to refer to faculty who were born to working-class parents, regardless of their present social status and identification. Another explained definitively that class is determined by the husband's or father's economic status alone, regardless of the wife's or mother's economic background. On the other hand, several contributors have theorized that the rites of passage of the doctorate restate one's identity and reformulate the graduate student into the intellectual elite. Others see the profession as a vehicle for social mobility without seeing such mobility as capable of eradicating prior social identity. Still others see class status as impervious to change. Within these different formulations, many of us have felt, with Richard Rodriguez, that we can no longer speak to our parents and our families; that we have been irrevocably changed by our doctoral training in a way that shuts down, rather than opens up, communication for us with those who have provided us with nurturance and role models.[26] Nor are we (precisely) playing Bourdieu's academic field to the extent that graduate school had promised us we might.

We offer this collection of essays not as a tangible answer to the dilemma of class, or of gender and class, or of gender, class, and the academy. We do envision it as a structure for conversation, and we hope the essays that follow will stimulate many others outside their textual borders.

Notes

1. We are using working definitions of ethnography particularly as employed by Clifford Geertz: "The aim is to render obscure matters intelligible by providing them with an informing context" (*Local Knowledge*. New York: Basic, 1983), 152; see also *The Interpretation of Cultures* (New York: Basic, 1973).

2. That is, radical chic can still denote high culture, however much it looks like and is derived from street culture.

3. In particular, we're thinking of the National Association of Scholars, formed, in its words, "to redeem American higher education from intellectual and moral servitude to forces having little to do with the life of the mind or the transmission of knowledge" (*Profession 89*, 49). For a brief but trenchant meditation on culture and intellectual elitism, see Andrew Ross's introduction to his *No Respect: Intellectuals and Popular Culture* (New York: Routledge, 1989), 1–14.

4. Pierre Bourdieu, a French sociologist, determines natural ease as the mark of the upper classes' social dominion over the lower. See *Distinction: A Social Critique of the Judgement of Taste*, trans. Richard Nice (Cambridge: Harvard UP, 1984).

5. Mikhail Bakhtin, "Discourse in the Novel," in *The Dialogic Imagination*, trans. Caryl Emerson and Michael Holquist (Austin: U of Texas P, 1981), 286.

6. Bettina J. Huber, "Women in the Modern Languages," *Profession 90*, 65.

7. *A Fact Book on Higher Education*, ed. Charles J. Anderson et al. (New York: Macmillan, 1989), 171.

8. Report of the Women's Committee of the American Studies Association, "Personal Lives and Professional Careers: The Uneasy Balance" (1987), 8.

9. Carol Gilligan, *In a Different Voice* (Cambridge: Harvard UP, 1982); Nancy Chodorow, *The Reproduction of Mothering: Psychoanalysis and the Sociology of Gender* (Berkeley: U of California P, 1978); Mary F. Belenky, Blythe Clinchy, Nancy Goldberger, and Jill Tarule, *Women's Ways of Knowing: The Development of Self, Voice, and Mind* (New York: Basic, 1986). See the annotated bibliography at the end of this volume for brief summaries of the theories involved.

10. For a supporting view of Gilligan, see Joan C. Tronto, "Beyond Gender Differences to a Theory of Care" *Signs* 12 (1987): 644–63. Also see Gilligan's early essay, "Woman's Place in Man's Life Cycle," in *Feminism and Methodology*, ed. Sandra Harding (Bloomington: Indiana UP & Open UP, 1987). For critiques, see the interdisciplinary forum in *Signs* 11 (1986): 304–33, and *Women*

and Moral Theory, ed. Eva Kittay and Diana Meyers (Totowa, N.J.: Rowman, 1987).

11. See characteristic remarks on the efficacy of southern university education in Christopher Jencks and David Riesman, *The Academic Revolution* (Garden City: Doubleday, 1968), esp. 174–75.

12. Maxine Hong Kingston, *The Woman Warrior: Memories of a Girlhood Among Ghosts* (1976; New York: Random, 1977).

13. Many academic parents might struggle to send their children to Ivy League schools because they are cognizant of the schools' value. (We might apply Bourdieu's analysis that groups with cultural capital tend to reinvest in cultural capital.) On the other hand, working-class families with comparable incomes might believe any graduate education is outstanding and opt for a public institution.

14. Jake Ryan and Charles Sackrey, *Strangers in Paradise: Academics from the Working Class* (Boston: South End, 1984), 77.

15. "Caste, Class and Canon," *A Gift of Tongues: Critical Challenges in Contemporary American Poetry*, ed. Marie Harris and Kathleen Aguero (Athens: U of Georgia P, 1987), 57–82.

16. See Richard Sennett and Jonathan Cobb, *The Hidden Injuries of Class* (New York: Vintage-Random, 1973) for a discussion of how working-class people often find white-collar work, which yields less tangible results than blue-collar work, unrewarding.

17. For a discussion of how the middle and upper classes used the working class as scapegoats during the 1960s—the very time when many working-class students were beginning to gain access to college—see Bob Blauner, *Black Lives, White Lives: Three Decades of Race Relations in America* (Berkeley: U of California P, 1989).

18. Henry A. Giroux, *Theory and Resistance in Education: A Pedagogy for the Opposition* (South Hadley, MA: Bergin, 1983), 234.

19. These state universities are those of North Carolina, Georgia, Vermont, Ohio, Tennessee, Maryland, South Carolina, and Transylvania University of Kentucky. From *Higher Education in Transition*, ed. John S. Burbacher and Willis Rudy, 3d ed. (New York: Harper, 1976), 145.

20. Dominick La Capra, "On the Line: Between History and Criticism." Reprinted in *Profession 89*, 4–9; citations from p. 5.

21. Fredric Jameson, America's foremost Marxist literary critic, for instance, leaves gender out in *The Political Unconscious: Narrative as a Socially Symbolic Act* (Ithaca: Cornell UP, 1981).

22. Nadya Aisenberg and Mona Harrington, in *Women of Academe: Outsiders in the Sacred Grove* (Amherst: U of Massachusetts P, 1988), discuss the

intense, often counterproductive attachment women have to their work. They do not, however, address gender-class dynamics. Attitudes toward academic work typical of women, we have found, are compounded by working-class backgrounds.

23. Michelle Tokarczyk notes, "I've had to confront anti-southern biases in some of my New York friends. With some pain, I remind them that Howard Beach and Bensonhurst are not in the Deep South."

24. Marx's early work was influenced by Hegel and the humanist tradition in which he considered the governing body of the state as alienating, or at least as emblematic of man's alienation from himself. Lenin differed in his thought concerning the state, seeing it as the product of class conflict, arising when conflicts cannot be disinterestedly ameliorated. Gramsci, the political theorist who works out the complexities of hegemony, sees the state as a complex interaction of the civil body and the political body. For a highly accessible introduction, see Robert Babcock, *Hegemony* (New York: Methuen, in association with Tavistock, 1986); citation is from p. 32.

25. Pierre Bourdieu, *Homos Academicvs,* trans. Peter Collier (Stanford: Stanford UP, 1990), 74.

26. Richard Rodriguez, "The Achievement of Desire," in *Hunger of Memory: The Education of Richard Rodriguez* (Boston: Godine, 1981).

Class Discussion: A Dialogue between
Kate Ellis and Lillian S. Robinson

ELLIS: Lillian, I wanted to ask you some things about class and your experiences as an academic. The reason I'm interested in doing this, is because I come from a very elite background and haven't always understood, as a feminist and someone on the left, how that would affect my teaching and my general place in academia. I know your background is very different from mine, but we've nevertheless followed, in many ways, a common academic path, so I thought you would be the perfect person to talk to about the difference that has evolved between you and me.

ROBINSON: But Kate, I don't think we *have* followed a common academic path, and *that's* the difference.

ELLIS: Are you saying that your life in academia has been different from mine because of the class position into which you were born?

ROBINSON: I was very surprised to hear you say that you thought our academic lives have followed a similar trajectory. What's followed a similar trajectory is our interests, but we both know better than to define our reality only in terms of what happens in our heads. We met as graduate student activists and we both got our doctorates specializing in earlier periods of literature. We were already doing radical criticism, but applying it to a male intellectual tradition. Then we both began working on feminist criticism and theory and also moved into studying popular culture. We began writing poetry around the same time, in the early seventies, and, in the last couple of years, we've both started writing fiction. Moreover, in the first year of the women's movement, we wrote a piece together with three other women. It was my first experience (maybe all of ours) in collective writing. So our intellectual trajectory has not been dissimilar, but our careers certainly have. You're a tenured professor at a public university, while I . . .

ELLIS: Yes, but you were at a public research university . . .

ROBINSON: For four years! And I gave that up, tenure and all! And I was wondering if one of the differences may be precisely that I did give it up. That my being prepared to take risks with jobs, with my career, may have something to do with a different sense of reality. A friend of mine has a line about me, "Oh, you chose to marry poverty." Even my choosing what, to his mind, is a low-paying profession, is something that he sees as a matter of choice. I've always been very irritated at that notion. Here's a man who inherited millions of dollars, and who has made a great deal more, saying to me, who inherited nothing except my labor power, and who has not been notably or at least consistently successful at selling this, "You've made this choice." But trying to be intellectually honest, as well as being irritated at his ability to wave his hand and characterize my life, I realize that I *have* made some choices. And perhaps the professional risk-taking, the absence of caution, is part of that. Now this is absolutely contrary to the stereotype that we have about working-class people and particularly working-class people in relationship to middle-class careers.

I've been told that I have a proletarianized approach to selling myself. For instance I was commenting recently on the fact that I get a great deal more money per public lecture than I used to and attributing that to inflation in the lecture market. It turns out there are still people getting the three to five hundred dollars that I used to get, whereas I now get twelve to fifteen hundred—some of the time, anyway. Somebody had to explain this to me—*who* you have to be to get that kind of amount. It never occurred to me that my skills were growing, because I have a kind of static sense of myself as a worker. So there are those two things that I think are definitely part of it.

I think my tendency to see the academic world as a workplace that is not intrinsically different from other places also may have to do with class background. Obviously, it's a combination of class background and politics.

But I don't know whether, given your class experience, you would have seen in the same light that I did, the story of a friend of mine who was offered a full professorship at an Ivy League university. He was invited, at the recommendation of several of the biggest men in his field, to apply for a senior position in a very prestigious department. The big shots told him they'd been asked to name the very best person for such a position and that they'd suggested him. So he went through the entire search procedure, including the interview (where he was told the paper he delivered was the most brilliant they'd ever heard from a job candidate) and was offered the position. They'd even reached the point of locating university-owned housing for him and his family; I remember one call where he told me the dimensions of the proposed living room and what he'd have a view of. And then, at the higher levels of the appointment process, at a committee he'd thought was not only ad hoc but pro forma, he was turned down. And since the department had apparently exceeded its authority by telling him he was hired and listing his courses for the next term, he had no recourse. The official reason (though I don't know how officially they *can* say a thing like this) is that he was too young for such a position. Which meant too young to have published the work that his professional peers and seniors believed placed him in the first rank. It's as if they were saying he was too young to be himself, since his self is that brilliant. Well, he's the one who's my friend and I do think he got a rotten deal. But (well, you knew there'd have to be a "but," since we're talking about class and the university as a workplace) somewhere along in the hiring process—I don't know exactly when—he learned that the department had originally written to those top people as part of *someone else's* tenure procedure. The other fellow was an assistant professor coming up for promotion to senior rank and they asked for an evaluation of *his* work in the context of who else—anywhere—might actually be better. So here was someone good enough to be hired six years ago and a perfectly acceptable candidate for tenure—if "perfectly acceptable candidate" had been the scale he was measured on. But no, the way the system works, he had no right to the job he'd been doing—at least, no right that weighed against the possibility of their comparing him with the Platonic ideal. And my friend came closer to the department's sense of that Platonic ideal, being best at what he does. So to some extent he was complicit in what was going on. He didn't think the internal candidate had any right to keep his job if it was decided that *he*—Mr. Platonic Ideal—was even more brilliant. He didn't question the way these hiring practices work— at least not until he became the victim of another unfair piece of the process.

In fact, maybe I'm questioning it as an outsider too. Not just one who's been burned by the academy's vision of itself, but one whose class assumptions inevitably make her an outsider. I mean, I look at the university as a workplace and I say what the *hell* kind of job is it, where someone with an excellent performance record—because I gather he had his supporters, too—can be thrown out after seven years because they believe someone else will be even more excellent? And what the hell kind of workplace is it where this rhetoric of excellence, of distinction, of brilliance is so ingrained that everyone assumes—at least, everyone who's signed onto the system—that we really are working in a meritocracy, with the *most* brilliant on top and so on down the ladder.

I don't know, maybe as a feminist you will see what I'm saying, because it's patriarchal, as well as archetypically capitalist. But it's muddied by the talk about brilliance, a belief in which to some extent I know I share. So I may talk about my skills that I'm selling and how I have a proletarian sense of them that makes me surprised when I realize that things like my lengthening list of publications aren't just an aspect of longevity but also account for pushing me to another, a higher job category. But I also know that part of what I sell *is* what the academy defines as brilliance—that and my personal charisma. And charisma—mine, anyway—is far from universal, so when it doesn't "take," I feel very empty and as if I have *nothing* to sell, whereas when it does take, I can get paid a lot for public lectures. And when I have jobs, they're endowed chairs and I earn twice as high a salary as you do. But there's no . . . no routine to it, and no sense of security.

ELLIS: One big difference between you and me is that as a woman coming from a family where women do not earn money—my generation being the first to do that, with me as the very first—I have a very peculiar relationship to my earning power altogether. It somehow seems mysterious to me that I'm actually earning money, and I would never assume that I would get another job unless I actually *had* another job. I don't see it as a part of the system that there are jobs, and once you lose one, you can go and get another one. Or at least I don't see myself as part of that system.

ROBINSON: Your position is a lot more realistic than mine has turned out to be. I haven't been able to go and get another one—a regular tenured professorship—either. But I think that your reasons are no more realistic and, as you point out, no less class bound than my own. I do assume that women work and that I will work at something or other and that I can always . . . I guess that's it. I have always assumed that I will not stop working at *something*.

ELLIS: What is it that you think you bring to the classroom?

ROBINSON: It's being prepared to take risks, intellectual risks first of all, and to encourage my students to take risks in what they think. But I'm not sure how far that goes.

Another thing is that students who have positive things to say about me on evaluations (which is by no means all of them) talk about warmth and directness and immediacy and humor. Of course, the Jewish stereotype and the working-class stereotype, both of which have some truth in them, suggest a great deal more warmth than upper-class WASP stereotypes do. I guess I haven't ever been in a position to adopt a professional identity—a *highly* professional one, in the classroom. A friend of mine told me she'd met the head of a search committee that hired me for a distinguished chair and he had a lot of kind things to say about me, one of which was about how I hadn't "lost the common touch." Apparently, it didn't occur to him that I may just plain *be* common!

ELLIS: I'm still thinking you and I seem to be contradictory in one respect that violates class stereotypes. People who have the tradition of economic security are supposed to be more, not less, willing to take risks. Supposedly, this is the reason some people are at the bottom, because they aren't willing to step out. It also explains why great risk takers, like entrepreneurs, can get rich.

ROBINSON: Well, who was jumping out of windows in the 1930s? Not unemployed workers, but Wall Street speculators who weren't brave enough to face life without their cushion of security. I agree that there is a cultural stereotype of the affluent as risk takers. Society does reward certain kinds of risks, but not risk-taking in your career. Risk-taking with material things, especially other people's money, livelihood, health and safety, is of course rewarded. But this is a society in which, metaphorically at least, risking your job is considered an act of desperation. For example, whistleblowers in a job where their expertise puts them in a better position to understand some potential danger than those whose managerial expertise is concerned only with the bottom line. Well, the popular discourse about that, about whether they should blow the whistle, is as if what was going to happen to them was some kind of fascist thing, as if they were going to be lined up against the wall and shot. "He could lose his job!" we say with awe.

I think that one of the many unexplored things about our generation has to do with what it meant for all of us to be raised by people who had the mentality of the Depression. It fits a sort of Laingian definition of schizophrenia, in that the immediately surrounding conditions absolutely contradict the words you're told represent the truth. So, whatever our class backgrounds, we were all taught certain things about the instability of economic security although we were surrounded by a society where in fact there were jobs. This was certainly the case all the way through the time you and I were in graduate school, that there were professional jobs in a growing area of both the culture and the economy. Any one of us in those years could look around and see there were jobs, there was adequate comfort, there were more consumer possibilities and hence more opportunities for self-realization through consumption. All of this while we were being told by our families, "You've got to save your money because you never know what's going to happen." Well, we thought we did know what was going to happen and it wasn't the Great Depression. On top of this, I got a second double message, growing up, which was that this is a highly prosperous society in which everything—which translated, once more, into opportunities for consumption—was getting better and better. While within my own family, which was being supported on Social Security Survivors' Benefits, that was not the case at all.

ELLIS: Do you think you can characterize yourself as a teacher in a particular way? Do you think you have insight that a teacher from a middle-class background does not? Is that one of the differences between us?

ROBINSON: No. I've taught students from a very wide range of class backgrounds, whereas you have had the same job for a long time. We were both preceptors at Columbia, but I've taught at perhaps a dozen institutions since then, and you've taught at one. It so happens that in my earlier years, both at Columbia and MIT, I taught students from ruling-class backgrounds—a Du Pont, an Auchincloss—as well as many, many students from comfortable, upper-middle-class, country club-ish kinds of backgrounds. I've also taught at institutions—public and private—where the majority of the students were the first generation of their families to go to college. Even at the elite institutions, I taught a few people from backgrounds like my own. Part of the difference, which increases every year we live, is a generational one. Thirty years ago, when I started college, I was on full scholarship at an Ivy League institution. But there were only a handful of very large scholarships. Not only did you have to get the idea of going to college at all, which wasn't taken for granted, and figure out how you could do it at some place that, unlike the colleges we now call CUNY, cost money to go to, but then you had to be one of those few awarded the opportunity to do so. Decisions had to be made about you by somebody other than yourself once you decided to make yourself something. There were no loans at all. There were no jobs of the sort that would really pay your way through, although it cost considerably less than it does now. (Tuition's gone up by a factor of ten, whereas most other things don't cost ten times as much as they did when I was an undergraduate.) Still, nowadays there are more students who get some kind of financial aid for higher education and couldn't go to college if they didn't—much of it in the form of big loans and grants that didn't exist in my day. And there's a wider range of motives for seeking higher education. Class mobility was so hidden on my agenda that I don't think I understood it as that. I thought I was looking for the truth and looking to develop myself in that search through the making and apprehension of art. And that just like the heroine of the Jane Austen novel, who of course must marry but who mustn't go out into the marriage market actively looking for a man, I would, as a matter of course, be rewarded in my search for truth and beauty by a job providing a certain degree of material security and even more prestige and respectability.

How does your family respond to the fact that you are a Ph.D. and a professor? Do they see this as prestigious or slightly absurd?

ELLIS: It's certainly not seen as prestigious. And I'm often amazed to discover that there *are* lots of people in the general public who think that being a professor is a big deal.

ROBINSON: What would have happened if you had been a boy? The fact that your father has three daughters is part of the ongoing drama of your upbringing that I do know a little about. Would it have been better or worse for a son of his to be a professor?

ELLIS: I'm the one of the three with the most academic degrees. . . .

ROBINSON: I was just thinking . . . just before you go on—my mother, even when she sends me a birthday card, addresses the envelope to

"Doctor." And she has my brother's Ph.D. framed on a wall in her apartment. (Mine is stuck in my desk drawer over there that I can't get open.)

ELLIS: I have mine somewhere. . . . My parents remind me of an ad for Chivas Regal. It's such a nasty ad. It says they *don't* do this and that and they *do* drink Chivas. And one of the things they *don't* do is brag about their children.

ROBINSON: You mean, this is the kind of people who buy the up-market brand of Scotch?

ELLIS: I once showed that to one of my friends and said, "I think this is a class issue being addressed here," because only upper-class people would not brag about their kids because they don't need to. Because all of them are going to be presidents of a corporation—they're all off to Harvard—they don't need to brag. They are able to send their kids to these schools and don't need to depend on scholarships. I've never been able to say my parents are proud of me for rising above the level of their expectation.

ROBINSON: But the way I read that, it's not only that the Chivas Regal drinkers don't brag about their kids. It's that they don't *feel* pride, at least not in that kind of achievement. Still, your parents *schlepped* out here to California for your son's graduation from Stanford.

ELLIS: Yes, they . . . those things can skip a generation.

ROBINSON: I see this to some extent as an ethnic rather than a class issue. The child of a Jewish parent wishes that the parents would feel precisely the same pride that they do but *shut up* about it! There are lots of reasons why it's embarrassing to *be* "My Son the Doctor," and one of them is that you have to live your professional life—or feel you do—in a discourse defined on the one hand by that brilliance thing and on the other by other people's WASP—Chivas Regal ethic of cool.

ELLIS: What if you're "My Daughter the Doctor"?

ROBINSON: That's different. Maybe. I've always felt that maybe this goes across class and ethnic lines, that there are two kinds of parents of adult children who are dissatisfied with their kids. One kind sends you a clear signal that if you did or were something else, you'd be satisfactory. You may even have a sibling who does have that life and seems to be getting parental approval. And then there are those of us who have the kind of parents that, whatever we did, it would be good enough. It's not just a question of expectations in a social or economic sense. It's who *you* are. Although some of it may have to do with things like whether and whom you marry, whether and how many children you have and how brilliant, beautiful, and successful *they* are. My ten-year-old son had occasion recently to write a "thank you" note to my mother, who'd sent him a present. And his second sentence after thanking her was, "And now I will tell you something you will like to hear." And he went on to tell her what his midterm grades had been, he had four "A's," two "A+s," and an "A−." Now, he knows that a grandmother wants to know that, because he's part of a culture where that's the function of a grandparent.

ELLIS: One of the fantasies I have about how being an academic from a working-class background would be different is that the issue of class could enter more directly into your criticism of the ways your students think. There are a lot of things about my students' thinking that bother me. Like it's hard to identify yourself as a feminist right now, and there are troubling issues about racism. I think a lot about how to raise questions of racism in my classroom. I don't imagine that these kids are the ones writing racist graffiti in the bathroom. . . .

ROBINSON: But *somebody's* doing it!

ELLIS: Somebody is doing it.

ROBINSON: Somebody in your immediate campus environment.

ELLIS: Yes, and some students also have a patronizing, superior attitude toward minorities, which comes from their definition of a feminist perspective, where women have to get their act together and pull themselves up as individuals. So the same is true of minorities. And one of the things they have not been able to imagine, from their upbringing or the culture, is class solidarity.

ROBINSON: So they can't imagine community?

ELLIS: No. I get very frustrated when I feel class relationships are a barrier to community, when I want to say "Look. You've got to stop thinking like this and you've got to start thinking this way." Though I've certainly developed certain methods for doing that, it seems to me if I were closer to their class position I would feel differently about telling

33

them that. It is similar to the difference between telling tales within the family and telling them outside of the family.

ROBINSON: I think that is part of the problem. The women's studies program that I used to work in at Buffalo was criticized, years ago, in one college issue of *Mademoiselle,* which was doing an article about women's studies. They claimed a feminist at another university said, "Oh, those Buffalo women, they're always talking about working-class this and working-class that." She claimed that students who come to college are upwardly mobile and they don't want to be reconfined in the working class, so it was wrong for us to do that. The implication was that any reference to "working class" is reconfining you and there can be nothing desirable or attractive about the environment from which you come. You *must* want to leave it behind. One way of getting around class issues with your students is by talking about ethnic differences among white working people. Because some students still have the sense that they're Italian, or Irish, or Jewish, or that one parent is one thing and one is another, so ethnicity made a tremendous difference in their parents' generation. You can ask if the assimilation of their parents into America has meant an erosion of those ethnic identities. You can suggest ethnicity may persist in discussions about things like parents having "backward" attitudes about whom their children marry or date.

ELLIS: That used to come up a great deal.

ROBINSON: And why shouldn't it? That's one of the main things on young people's agenda, first of all, and it's also the thing their parents are afraid of—interracial sexuality. Maybe they're even still afraid of interethnic sexuality.

ELLIS: With somebody in a class lower than you?

ROBINSON: I think. I don't know. In terms of marriage, probably. Going with somebody who is never going to "make anything of themselves"— who didn't go to college—I think, is the way it would be seen. You may very well have students who have an old boyfriend from high school who didn't go to college. . . .

ELLIS: I have one Greek student who was in a relationship with a Hispanic.

ROBINSON: I had a Chinese male student who is the only one in his family to go to college. He was the regular undergraduate age, but was already married and his wife became pregnant during the course of

34

the semester. He was about to graduate and they had not planned on the pregnancy but there was no question about their going ahead with it because they had been planning to have children very soon. He told me that his parents, who are not expressive people generally, had expressed tremendous pleasure. He was the youngest of a quite large family and the others hadn't been to college and had established their families earlier, so I said, "This isn't even a first grandchild." He said, "Yes, but it's the only *Chinese* one." None of his siblings had married a Chinese, and therefore he was the only one who, to his parents, really counted in terms of a grandchild. We had been reading some stuff about adolescent conflicts with immigrant parents where the issue of marriage arose, but not the issue of intermarriage. Intermarriage, however, had come up a great deal during class discussion, and he had experienced that.

Also, I was telling him about how I felt as a prospective mother myself—ten or nine years earlier—and how it feels to watch your children grow. He replied, "I wish my parents had said that. The way they say it is, 'Oh, you never gave us any trouble, your brother was a lot of trouble.'" It was always in those terms. We had been reading Maxine Hong Kingston and talking about what she has to say—her perceptions about directness and indirectness in language—but I tried to indicate to him that there was a class as well as an ethnic element to this, that very often working people will express relationship things indirectly. They fear saying too much. That's the other side of that bragging-about-your-children business, which is saying too much directly *to* them. That is a class thing.

I think our approach to students like this has to do with certain assumptions that are built into humanistic studies in a capitalist society. A lot of today's students from backgrounds like my own are majoring in business, or planning to enter business when they graduate. They think that kind of success is why you go to college and they regard our humanities courses as hoops that you have to jump through on the way toward getting that degree. The stereotype is, of course, that the only students who are looking for marketability are those from working-class backgrounds who are the first generation of their family to go to college. The public institutions supposedly exist to serve that population with those motives. But I've had exposure to the same attitude from students from highly privileged backgrounds.

ELLIS: Students who should have great intellectual freedom?

35

ROBINSON: I give you Dan Quayle. I have never met anybody like that personally. I've never known anyone like that socially. I've never had a colleague like that. But the vibes I get from him are of a certain kind of male student . . . the one who comes up to explain that he hasn't gotten a paper in. His excuse—that he was participating in a golf tournament or he went home to study for his CPA exam—is an insult to you, and he doesn't even *understand* that it's an insult. There's the privileged male's expectation that the other person will see the reasonableness of his point of view and share his opinion that the course in poetry is a lot of bullshit, which he's only taking because he has to have *some* literature to graduate. I have taught very fine students from upper-class backgrounds, and I have also taught many who have at least learned that your values are different, particularly with the studious female teacher versus the wealthy, ambitious young man. But I see the Dan Quayle student as the one who isn't even smart enough to have figured that *you* don't think the humanities are bullshit.

When I was at Brown, I had contemporaries whose fathers were embarrassed at their sons choosing to major in something like classics or English. And this was at an Ivy League university first of all, one in which it was impossible to major in anything that was very practical. (Although, I suppose you could study engineering.) In fact, when I was an undergraduate, the "C−" student types among the "girls," as we said then, majored in art history while the boys majored in political science. Philistinism was required for males from a certain background, while culture was transmitted on the female line.

ELLIS: What did they do after graduation?

ROBINSON: The men would go into their fathers' businesses or some-body else's business, and the young women would marry and be patrons of the arts, perhaps be on the board of the local museum. But they would not *become* art historians which is, after all, a very hard thing to be. In fact, they would have an appreciation of art but would not be able to make something themselves. They weren't the art studio majors, who were a different sort of person.

ELLIS: I think some of them did become art historians. There is a sense that women can be presumed to have some authority in art history and literature. But art history costs a lot of money to pursue. You have to spend the summer in Italy, and so forth and so on, and you can't always get a grant to do it. If your father has money, you can do those things and acquire the kind of information you need for art history—a second and third language, and so forth. But if your family doesn't have money, you can't.

ROBINSON: But we're assuming, of course, a scholarly motivation to study art very similar to the scholarly motivation to study literature. As you know, I did a graduate degree in art history as well as in comparative literature and encountered scholars of art, some of whom were, indeed, the children of bankers. They were not at all like the art history majors that I'd known as an undergraduate, who were art appreciators but just did not have the degree of rigor needed for advanced study. I hadn't even known at first that it is, in fact, a discipline of incredible scholarly rigor.

But I've been thinking about what you said about your students and the attitude of individualism, the idea that getting away from your background is a desirable thing and that social mobility is at odds with connectedness. This is the theme of a book that I often teach in humanities classes, Richard Rodriguez's *Hunger of Memory*. Although I dislike that book intensely, I'm also moved by it, so I see why my students are moved by it.

I wonder how many of our students really internalize that process that we're talking about and how many of them talk about it because they think it's what *we* want to hear. It's so much in the tone of society and the dominant ideology that they are showing that they have mastered it. Meanwhile, in fact, they do remain attached to their backgrounds in ways that they're not "supposed" to. They might be open to a vision of sisterhood, let us say, or some other kinds of solidarity, even though competition and self-development are *supposed* to prevail. I postulate this partially on the basis of their response to Rodriguez. Of course, he's an extreme case because he confuses what is, in fact, a common process with what happened in his particular class and ethnic case. Everybody in our culture grows up and leaves a family in some sense. But these ordinary developmental stages are to him so internalized as his own personal cross to bear, that he has to see himself as either completely "in" or completely "out" of the family-community world or the university-competitive world.

ELLIS: Let's move on to something else. I have heard from Adrienne Kennedy about her supportive relationship with her mother. This is something so far from my experience that I can't imagine it, can't envision the continuing nourishing connection between her and her mother that she speaks about having made her life possible.

ROBINSON: Yes, I've heard black colleagues, feminist literary critics of our generation, talk exactly that way about their mothers. And I did write a review of a book some years ago (the first one I ever did for *Women's Review of Books*) on a collection of oral histories of what were called "lower-income women," most of them working poor. A great many of them talked about their mothers and their connection with their mothers, and sometimes about their daughters and their ties to them. But the psychologist who wrote the preface to the collection talked about the differentness of these women *not* being alienated from their mothers. She wrote about alienation almost as if it were natural, because it's the middle-class norm. Generally speaking, I have a sense that in working-class (particularly ethnically identified working-class) families and black families, women don't refer to their mothers as a joke or in terms of differentness. Yet I'm fairly alienated from my own mother, and at that MLA session on working-class women in the academy, a lot of people were talking about not necessarily emotional alienation but about having been forcibly cut off from their mothers' language. I think that the difference is between these women who reject their mothers' lives for themselves (and who therefore seem to be rejecting their mothers) and women, usually working-class women, for whom options of becoming something other than their mother aren't available. And when you find working-class women whose lives are very different from their mothers', in many cases it means that their mothers have deliberately worked and supported their daughters to make sure their lives *are* different. So rather than its being a normal developmental thing that you reject who your parents are, who your mother is specifically, what you reject is her way of experiencing a woman's life. You know that the Yiddish theater has only one basic plot, that of children rejecting their parents. (For instance, the Yiddish *King Lear* is not a translation of *Lear* at all, but a modern Jewish immigrant story.) Who is the serpent's tooth after all? The child who betrays by assimilating—doing the very thing they have worked their fingers to the bone so that they *could* do. What the parents worked for, of course, was for the child to achieve that which no one in that family had ever achieved before—be it security, degrees, income, the trappings of middle-class life—while remaining entirely within the values and confines of the family. So you were *bound* to betray them, one way or the other.

Did you have any sense when you were growing up of what your mother wanted you to become? I mean, in contrast to all of this.

ELLIS: Yes. My mother used to tell us a fairy story about our weddings and who we married. The type of men and the type of weddings, according to our roles.

ROBINSON: Did she assign you those roles?

ELLIS: Yes. I was sort of the nonconformist. And that meant eloping to marry a movie actor—and living happily ever after—instead of having a large traditional wedding.

ROBINSON: But, you did have a large wedding.

ELLIS: Not by her standards.

ROBINSON: Well, you wore your grandmother's wedding dress, though you were pregnant, and your sister had a more conventional big wedding but married a black man. I guess there were some variations in the plot: You weren't exactly preparing to live happily ever after the way it was in her narrative.

ELLIS: That's true.

ROBINSON: You certainly didn't have to be directly told, for example, that you're supposed to be a virgin until the wedding night and that the groom's supposed to be white. The other possibilities didn't come up in your mother's worldview. I bet she told you the stories of weddings but not the stories of marriages.

ELLIS: No, she didn't tell us stories of marriages. She just wanted us to be happy.

ROBINSON: So in telling you stories of different possible weddings, your mother was saying that you were all going to get married to somebody appropriate to each of you and also acceptable to your parents. Which would lead to happiness.

You once told me that happiness in her wedding narrative involved the purchase of monogrammed linen, and so forth, the acquisition of things. That didn't mean that her daughters were going to be housewives so much as "chatelaines." What you were going to *be* when you grew up was married women of your class. And the major job of such a woman is what? Being a hostess, being a companion and support for her husband, socializing her children, doing good in the community, being a responsible citizen, and being involved in volunteer work on the boards of things. So that's what you were supposed to do. Neither you nor any of your sisters became that. You became a professor, and I know your younger sister is with the World Bank, and the middle one is a social worker, isn't she?

Of course, higher education would be part of your preparation for that life your mother pictured, but not preparation for a profession. Still, she never communicated outrage at your choosing to go to graduate school or anything like that. And if you had . . . oh, I don't know, been like one of those women in the female career novels who have gone into a managerial position in the entrepreneurial life and made a tremendous amount of money, would that have been more or less acceptable to your family?

ELLIS: I don't think so.

ROBINSON: It occurs to me that lots of people who are a disappointment to their parents know it. I come from a background where moving into the world of the university is moving up in class because the profession is seen as secure and providing a high income compared to what I was used to. But part of the class status also derives from the prestige that comes from culture. I've been traveling around doing guest lectures about the literary canon as a secular religion and I came to this realization through thinking about male professors and writers like Allan Bloom and Saul Bellow who have uncritically allied themselves with the canon and the great male minds of the past. The way they have done this involves social mobility, not in a vulgar sense but in precisely a sense that eschews the vulgarity of poor and immigrant and outsider backgrounds. I've been trying to see not only the nature of the ideas they hold but the way in which they hold them, and what their attitude is toward that which is outside the canon, which is kind of a secular religion. In the process, I've had to examine my own approach to the stuff that we teach, both canonical material and material that enriches the canon, multicultural and women's writings. This new material reflects lives like my family's and like our students' much more than the historical tradition does. We should keep in mind that people like Bloom didn't necessarily enter academic life in order to be a big success.

But then again it depends on your definition of success. In Jewish tradition, there is something called *yichus*, which is "status," but status according to spiritual merit, which in the European Jewish tradition is demonstrated through the intellect. That's familiar to us in the academic world—at least we *think* that's where prestige is located—but very different from the way it is in the society that supports the academic world. I think we who have taken the academic world on its own terms are always surprised when we discover the extent to which the academy resembles the rest of society.

ELLIS: Can you say more about that?

ROBINSON: Well, the academic world was supposed to be a retreat. It was supposed to be based on better values. The smarter you are, the better you'd do, according to our definitions of prestige.

Recently I took my son, Alex, to an academic conference with me. I told him that some of the people sitting around the dinner table with us were very famous. He said, "Oh, who?" So I said, "Well, Cliff," who was Clifford Geertz, and "Liz's husband," who was Carl Schorske. Well, my son was about to go see Kareem Abdul Jabar play basketball. That's famous to him! But that's famous to the rest of the world too! And, one of the things about Kareem Abdul Jabar, in addition to his being a very good basketball player, is that he makes a lot more money than any academic, even Allan Bloom with a best-seller. Money is the yardstick according to which many other things are measured, although in social terms the measurement is often masked as old family, or cultural refinement, good manners—knowing how to behave is crucial. You once told me about how a colleague socialized you to the academic world, took you to a conference and told you how to talk to the people who were part of academia. You said it was very similar to the way your mother told you things before you went off to the first boy-girl parties in dancing school. The only difference is that instead of saying, "Where do you go to school?" and then seeming terribly interested in what sports they play, you're supposed to ask, "Oh, where do you teach?"

ELLIS: Yes. Yes.

ROBINSON: And obviously with this comparison you were expressing your discomfort with having to translate what your mother had taught you into terms that weren't sufficiently different.

41

ELLIS: I didn't want the academic world to have anything in common with my mother and her expectations.

ROBINSON: I've given some thought to this idea from another point of view because I think of myself as somebody who basically does not know how to act. I am sometimes told that I am a crude, blunt person because in delicate situations, I will say what is on my mind. But in some social situations I do very well. A few years ago, I was being interviewed for a deanship at an institution where I know two senior women on the faculty, one of whom was on the search committee and who was telling the other one, over dinner in my presence, about how well I had done in the chit-chat aspects of the interview. She said, "Y'know, Lillian can talk to those guys!" The one who had not been present, immediately said, "Oh, I know what you mean!" She then talked about how she had flown to the state capital to testify about a matter of professional concern. The hardest part of the experience, she felt, had been not testifying before the legislature, but having to make small talk with her dean, who was also testifying, on the plane. The other one was completely sympathetic, "Oh yes, that would be awful, I *never* know what to say to these guys." Well, I do know what to say to these guys. I couldn't think why—I certainly have less in common with them, if anything, than these women do. Then I came to an explanation that I think is based on class background. Both of these women are the daughters of upper-class professionals. One has a father who is a doctor; the other's father is a lawyer. These women chose the academy as a profession to which they were temperamentally suited, which is to say one that involves being by yourself in a library and having interactions with students and colleagues which are based on subject matter. Both of them happen to be extremely good teachers. It's not that they don't like human intercourse. It's that they want a certain authentic kind of human intercourse, and not other kinds. What I'm saying is that they grew up thinking they could choose a profession on the basis of their interest in the content and its temperamental suitability. Whereas for me, anything that I chose, any profession I entered, would mean wearing a mask, pretending to be and eventually becoming somebody other than myself. I had been very much aware during that job interview, and even more so when I was brought back for a second one. The second interview was longer, and I realized at the end of it that I had said almost nothing in the entire time that reflected myself. I began wondering whether I could stand being that alienated. As a teacher and a writer, I may be wearing a mask of being a middle-class professional, but I'm also saying things I very much believe in. Whereas, of course, as an administrator, I was almost totally behind a mask. Now some (in fact I think most), women from working-class backgrounds talk about the academic world as an alien place. I hear about this particularly from graduate students who are beginning to learn there is something beyond the content, beyond the work itself. They say they think they don't belong, they feel they can't ever fit in, that they don't know, in the very profound sense, what fork to use. The people who talk most about it are the people who are conscious that they're not going to do it, not going to make it. But I talk about academic rituals as something I've mastered, though generally speaking, I think the people who have mastered them don't talk about them.

ELLIS: I wonder if those who master the rituals have had role models.

ROBINSON: Once I was explicitly asked to be a role model. A student who graduated from the program I taught in went off to graduate school and was having what grew into a fairly full-blown nervous breakdown. A friend of hers said that they wanted to talk to me about what was happening to her; they had chosen me very deliberately. I was by no means the faculty member that she was closest to, but the other student said to me "You're the only woman we know from a working-class background who's entered the academic world and has not gone crazy." Well I thought I was pretty crazy at the time, but it was other things that were what was making me crazy. Occasionally, some friend of mine will tell me about having taught the daughter of some famous woman scholar. By and large *our* students are not the daughters of our colleagues, and they don't know how to be in the academic world as a woman specifically. They look to us for some kind of explanation of how you go about doing it, because they know it's different for women. I'm often called upon for this, and it seems ironic because I don't consider myself a success. But it turns out that my students can't see the difference. Also, I don't know . . . what is the advice one gives? What is the right thing to say if you are explicitly approached? I'm asking you this as a real question, not as a rhetorical question.

ELLIS: As a person who comes from a middle-class background I'm not sure what advice I'd give other than to share my experiences as a woman.

ROBINSON: I guess the message you can't explicitly say is "Don't lose the strengths you have, in acquiring other ones. Don't lose yourself in trying to fit into academia."

I think that what we're really talking about communicating is the notion of connectedness. There is incredible power in the individualistic ideas of the dominant society, but you can try to communicate that connectedness as a real strength in the lives of working-class women. And they needn't leave that behind. Parenthetically, one of the first ways in which I was involved in expressing solidarity with my colleagues (other junior faculty) had to do with organizing around salary inequities. What we wanted was for the department to establish a step system for junior faculty, similar to what exists at public institutions, which would mean equalization, of course. We decided to threaten them by publishing our low salaries, at least by putting up a poster with everybody's salary, degrees, and length of service. Then we realized that in order to be able to make good on this threat, we'd have to tell *each other* how much we earned. This was 1969–70, when everybody around the table knew practically everything about each other's sex lives, but these people from middle-class backgrounds were almost incapable of— it really caught in their throat—saying the dollar amount they earned. And, of course, the department was relying on this reticence. That's something that's very foreign to people from working-class kind of backgrounds; they're very open about salaries, and money comes into the agenda differently.

ELLIS: It was considered very vulgar in my family to talk about money. But I'd like to talk a little more about role modeling. I remember a colleague who came from a middle-class background saying that his family's friends, and his family itself, lacked compassion for those who failed, because *they'd* set goals and succeeded. In my family, failure is always your fault. You have all the advantages, so failure is always inexcusable.

When I think of what I would want to do as a role model for students, it would come out of my consciousness of class, and it would lessen fear of failure and the fear of competition that often goes along with it. I'd like to set up an atmosphere in academia where people can collaborate and contribute to one another, where what you know and what I know, and what this other person knows is not some sort of chess game to see who's going to end up with the most pieces.

44

ROBINSON: But the academic world tells us we are playing that game, and at the same time, it holds a fundamental myth about itself—that it's a community of scholars. And there *is* a great deal of intellectual generosity in the academic world, but along with it are dishonesty and theft, theft so serious it almost amounts to professional murder.

ELLIS: But you can't just ask for information. There is something shameful about it. So you research for days, weeks, or months in the library, and then present yourself in a graduate seminar as somebody who knows more than anybody else there, and someone who doesn't need to get any more information. You have it all, and you can put down anyone who didn't realize some minor point about Ben Jonson.

ROBINSON: It's not just faculty. In the academic world, competitiveness is acute among graduate students who are competing for Daddy's favors . . .

ELLIS: Yes.

ROBINSON: . . . which are real material favors as well as love or esteem.

But what I do like about the academy is that you can go next door to somebody whose political views may not coincide with your own or to someone you may not care for personally and say, "Can you summarize the theory of the king's two bodies?" And the person will do so and *then* say, "Why do you want to know?" And you'll say, "Well, I think it might have some connection with what I'm working on." And in fact, that very question "What are you working on?" is an opening to conversation.

Incidentally, one of the big differences between academics and almost everybody else in society is the way we use that word "work." I made up a dialogue that was part of the beginning of a lecture I gave about connectedness among women who work together, primarily in proletarian jobs. I started out talking semantically about the different uses of the word "work." In my imaginary dialogue between two academics, one of them says to the other, "Did you get much work done over the vacation?" And the other one says, "Yes, but I haven't done a thing since I got back to campus." And the first one replies, "I know what you mean. I was on leave last spring and got a tremendous amount of work accomplished, but as soon as I came back they made me the head of the search committee; you know, we have three retirements in my department." The second one stops and thinks for a moment to figure out who's leaving, then says "Retiring? At least they'll get some work done." The academic notion of the vacation, the leave of absence, the retirement as sites for doing some *work* is really quite peculiar.

ELLIS: Yes.

ROBINSON: We contrast this work to that for which you receive your paycheck. The distinction goes beyond job satisfaction or the lack of it. It involves what you think your real work is. That real work is something to be proud of and to be desired, and not only because it carries with it ancillary material rewards like tenure, which is not necessarily based on what you get your paycheck for. Real work, to the academic, brings real status. But the perspective of the outside, say the perspective of our two families, is that you go through an educational process and then you get a job in a particular institution and then you are a professor. However, from inside the profession we know that there are "big shot" professors, and "medium-big shot" professors and "obscure" professors. I guess to your family they're all "obscure" and to my family they're all "big shots." Yet no one—only the most vulgar in graduate school—would have said, "I'm going to be a famous professor when I grow up," although we all got socialized to the academy's own class system, without seeing how it both replicated and coexisted with the *real* class system we thought we'd come away from.

Belonging

"What's a Nice Working-Class Girl Like You Doing in a Place Like This?"

IN AMERICA we are taught, from our earliest years, that upward mobility is the essence of the American dream. Growing up in a white working-class family, I equated such mobility with the "good life," "making it," and middle-class respectability. Like many of my peers, I saw education as the key to actualizing my vision. It was clear that I not only wanted to move up, but out. By getting a "good education" I would be able to leave my past behind and create a life for myself which was radically different from that of my parents.

During those early years, my own classism prohibited me from questioning the "dream" or the "rewards" education would bring. I was also unprepared for the marginality and estrangement I would feel as my "dream" came true. These feelings initially surfaced during college and only intensified as I moved up the educational hierarchy. Thus, the more "successful" I became, the more marginal I felt.

For many years I saw this pattern as indicative of my own personal inadequacies rather than as a function of the ways in which my gender and class background shaped my experience within academe. In other words, I lacked what C. Wright Mills called the sociological imagination, or the ability to see that my private troubles were intricately linked to larger social forces. A key barrier to developing this awareness was the invisibility of other faculty who shared my class background. Without the knowledge that there were others "like me," it was difficult to move beyond a self- or victim-blaming perspective. It was only by breaking my self-imposed silence and sharing my experience with others that I began to realize I was not alone. By coming out of the closet, I soon discovered that what I had viewed as personal problems were, in fact, common struggles.

As I spoke with other women like myself, it became clear that these struggles were directly related to the dual nature of our class identity. On the one hand, we had, in many ways, become middle class. Our education, occupation, and income were indisputable markers that clearly separated us from our families of origin. Yet our subjective experience of class was not that clear cut. Despite our objective position in the class structure, many of us did not feel middle class or as if we really belonged in the world we inhabited. What we were keenly aware of, which many of our middle-class colleagues failed to understand, is that "education and a good job don't turn a black person white and they don't negate a white working-class person's background" (McKenney 147). As a consequence, a part of our identity was middle class while another part remained back in the working-class world of our roots.

Thus, as upwardly mobile working-class women, we lived in two culturally distinct and, at times, contradictory worlds. One consequence of this multiple consciousness was that we often experienced ourselves as outsiders, both within the middle-class world of academia and within our families of origin. As members of what might be best described as a transition class, we saw ourselves as living on the margins of two cultural worlds but as members of neither.[1]

We also felt that this sense of marginality was augmented further by our gender. As women, we were well aware of our anomalous position within an institution whose structure and ideology reinforced patriarchal values. As a consequence, we frequently saw ourselves as outside the mainstream of university life, alienated and invisible.[2]

In this chapter I examine the personal and professional struggles faced by female academics from the working class as they try to cope with their marginal status and the psychic disequilibrium created by upward mobility. Given the dearth of literature on this topic, I will draw on my experiences and those shared with me by other women faculty. Like myself, these women are white and all are in their mid-thirties to early forties. The ambiguities and ambivalences with which we are most familiar shape the central themes of this chapter. How these themes might differ for male academics from the working class, or for other racial and age groups, are issues that remain to be explored.

Central to any discussion of social class is the profound effect it has on our perception of the world as well as of our place in it. When we identify ourselves as being in one class or another, we are making a statement about what we view as our objective position within the class structure. However, class is more than an abstract category or benign label assigned to self or others. Each class has a distinctive social existence, a culture that creates a sense of belonging among its members (Ryan and Sackrey 107). This culture shapes how we speak, walk, dress, eat, our sense of control over our life, our values and attitudes regarding work, family, intimacy, money, leisure, and education.[3]

Within American society, however, each class culture is not equally valued. Specifically, the norm, the standard of acceptability and respectability, is middle class. Thus, to be from the working class is to be defined as "less than," inferior, subordinate. As many feminists have noted, this pattern of responding not only to class but to all human differences in dualistic and hierarchical terms characterizes much of Western thought. Representing what may be called a patriarchal consciousness, this mode of thinking "conditions us to see human differences in simplistic opposition to each other: dominant/subordinate, good/bad, up/down, superior/inferior" (Lorde 114). Within this framework, those who lack privilege and power become "other," the outsider whose experience is ignored, devalued, or erased.[4]

For members of the working class and other subordinate groups, this reductive response to human differences often leads to internalized oppression. This refers to the "incorporation and acceptance by individuals within an oppressed group of the prejudices against them within the dominant society" (Pheterson 148). And, as Pheterson notes, internalized oppression is likely to be associated with feelings of inferiority, self-hatred, self-concealment, and isolation (148).

What are the consequences of these cultural patterns for academics from the working class? First, they strongly affect how such faculty perceive themselves and their place within the academy. Given the middle-class values and assumptions that permeate university life, academics from the working class are constantly aware of their differences from the norm.[5] The taken-for-granted reality that "everyone is middle class" typically structures the curriculum as well as conversations with colleagues and administrators. Within this environment, it is not surprising that, as Ryan and Sackrey learned, working-class faculty often view themselves as outsiders or as marginal members of the academy. For female academics from the working class, this sense of not belonging is augmented further by the masculinist culture and male-centered nature of the university.[6] Well aware of their outsider status, both as women and as members of a culturally devalued class, many silence themselves. While this strategy enables them to "pass" as middle class or appear as an insider to others, "passing" is not the same as belonging. Thus, silence may protect working-class faculty from being "discovered" by others, but it does not eradicate their cultural heritage and the feelings of estrangement that stem from it.

Second, due to internalized oppression, working-class faculty may be more likely than their middle-class colleagues to have serious doubts about their self-worth, skills, and ability to perform or succeed. Objective evidence of professional success often does little to ameliorate these doubts and, in fact, frequently has the opposite effect. This theme is aptly illustrated by the following experience shared with me by a well-known women's studies scholar. Although she had published five books, she experienced a great deal of difficulty completing and submitting the final draft of each one. In her words, she feared "letting go" of her work because she knew this would ultimately lead to her being "judged by others and put on trial." Though her work was always well received, each time she neared the completion of a new book, she would begin to define her past successes as a fluke; she had just gotten "lucky." This time, however, it would be different. Her ultimate fear would become a reality. Others would finally discover who she *really* was: "a working-class kid who managed to con everyone into believing she was good enough, smart enough, and so forth." Although she always managed to overcome this fear and submit her work for publication, doubts regarding her self-worth remained. Accordingly, whenever a new challenge or project arose, the cycle would repeat itself.

The fear that others will discover one is a fraud or impostor is quite common among first-generation professionals, including academics from the working class.[7] Having internalized the classism of the larger culture, such faculty may find it difficult to accept praise from others and they often deny their own competence. Accordingly, they attribute success to external events such as luck rather than to personal skill or ability. Ironically, as their professional achievements increase, working-class faculty may feel more than ever that others have a false impression of them. And, this in turn, can heighten their fear of being "discovered."

Another issue that may arise concerns the symbolic meaning of one's work or professional success. For often what is defined as "success" within the middle-class world of academia becomes yet another manifestation of separateness and alienation from the working-class world of one's roots. Accordingly, the more one succeeds, the greater the social distance from one's class of origin. Given this dynamic, there is often a desire for and simultaneous fear of such "success" among working-class faculty. This double bind can lead to confusion and ambivalence regarding what others in academe take for granted as indicators of professional success (e.g., completing a dissertation, publishing, receiving tenure). Working-class academics may therefore experience more difficulty reaching professional goals than their middle-class colleagues. And, once achieved, such success can raise new existential dilemmas. This theme, as well as the class-based contradictions associated with academic success, has emerged repeatedly in my conversations with others. For example, during a recent conference, I heard a working-class faculty member discuss her response to receiving tenure. For years she had thought this rite of passage would mark the beginning of a new life. Self-doubt and anxiety would no longer characterize her experience within academe. After all, she would have "made it" and finally proven herself. She soon discovered, however, that tenure was a mixed blessing. It secured her place within the middle-class world of academe, but by doing so, raised a plethora of new questions: Was she now one of "them"? Had she finally become a full-fledged member of the educated elite, a group her family referred to with disdain, yet often admired and wanted to emulate? Had she betrayed those she left behind? Would her newly won status separate her even more from her family of origin? What *did* this rite of passage mean in terms of her self-definition? As I listened to her remarks, I remembered having similar thoughts while writing my dissertation. In fact, these thoughts were a large part of why I feared completing it. Thus, for working-class academics, whether beginning or at later stages of their careers, professional success can create identity confusion as well as heighten feelings of estrangement.

The feelings of marginality and alienation experienced by working-class faculty within the academy may also permeate their relationships with significant others from their past, particularly family members. As one interviewee in a recent study of working-class academics noted: "Years of living a university life have isolated me from my working class origins. What do we have in common, what can we talk about? Their interests are not my interests, their values are no longer mine" (Ryan and Sackrey 138). Given the centrality of kin in working-class culture, such isolation can create a great deal of anguish.[8] In addition,

53

because women tend to define themselves in more relational terms than men, estrangement from kin may be particularly difficult for female academics from the working class.[9] Such women learn very early in their careers that their life-style, general interests, and work are largely incomprehensible to their families. Although family members may try to understand this "new" life, the pain is, in many ways, that they can't. Attempts to explain one's life-style and work often only broaden the chasm and, in the end, it becomes painfully clear that they are living in radically different worlds from one another. For example, during a recent conversation with my mother, I began discussing a conference I planned to attend on the West Coast. She immediately asked what people did at a conference and I explained that they present their ideas and talk about them with others. She then asked whether I knew any of the people who would be there and I said a few, but that hundreds would be attending. Her response: "You mean to tell me that you are going to travel three thousand miles to talk to people you don't even know?" I meekly replied "yes."

Thus, even on the most rudimentary level, working-class academics frequently lack the familial support and validation of self that is taken for granted by many of their middle-class colleagues. As a result, they often feel like outsiders at home as well as within academe. Consequently, interactions with family members may be strained and, at times, painful. In sum, working-class faculty may feel estranged regardless of where they turn for validation: to their families, their colleagues, or their work.

How can these feelings of marginality and estrangement be reduced? How can working-class academics begin to integrate the divided or split sense of self that arises from belonging (yet in some fundamental ways, not belonging) to two distinct class cultures? As members of a transition class, it is likely that working-class academics will always feel marginal to some degree. However, if this outsider status is to become a source of empowerment rather than a source of internal conflict, it is imperative that such faculty begin to validate the working- and middle-class parts of themselves. To do so requires that they recognize and confront the ways in which they have internalized the classism of the larger society and, thus, their own oppression. This process is essential if working-class academics are to reclaim their power and develop an authentic or integrated sense of self.

For me, learning to claim and appreciate my bicultural identity has been an arduous process and one that is far from complete. As a marginal member of two cultural worlds, I have been forced to confront the issue of difference in ways that a more comfortable status might have diffused. The most difficult aspect of this process has been coming to terms with my own classism. Doing so, however, has provided the opportunity for me to challenge personally the dualistic and hierarchical thinking that underlies our cultural response to difference. Thus, rather than asking whether I am working class or middle class, I have come to recognize that I am both. Although this reconceptualization of self may not appear revolutionary, in many ways it is. For this type of integration to occur, academics like me must move from a denial of our history to an acceptance of it. Because many of us have learned to negate our class background in order to survive, this radical shift in perspective will be a difficult transition. Once achieved, however, this new awareness can be a valuable resource. Claiming one's past can renew the self as well as stimulate intellectual energy. It might, for example, trigger new research issues or provide the stimulus for a radical revision of our courses. In each case, one's history becomes a resource and an integral part of one's work, something to learn from rather than deny. This shift in consciousness may be particularly significant for working-class students in our courses. When we claim our past, we validate theirs and, more important, we empower them to do the same.

It is important to recognize, however, that learning to reclaim and value one's working-class heritage can be just as difficult for working-class students as it is for faculty with similar backgrounds. Those of us who decide to make social class differences an integral part of our courses and/or to "come out of the closet" need to be particularly cognizant of this fact and of the effect it may have on classroom dynamics. Denial, feelings of personal inadequacy, or embarrassment as well as a fear of being "discovered" may, for example, cause some students initially to distance themselves from discussions of working-class life. In contrast, others may find the heightened class consciousness produced by such discussions to be a source of validation and central to their self-empowerment. These qualitatively different responses can create tension within the classroom, particularly if students articulate their feelings and concerns. In addition, this volatile situation may be exacerbated if middle-class students deny or minimize the im-

55

portance of class differences and/or their own class privilege. These different student responses can create a highly charged and potentially divisive classroom environment. If, however, we structure our courses in ways that emphasize and affirm the importance of diversity, students will be less likely to view such differences as divisive and more likely to appreciate and learn from them.[10]

As we continue our struggle to make ourselves whole, we need to remember that, regardless of how "integrated" or "successful" we become, to some degree we will always be marginal members of the academy or "outsiders within."[11] We may, at times, deny our history, but it is clear we cannot erase it. We can, however, use our "outsider within" status to challenge the institutions of which we are a part as well as to transform conventional ways of knowing within our respective disciplines. Thus, instead of denying our cultural heritage or pretending such differences are irrelevant, we can work to "conserve the creative tension of outsider within status by encouraging and institutionalizing outsider within ways of seeing" (Collins 29). For this to occur, we, as working-class academics, must "learn to trust our own personal and cultural biographies as significant sources of knowledge" (Collins 29). By doing so, the unique standpoint and critical consciousness engendered by our marginality will become sources of power and vision. By learning to value the ways in which we *are* different from many of those in academe and by actualizing the creative potential of our "outsider within" status, we will have fully claimed ourselves.

Notes

1. This classic definition of marginality has most often been used to describe the experiences of racial and ethnic minorities. See Park; Almquist (esp. 434–35). For further discussion of marginality in reference to academics from the working class, see Ryan and Sackrey.

2. It is important to note that this pattern was mentioned most often by those women who defined themselves as "strongly female-identified." In essence, this meant they "had not been co-opted by the system" or become what many referred to as "male-identified." Their use of the latter term was similar to Rich's description of the token woman: "Losing her outsider's vision, she loses the insight which both binds her to other women and affirms her in her-

self. Tokenism essentially demands that. . . . she perpetuate rules and structures and criteria and methodologies which have functioned to exclude women; that she renounce or leave undeveloped the critical perspective of her female consciousness" ("What Does a Woman Need . . ." 6).

3. The contrasting realities of middle- and working-class cultures are highlighted by a number of authors. For example, in her autobiographical essay, Berson provides an excellent discussion of middle-class privilege as well as of the stark differences that exist between class cultures (60–62). See also Sennett and Cobb.

4. For a discussion of the view of the working class as subordinate, see Reid and Bunch; Hughes; Gowens. For more on the concept of patriarchal consciousness and its effect on how we respond to differences, see Gardner, Dean, and McKaig.

5. Working-class students are similarly cognizant of their difference from the norm. For an analysis of the culture shock experienced by such students and of how universities reinforce a middle-class consciousness, see Brown (16–18) and Gardner, Dean, and McKaig (68–70).

6. Over the past decade, there have been numerous feminist critiques of the university's androcentric structure and ideology. Rich, for example, presents a thought-provoking discussion of these issues in her now-classic essay, "Toward a Woman-Centered University." See also Gearhart.

7. Clance provides an excellent overview of the impostor phenomenon, including its particular relevance for first-generation professionals. For a discussion of how the impostor phenomenon affects academics from the working class, see Ryan and Sackrey.

8. The more exclusively kin-oriented nature of family life characteristic of the working class has been documented by numerous studies. See, for example, Rubin. For an excellent summary of this literature, see also Allan.

9. For further discussion of gender differences in identity formation, see Chodorow; Gilligan. See also di Leonardo.

10. For more on student responses to social-class differences and teaching strategies designed to encourage a greater understanding and appreciation of diversity, see Gardner, Dean, and McKaig.

11. Although the concept of "outsider within" was coined by Collins to describe the position of black feminist scholars, it can also be used to refer to other marginal members of the academy such as black men, working-class individuals, white women, religious and sexual minorities, and so forth (29). Similar to the position presented here, Collins argues that a marginal or outsider status can be a source of power and creative insight. For more on this theme, see Lorde: Rich, "What Does a Woman Need . . ." (1–10).

Works Cited

Allan, Graham. *A Sociology of Friendship and Kinship.* Boston: Allen, 1979.

Almquist, Elizabeth M. "The Experiences of Minority Women in the United States: Intersections of Race, Gender, and Class." *Women: A Feminist Perspective.* Ed. Jo Freeman. 4th ed. Mountain View, CA: Mayfield, 1989. 414–45.

Berson, Ginny. "Slumming It in the Middle Class." Bunch and Myron 56–62.

Brown, Rita Mae. "The Last Straw." Bunch and Myron 13–23.

Bunch, Charlotte, and Nancy Myron, eds. *Class and Feminism.* Baltimore: Diana, 1974.

Chodorow, Nancy. "Family Structure and the Feminine Personality." *Woman, Culture, and Society.* Ed. Michelle Zimbalist Rosaldo and Louise Lamphere. Stanford: Stanford UP, 1974. 43–66.

Clance, Pauline Rose. *The Impostor Phenomenon.* Atlanta: Peachtree, 1985.

Collins, Patricia Hill. "Learning from the Outsider Within: The Sociological Significance of Black Feminist Thought." *Social Problems* 33.6 (1986): 14–32.

di Leonardo, Micaela. "The Female World of Cards and Holidays: Women, Families, and the Work of Kinship." *Signs* 12 (1987): 440–53.

Gardner, Saundra, Cynthia Dean, and Deo McKaig. "Responding to Differences in the Classroom: The Politics of Knowledge, Class, and Sexuality." *Sociology of Education* 62.1 (1989): 64–74.

Gearhart, Sally Miller. "If the Mortarboard Fits . . . Radical Feminism in Academia." *Learning Our Way: Essays in Feminist Education.* Ed. Charlotte Bunch and Sandra Pollack. Trumansburg, NY: Crossing, 1983. 2–18.

Gilligan, Carol. *In a Different Voice.* Cambridge: Harvard UP, 1982.

Gowens, Pat. "An Impoverished Feminist Clarifies Class." *Sojourner* August 1986: 14–15.

Hughes, Nym. "Why I Can't Write About Class." *Fireweed: A Feminist Quarterly* 25 (1987): 21–24.

Lorde, Audre. "Age, Race, Class, and Sex: Women Redefining Difference." *Sister Outsider.* Trumansburg, NY: Crossing, 1984. 114–23.

McKenney, Mary. "Class Attitudes & Professionalism." *Quest: A Feminist Quarterly* 3.4 (1977): N. pag. Rpt. in *Building Feminist Theory: Essays from Quest.* Quest Book Committee. New York: Longman, 1981. 139–48.

Mills, C. Wright. *The Sociological Imagination.* London: Oxford UP, 1959.

Park, Robert E. *Race and Culture.* Glencoe, IL: Free, 1950.

Pheterson, Gail. "Alliances Between Women: Overcoming Internalized Oppression and Internalized Domination." *Signs* 12 (1986): 146–60.

Reid, Coletta, and Charlotte Bunch. "Revolution Begins at Home." Bunch and Myron 70–81.

Rich, Adrienne. "Toward a Woman-Centered University." *On Lies, Secrets, and Silence.* New York: Norton, 1979. 125–55.

——. "What Does a Woman Need to Know." *Blood, Bread, and Poetry.* New York: Norton, 1986. 1–10.

Rubin, Lillian. *Worlds of Pain.* New York: Basic, 1976.

Ryan, Jake, and Charles Sackrey. *Strangers in Paradise: Academics from the Working Class.* Boston: South End, 1984.

Sennett, Richard, and Jonathan Cobb. *The Hidden Injuries of Class.* New York: Vintage-Random House, 1973.

Who Am I Now? The Politics of Class Identity

I HAVE recurring dreams. Although the details change, my dreams generally portray my inability to feel at home in middle-class environments and my fear of betraying working-class friends.

In last night's dream I am living in Paris with a rich family and teaching at a university. On a sunny day I am riding my bike to the museum dressed in very pretty clothes and feeling happy. As I approach the museum a gardener looks up and we recognize each other. He is a friend of my parents. The gardener looks back down and without a word returns to his work. In one glance the gardener has called my bluff. I am reminded of who I am and how false the illusion of happiness based on privilege is. Because of my class background, I will notice working-class people; they are not invisible to me, and so I am reminded of privilege based on inequity.

In the dream the gardener had looked at me like I was part of the occupying forces, part of the crowds that enters the museum in their leisure time leaving trash for him to clean up. He did not give me the impartial look one gives a stranger. His glance communicated that he knew me, but didn't know if he wanted to.

Such is the general theme of my dreams—that I have betrayed my family and friends of origin by entering a world of privilege. And that any happiness based on the privilege of having things is an illusion when others live without so much.

My dreams often play out the dilemma I face coming from a working-class background and now, late in life, finding myself in a middle-class enemy camp of academia. I fear that my life has changed so much that my own people will not care to recognize me. I fear becoming oblivious to my privilege based on education (and in this country education itself is a privilege, not a right). I fear becoming no better than middle-class people who would look down on my family. I am afraid that by possessing the privilege of education I can hurt those I care about, unintentionally.

In the second part of this same dream I turn away from the museum after the encounter with the gardener and return to the home of the rich family I'm living with. I walk into the entryway of the house noticing all the space and beauty; marble staircases like ones I've scrubbed. But I feel unsafe in the house and don't want to stay. So I sort through the mail on a table taking some high-fashion magazines with me for my mother, knowing how she always liked Hollywood gossip magazines and thinking, "wouldn't she have fun looking at these?"

Another theme in my dreams highlights how unsafe I feel in middle- and upper-class settings. I often want to resolve these situations where I feel caught between worlds by taking something from the settings of privilege back to my family, my original community, something they would enjoy. But here is the dilemma—once you get into that setting of privilege, what is there that you can take back which would be anything more than a curiosity (i.e., high-fashion magazines)? What can I glean from the privilege of education that can be of use to my family and friends?

These dreams of visiting rich families are ironic because as a little girl I spent hours fantasizing that I had actually been adopted by my mother and that my real parents were very rich and would someday find me. I started hating my mother when I was about nine for the kind of life we had to lead on welfare. I don't remember hating her before I began to realize how little we had compared to some other kids in school. My clothes clued me in to my beginning recognition of my class position, since some kids had a semblance of matching outfits from Penney's or Sears and seemed quite well dressed compared to me in the hand-me-down clothes I got from aunts and neighbors.

Close to this same period, I was pushed further into misery when I discovered upper-middle-class people who I understood to be rich people. In our town there was a Santa Claus Lane, an upper-middle-class area of town that had decorated houses with lawn displays and Christmas lights. Families loaded up in broken-down station wagons like ours paid to drive through. Seeing houses like these made me truly miserable.

My mother pushed me toward a life of higher education very early, in the same way that if we had been Catholic she might have advocated the profession of a nun for me. She just wanted different choices for me than those she had had. My mother had been kicked out of high school at fifteen when she became pregnant with me. My mother, who was divorced in the 1950s at age twenty-one with no high school diploma and four children to support, understood only too well the need for my independence, an independence that she thought only an education and a career could give a woman. The high point of her dream was that I would become an elementary school teacher, one of her few models of an educated woman.

My mother and the other women in my family were highly respected for their intelligence and survival skills. I was totally indoctrinated by them with the idea that I possessed extraordinary intelligence and creativity. Because she was busy with diapers, bottles, and jobs, I have few distinct memories of interacting with my mother. But I do remember her praising my academic skills. One of the few memories of closeness I have with my mother is of her rewarding me with a pencil and plastic cup when at age four I wrote my whole name for her. I was encouraged to write stories and plays and she bragged to friends about my works. My parents transformed the garage in one of our old houses into a schoolhouse so that I could play the role of teacher to my captive siblings. At every turn my mother enhanced the formation of my identity as a smart, in-charge, capable, creative young girl. In this way she handed me a self-image that might enable me to strive toward that goal of becoming an elementary school teacher.

It was mandated that I was to go to college. Because of my mother's attitude it never occurred to me that I wouldn't. My mother didn't know many details of how you got there but she did review the college catalogs I brought home from high school and seemed to live vicariously through the possibility of my achieving a college education.

Although we lived just blocks away from the college campus in our town, I visited it only once, when my stepfather took me to sell Girl Scout cookies to the girls in the residence halls. My stepfather was very respectful toward these young women. My family had an interesting mixed attitude of fear and respect for specific people they might run into who possessed education and money, but disrespect in general for the rich and what they did to the poor.

We did not have the money to buy a lot of books, so my mother and aunt walked us regularly to the library to check out books. I was quite thrilled and felt so important and learned on my ninth birthday when I received a set of Golden Book encyclopedias bought week by week at the local Safeway grocery store by my great-grandmother. It was as fancy to me as a leather-bound set of the classics might have been to another kid. I always meant to read through all twenty-six volumes, but kept forgetting my place and starting over again with the first volume "A" and "aardvark."

We had enough books in our home to fill a bookcase; in our neighborhood, this was an accomplishment. These books made me feel very special, even though they were discarded library books, Golden Book encyclopedias, and trashy novels. Possessing books was a rarity, something special, the way possessing a Picasso might be in another neighborhood. My mother placed a high value on reading, but it was rather indiscriminate: Zane Grey novels and lots of movie magazines. My close relationship with books set me apart from other girls in school, who were busy with boyfriends and makeup. Although my bookworm habits were largely encouraged by my family, they often complained that I spent too much time alone in my room, so I was required to sit out in the living room and watch TV with everyone else for at least an hour a night.

By the time I entered junior high my mother had remarried and we moved into a "better" (i.e., lower-middle-class neighborhood). I was very ashamed of my parents and our tattered furniture and "beater" car. We couldn't afford carpeting in our home, so we went out to garbage bins behind carpet stores and heisted their remnants to make patchwork carpets. There was a class mixture in this neighborhood. Some worked in gas stations, as truck drivers, like my stepfather, or as file clerks, like my mother. Others worked as low-level professionals.

One family goal for girls in my setting was that they have good reputations and make good marriages. My parents were very vigilant about my reputation—to the point that I was actually afraid of boys, so I really didn't date until college. My mother took conscious actions to insulate me from her fate and the fate of other young girls around me: early marriage and pregnancy. I did well in school, and I was perceived as being special because I was to go to college. I was allowed to keep up friendships with some of my girlfriends—for instance Bonnie Witcher, who married at fifteen with me as her fourteen-year-old bridesmaid, or Linda Gonzales, who at twelve was sleeping with boys and had scars across her wrists from suicide attempts. These friends were allowed because they were the exception to the rule and I was probably being a "good influence" on them. I might occasionally befriend these girls but my mother made it clear that my circle of friends and my closest friends were to be girls like my best friend Nancy Sakaguchi, also a good student and "good girl." Our poverty also insulated me from early dating. My family did not have money for clothing. I could never achieve a datable look in second-hand clothes from an older aunt. In high school I remained an egghead student and I did not have a date until my senior year. By then hippie clothes had become fashionable so clothing codes relaxed a bit and acceptable clothes became somewhat more affordable, although the right kind of jeans weren't on K mart's and Penney's racks.

Among the many benefits of a good reputation was the assumption that it would lead to a good marriage. A bad reputation for a girl guaranteed that she would not be able to marry well or marry upward. To marry upward, besides a good reputation and extreme good looks, one also needed at least a modest degree of higher education—more than tech school or community college. In junior high and high school I was placed in advanced, honors, and college-bound classes, but most of the people in these classes were higher in the class hierarchy than I. None of my friends, except Nancy Sakaguchi, were in these classes. It was a given in my family that I had to achieve an A average to get a scholarship. A B on my report card was equivalent to an F.

Right out of high school I had a college scholarship, but I was not drawn to "the classics." The material taught in college classrooms was written mainly by, for, and about white privileged males. It provided me with few opportunities for self-discovery. I later found that mothering and organizing at work offered richer learning experiences than studying footnotes.

In college, just as in honors classes at high school, I continued to be in places where my friends weren't. It was lonely and isolating and it was hard to maintain the friends I had who were working or at the community college. In a way it was only natural for me to be in college—I had been prepared for it like the priesthood. But it was also unnatural to be there, away from people I knew. I lasted one year before I quit to work and marry. Although at twenty I had what would be considered a good marriage because my husband was a nice, sober, hard-working man, my mother was very disappointed that I had not finished college but married a gardener with little education or apparent future.

In my extended family, adults place great value on children in the family. They measure the success of their lives by having good produc-

tive children and grandchildren. The way that one lives her life therefore carries great importance since it reflects on her family. In many
ways one's life represents the accumulated interest and investment of
parents, grandparents, and other family members. Children are cher-
ished in my family. Jobs are just the means that allow you to provide the
best you can for your children. Being a mother and having children
seemed a more important and rewarding goal to me than getting an
education. Two weeks after my first wedding anniversary my first son
was born.

My life echoed my mother's when, at age twenty-three, I became a
single parent with little education and few skills. I often felt ashamed of
my living conditions as a single parent. I would buy lots of books at the
Salvation Army whose titles I recognized as classics. They would sit as
decorations on my bookshelves indicating a level of reading compre-
hension I wanted to reach someday.

My route to academia was very indirect and "nontraditional,"
which is much more common for working-class people, if they ever take
it at all. I had children and a variety of jobs for years—clerk, waitress,
factory worker, oil refinery crew. It took me twelve years to complete my
bachelor's. I was depressed at my graduation ceremony—here I was with
all these young kids who were receiving their college diplomas as if it
were perfectly natural rather than a decade-long struggle.

My family was very proud that I went on for an M.A. and Ph.D., but
they couldn't quite understand why I would. It was odd and foreign to
them, no one they personally knew had done such a thing. When I
finished my Ph.D., my grandparents thought I had just finished my M.A.
They weren't sure what the difference was between the two.

There were so many hurdles to get past before reaching Ph.D.
status. I actually turned in my Ph.D. application late. I couldn't imagine
that I would be smart enough or good enough to go that far. It was so
hard to muster up the self-confidence to state why I should be in a
graduate program.

Access to higher education is very limited for poor and working-
class students. Education under these conditions is only an option if one
takes out loans that have to be paid back. My college loans are as big as
many home mortgages, and so are the monthly payments. In retrospect
my education was a very expensive luxury, although I wanted so badly
to get an education that at the time it felt like a necessity. I had no

65

savings, no decent car, furniture, or clothes when I started graduate school. I had no family I could depend on for help. I was a single parent and my part-time day-care costs were higher than the rent some of my fellow graduate students were paying. Yet TA positions were not based on need but on the old boys' network. I was the only single parent in the political science department at a very large university, but I had a TA position for only one quarter of my four years there. I was very fortunate that the women's studies department was more supportive, employing me every quarter, but because I hadn't been a TA in political science, I had no competitive edge in applying for jobs after graduation. Unlike other graduate students, my study time began after my children were in bed—sleep was a luxury. The weight of work and study loads in graduate school, working with less money, sleep, and support than other students, was extremely stressful. At one point I became clinically depressed—a well-meaning psychiatrist suggested antidepressants or quitting school. I rejected both. My main motive was to find a better way to support my children. Quitting school was a luxury I could not afford.

I AM NOW with a partner from a class background similar to mine who has one year of community college education. We are very close for a variety of reasons but there are times when I am painfully reminded of the difference education can make. I'll look at her misspelled words on the grocery list and be quietly faced with a reflection of myself just a decade ago. But education is not a measure of intelligence. My parents and grandparents have no education beyond grade school or high school, yet they are among the most intelligent people I know. Education, though, does give one privilege. Those little initials behind one's name (M.A., Ph.D.) bring a lot of benefits and status. The ability to gain these letters is predominately a reflection of class background.

As a single-parent graduate student I had to frequent the food bank and to do this meant standing outside in line on one of the busiest streets in the university district. Sometimes other graduate students would walk by or be the ones who passed out the groceries to me. At a certain point I became afraid that students I was teaching would see me, so I tried to go to the lines as seldom as possible and as early as possible. If my status as welfare mother was recognized by my students, I would receive more hassles in the classroom and lower teaching evaluations.

In graduate school verbal cruelty seemed to be the rule of the day. In the factories I've worked in, if you talk down to another worker you can expect to be "punched out." The basic operating procedures of academia and graduate school are offensive to me. They are based on competitive game playing, which in working-class settings would make you an outcast. Competitions among graduate students and faculty to out-ego each other were hilarious at times. In my previous work environments this type of behavior had specific names: "brown nosing," "kissing ass," and so on. In graduate school I was expected to shift cultural gears and act in these ways on a regular basis in order to receive a high grade or respect from my peers. I remained one of the quieter members in group settings, whether committee meetings or classroom.

I often felt isolated as the only working-class person in various situations. I received a fellowship in graduate school and had to attend a banquet at a country club. I had never been to a country club in my life. It was hard to find something to wear. I purchased the best blouse I could at a second-hand store; my girlfriend, Laura Esparza, sewed my skirt; I bought my oldest son a new suit at Penney's and pulled into the parking lot of the country club in a very beat-up car with bumper stickers that read "The world can no longer afford the rich" and "End Racism." Coming from a working-class background guarantees that you will feel uncomfortable in middle- and upper-class settings. The evening was painfully amusing; I was a stranger in a strange land.

By entering academia, I sometimes found myself tossed into class settings I would have preferred to avoid. As a graduate student I was sometimes invited to meet important scholars at nice restaurants or receptions. I was seldom able to work up enough courage to overcome the difficulties these settings presented. Keeping up a different set of "manners" and pretentious small talk is an exhausting experience.

Middle-class dress is the standard in academia. When I worked at a fish factory or oil refinery, there were dress codes for work. Now in academia the dress code is largely middle-class preppie or middle-class hippie chic. It is much more difficult for me to dress in jeans and sweatshirts like middle-class white male colleagues and be treated respectfully by students and peers alike. I feel a need to dress up and look professional to maintain what I experience as a tenuous position.

While I was on fellowship in London a friend and I were looking one evening for a place to eat. I followed her lead into what turned out to be a very exclusive restaurant. Although we were both dressed casually, I sat down in shock, humiliation, and tears. It was totally intimidating for me to walk into a setting like that. I had a sense of not belonging because of who I am. It was painful for me to be there. I will never feel comfortable in extravagant classist settings and I feel no compelling reason to subject myself to those situations. I still shop largely at Penney's, but I do look for labels when I go to second-hand clothes stores. Looking for labels is learned class behavior. Until I entered the academic workplace, I never knew labels had any function beyond giving cleaning instructions.

Because of my education and job, I often have little control over the worlds I enter socially. So I continue to live in two worlds, aware of the violence between them. Academe is a new place of loneliness for me. Most academics from working-class backgrounds end up on the bottom of the academic heap. They receive little guidance or mentoring from professors, which is particularly detrimental because their network of family and friends is not connected to academia. They are expected to know instinctively how to do all the things that one does in that world. Access to education and to decent jobs is based on inherited advantage. If one has no familiarity with academic models of professionalism she is at a great disadvantage. The modus operandi among middle-class careerists is based on competition.

Career consciousness is a skill learned in middle-class families. In working-class families people are more concerned with getting and keeping jobs. It never occurred to me when I won scholarships to attend institutions of higher learning, that it made a difference which school I went to. A B.A. was a B.A., right? And when hunting for my first teaching job it still didn't seem important to pay attention to where I taught, as long as I had a job. Because of the way we are socialized the working class produces very poor careerists. Our network of friends are seldom connected to academia. I hate that I am still intimidated by the same sorts of privileges that have intimidated my parents: those of education, titles, and settings.

I used to think that I was very shy, but over the years I've realized that I only have trouble in middle-class settings. The worst for me are the academic meetings where I'm surrounded by middle-class people whose speech and behavior dominate the meetings. It's like never getting out of graduate seminars. There is an underlying assumption that people of color and women don't belong in academia and are there as a result of affirmative action. The way one acts and talks can give away class background.

68

I now have many conflicting feelings about working in an institution which is supposed to separate working people from the middle class. Traditionally, the B.A. or M.A. was a degree of class certification. I work with a number of students from working-class backgrounds who have come to college hoping that education will lead to the good life. But most of the education they receive in university settings will serve only to perpetuate dominant values. The culture of most working-class kids places them at a disadvantage in an educational setting. Most privileges are the result of class advantage, and in order to gain these privileges, the working-class students must be willing to become middle-class impersonators. They have to learn not just the course content, but a new culture as well. Students from middle-class backgrounds have a jump on them.

As I came closer to completing the work toward my Ph.D., I started to worry about what my class background was. The thought that I might not be working class had never occurred to me before. Something about obtaining that piece of paper and having an official job title was frightening because they seemed to have the ability to change my identity. Becoming a traitor to my class was a frightening possibility. Tillie Olsen has stated that with race and class there's no such thing as passing. I generally agree with her statement, but because class has both economic and cultural dimensions, I am concerned that I may lose my ability to recognize fully the privileges I now have.

What determines class identity? It's not sheer economics because I earned substantially more on an oil refinery crew eight years ago than I do now in academia. It's more than income; it also has to do with the range of choices one has in life.

I come from white working class. This is true in terms of my family of origin and because I have also spent my adult life as a single parent, welfare mother, and factory or clerical worker. For the first time in my life I've begun to question my class identity. I entered academia when I was in my late thirties and I struggled to stay. I've obtained education far beyond the level of others with my class background. I worked two jobs and raised children as a single parent for years while I was also in school. My children and I survived the enormous economic and psychological stress that is the lot of anyone who enters an environment that is unfamiliar and—in a sense—even forbidden.

This is not the first time I have gone into a hostile environment. In the mid-1970s I worked in nontraditional blue-collar jobs in an attempt to support my children. I encountered substantial sexism. I was not supposed to be in that male work setting. In the early 1980s I entered graduate school and the world of academics in an attempt to find a "better" way to support my children. I encountered sexism, heterosexism, and classism at every turn. I was not supposed to be in that middle-class work setting.

I feel that I must acknowledge the incredible privileges I have acquired as a result of the educational and job status I have achieved. At the same time I feel great anger when middle-class academics circle me ready to crown me with a new class status. What do you call a working-class person who is uppity enough to get a good education? Middle-class people may become confused when working-class people gain educational and job benefits they are used to monopolizing. With classism intact, they would have either to think less of themselves for working the same job as someone from a different class background, or to think more of working-class people by elevating them to middle-class status. Thus when working-class people enter a middle-class environment like academia, they are defined out of existence. Since we seem to "talk like" or "think like" educated people, we must be middle class. But someone from a middle-class background in the same job will not have the school loans and family responsibilities I have. With fewer credentials they will be viewed more favorably. It never fails to amaze me how just acting with dominating, elitist classist attitudes is described as being "brilliant." In graduate school any male who acted like a "prick" was viewed as being very intelligent, as was anyone with a classist attitude. Out at the factory the same type of behavior would be stupid, arrogant, and egotistical.

The second I have conferred upon me an appropriate job title the middle class is anxious to claim me as one of its own. Is being middle class contagious? Can you catch it by working with people who are? The most ethical response that I've been able to come up with so far about my class identity is simply to state that I was raised and spent the majority of my life as working class or poor, but that as to what I am now, I don't know. If I were to define my own identity I would say that I'm a working-class person who has privilege due to my education. When I expressed my fear that once I got an official piece of paper (Ph.D.) I would become middle class, my friend Gloria Yamato just laughed and told me that I am merely what a working-class person with an education is like. Still, I think I have something like heterosexual privilege now due to education and job title. I think that I sometimes can pass in terms of class, and this scares me. If you are a professor, most people will assume you *have* to be middle class.

Class is complex and has different meanings and experiences in different settings. There is a difference between the urban working class and the rural working class. Class is defined differently in African-American, American Indian, Asian-American, and Latino communities. There is a very complex system of class differences and privilege among the working class. Within the white working-class community, members of my father's family were solidly working class because they had unionized jobs and owned a modest house and furniture. My mother's family was working poor, composed mostly of female-headed households where women worked as barmaids, waitresses, and in service occupations. I have had enormous privilege by being white within the working class. It has been a struggle to pursue my educational goals but because of the privilege that comes from being white, some things have been more possible for me than for other friends and co-workers.

I also had the advantage at one time of heterosexual privilege, which counts for a lot when you're a woman. Heterosexual privilege directly contributed to my ability to attend graduate school. My second relationship was with someone from a middle-class background who understood and supported my desire for education. I was in this relationship during the last year of my undergraduate work and the two years of my M.A. and when I made the decision to go on for my Ph.D., my partner, who had gone as far as the M.A., was not particularly supportive of this last step because it meant I would have more education than he did. The relationship ended. My middle-class partner earned less money than my working-class husband, but there was a value placed on education. Being heterosexual allowed me the possibility of attaining some privileges outside my class through a male partner. Being connected to middle-class white male income brings some class privilege. Heterosexual privilege in and of itself may not carry economic benefits for women of color or for white women not connected to white middle-class men.

I have a lot of conflicting feelings and a lot of guilt about my upward mobility in terms of status. I feel that my working-class background marks me in academia and that my middle-class education marks me in working-class settings. I sometimes feel like an impostor in both camps. I do not feel that I don't belong in working-class settings but I seldom feel at home in middle-class situations.

When I worked as one of the first women on an oil refinery crew, there was an understanding that only one woman was allowed on any single crew, so women never got to work with each other. The underlying reasoning was that we weren't competent and didn't really belong there. If there were more than one woman per crew it would mess things up (yeah, like challenge some stereotypes). I have few working-class allies in academia. The more prestigious a university, the fewer faculty from working-class backgrounds are there, so those who do make it lack mentoring and with it the knowledge about what things look good on a resumé. I also lack money and time to spend on extra activities to boost my academic profile. No matter how qualified we are, those of us from working-class backgrounds are seldom viewed as being as competent as someone with the proper middle-class speech and mannerisms.

In academia I usually feel safest teaching and doing research. I actually love those parts of my job. I often feel unsafe or have a sense of not belonging in meetings, committees, and socials. I don't always understand the rules of middle-class academia that others seem to know.

I thought my education would take me away from assembly-lines, but I'm caught now on an academic treadmill of research, publishing, and teaching. At least when I worked at the factory my hours were set; my home life and work life were separate. Now they blend together and I work seven days a week. In what used to be my leisure time, I'm writing articles while my children run around in the house.

For the most part, I focus on the things that bring me joy: teaching, research, my children, grandchildren, other family, and friends. I try to ignore the middle-class game-playing bullshit that goes along with the job. I know perhaps I should concentrate on changing the rules, but frankly I'm vastly outnumbered and I can think of many more interesting things to do with my time. Some at work may think I'm distant or uninvolved. Like others with a typical country-club mentality, it's hard for them to figure out why I wouldn't want to belong. Academia was supposed to be my way out of the factory. Now, I wonder what will be my way out of academia?

Writing and Teaching with Class

As a novelist who writes about working-class lives, I often find myself at odds with the academy and with mainstream American publishing. When working-class people aren't ignored in current literature, they are portrayed as "other"—either as characters who "used to be" or as caricatures fundamentally alienated from the essential New World possibility. I get cranky about what does get published and heralded, and angry about what doesn't. For writers from working-class families, the making of art can be a cultural disenfranchisement, for we do not belong in literary circles and our writing rarely makes it back home. Those of us who write about our class heritage experience a variety of censorship and self-censorship.

In this chapter I will explore the experiences of the "working-class writer" in the academy from two foci. First, I will consider the creation of the books themselves and their critical reception. Then I will examine the place of the writer as teaching worker in the university. I have chosen to start with the writing because my fiction is my "professional contribution," parallel to my academic colleagues' scholarship. The obstacles I encounter from publishers and critics in the making of working-class literature reflect problems encountered by scholars creating criticism about working-class literature. They also mirror some of the frustrations of my working-class students. Finally, it is appropriate to begin with the writing and then move on to the teaching because one usually has to publish fiction before one is asked to teach fiction-writing classes.

Every day I wonder whether writing is a form of lunacy or betrayal. One of my parents didn't go past grade eight and the other didn't finish high school. My mother works in an all-night coffee shop and her goal for me has always been "to get a good job at the telephone company." She still doesn't understand my work and worries—justifiably—how I make a living from writing. There were few books in our house, no symphonies on the Victrola, no high drama except at the Sunday dinner table. One of my brothers grew up to be a carpenter. The other works for a maritime union. So I've always carried that Miner suspicion that laboring with words is not real work. I ask myself: Does writing mean anything? Do I have a right to feel tired at week's end? Shouldn't I be doing something useful?

I decided to talk with other women who grew up working class about reading, writing, and attitudes toward work. I talked with poets and novelists whose parents were waitresses, builders, typists, migrant farmers, and mechanics. I chose writers from "the first generation" Tillie Olsen discusses in *Silences*, people who emigrated from their working-class households into the professions (262). Many were, like me, the first to go through college, surprising everyone by becoming something as exotic and impractical as a writer. Many no longer call themselves working class, given their current possibilities and privileges.[1] Yet the art remains influenced by childhood experience. Despite obstacles, everyone was adamantly grateful to families for a certain kind of vigor and common sense. Our conversations turned on the treatment of our books in the American library scene and on our personal experiences of cross-class immigration.

Americans pretend we are a classless society. Everyone is potentially middle-class. Like Original Sin, working-class origin is a state from which we are saved—by working hard and being good (Americans). Working class is a past we acknowledge only when we want to demonstrate how far we have progressed. During the last ten years American fiction has turned intensely solipsistic. We read endless odysseys of lawyers and doctors and teachers paddling through psychotherapy, divorce, bankruptcy, and religious crisis. Some of these books are fascinating. But they do not define the parameters of serious literature. Reading the *New York Times*, one is tempted to think that the archetypal American journey is "Ennui in Westport." Critic Diane Johnson has named such work "fiction of the self" (15). Indeed, it is a fiction of the middle-class self. In contrast to more voguish literary obsessions with *isolated* relationships, working-class novels rarely situate characters alone. More likely, characters are portrayed in the workplace, in union meetings, in neighborhoods.

As Joyce Carol Thomas tells me, "It's easier to find material from middle-class life in contemporary American literature—perhaps because publishers are from that world. We're all more comfortable with what we know." Thomas's *Marked by Fire* is a dramatic novel about a black girl in Oklahoma. She considers it serious adult fiction, but when it failed to sell to that market, she was forced to publish it as a "young adult novel." It later won two American Book awards.

Marge Piercy observes, "There's a prejudice that the lives of people who have less [are] less interesting. A prejudice that people who have less, think less and feel less." Piercy's novels open a light on her own youth in the Detroit streets, perhaps none more hauntingly than *Braided Lives*, which traces the hopes of two working-class students at the University of Michigan in the 1950s.

There's working-class and there's working-class. You have a very different sense of identity, possibility, disadvantage, and advantage depending on such factors as race, ethnic group, sex, and region. Class bias is different from racism and many writers of color face a double jeopardy.

JOYCE CAROL THOMAS says, "It's dangerous to put all blacks in one class. Of course what distinguishes blacks from whites is that for most of us somewhere in our near history is a working-class relative, within one or two generations."

Certain kinds of working-class labor are typed by ethnic group. Gloria Anzaldúa writes movingly about her family's experience as agricultural laborers in the poem, "sus plumas el viento," from *Borderlands/La Frontera*.

> cutting   washing   weighing   packaging
> broccoli spears carrots cabbages in 12 hours 15
> double shift the roar of machines inside her head.
> She can always clean shit
> out of white folks toilets—the Mexican maid.   (118)

Anzaldúa's book, like the work of many marginalized writers, is published by an independent press, in this case, Spinsters/Aunt Lute Book Company in San Francisco.

Censorship in mainstream publishing houses and the review media is legend. The often unconscious dismissal of working-class writing at the editor's desk is a pernicious sort of censorship because it is subtle and often hard to document. But we can piece together the personal stories. And they are not just women's stories. After a substantial track record, William Kennedy submitted *Ironweed*, his novel about an ex-

75

ballplayer and part-time grave-digger, for a year and a half before it was accepted by Viking. Later *Ironweed* won a Pulitzer Prize. Novelist Doro- thy Bryant was told that *Ella Price's Journal* didn't have enough interest to sustain a novel. "Later I found out this was the only novel about a col- lege reentry woman that was not about an upper-middle-class woman." Once the book was published, it went on to sell eighty thousand copies and Bryant was invited to address groups of working-class women at community colleges in different parts of the country.

Of course writers from all backgrounds complain about rejection. What unifies the response of these writers is that they were informed the subjects of their work were uninteresting or not appropriate literary material.

When such books do traverse the publishing hurdles, few win the Pulitzer Prize. More likely, they encounter ignorant or hostile critics. Many of the writers I interviewed referred to "better days" in the 1930s and 1940s. Before the Cold War, radical artistic solidarity flourished, but McCarthyism silenced much literature about union struggle. Many authors were blacklisted and others, like Agnes Smedley, forgotten. (By the way, I'm grateful to see that The Feminist Press has resurrected some of these books.) For the most part that old fellowship of hope is taken less seriously now and contemporary literature is marinated in cynicism.

Studs Terkel tells me, "The problem is the whole climate of the country. Never before has labor been held in such ill repute. You have young kids today who are critical of the labor movement yet they don't know that it was because of labor organizing that we got the minimum wage. They don't know about Haymarket. They don't know about the Memorial Day Massacre of 1937."

Perhaps a deeper problem than the external censorship of pub- lishers and critics is self-censorship by writers who never imagine the possibility of publishing or by others who omit material to accommo- date editors. At best the class bias makes authors from working-class families angry and provides a momentum to "catch up." At worst, it paralyzes writers with doubt. As Tillie Olsen says, "There's little to validate one's own sense of reality." Self-censorship in working-class art exacerbates the effect of outside censorship. You think you are a poor writer. You think you are crazy for wanting to describe such people, your people. Self and outside censorship make you aware that class denial is seamed into the American cultural psyche.

The very content—descriptions of waitresses and secretaries and construction workers—is passing family codes to middle-class outsiders. Of course anyone who writes faces issues of confidentiality. But class compounds the dilemma because of the power inequity between the working-class characters and the often middle-class audience. For some working-class people the secrets seem all they have. Thus writing about them feels like betrayal.

Or desertion. Moving from this background into the professions is an immigration. Writing is particularly alien because it embraces literacy, sometimes the major obstacle to parents' success. Certain cultures emphasize reading more than others, but for many working-class people, becoming a writer is like moving to a country where a different language is spoken. Your family cannot reach you. Gradually you lose touch with them. Soon you become a stranger, a descendant before your generation. Writers from middle-class or upper-class families also protest, "My parents don't understand me." But the rift between writer and working-class parent is more profound than the friction between an artist and the parent who wants to pass on the family law shingle. In becoming a writer, the working-class person makes an irrevocable shift, moving beyond the family's imagination.

Maureen Duffy discusses this in the introduction to the new edition of *That's How It Was*, her passionate novel about working-class childhood in England during World War II: "As I had gone along with the educational process my goal had receded toward the glorious heights of ambition to go to university and be a writer. This last I hadn't really confessed to anyone. I disguised it under the professed intention of becoming a teacher. It was asking a lot to be the first of the family to go to university. Then to propose to throw away everything that had been struggled for in the vain hope of being that most despised thing, a poet, was unmentionable."

Sherley Anne Williams, who writes poetry, drama, and fiction tells me, "My family doesn't understand why I spend long hours in my bedroom writing. They think it's self-indulgent." Williams calls herself "pre-working-class" because she was raised on welfare by a widowed mother.

Tess Gallagher's fiction and poetry often draw on the lives of her farmer mother and longshoreman father. Her work is threaded with the painful distance between her life and theirs, such as in the poem, "3 A.M. Kitchen: My Father Talking,"

I quit the woods. One day just
walked out, took off my corks, said that's
it. I went to the docks.
I was driving winch. You had watch
to see nothing fell out of the sling. If
you killed somebody you'd
never forget it. All
those years I was just working
I was on the edge, every day. Just working.   (30)

Gallagher tells me, "My father shook his head when I said I wanted to be a writer. He thought I was mad. My mother told me I was just nervous and she taught me to knit. They took it seriously when I earned some money. I made $350 for a poem in the *The New Yorker*. I got a steady job teaching. They knew I wasn't going to be destitute."

My own experience is similar. My mother still wants me to get a real job. My father, who is retired after forty-four years in the merchant marine, has never read my work. When I visited recently, the only book in his house was the telephone book. He asked a neighbor to read my new novel and tell him about it. My brother, the carpenter, thinks I'm crazy to work without a contract. How can I put four or five years into a novel when I don't know if anyone is going to publish it? He wouldn't install a kitchen without a contract. My brother, the union representative, thinks I'm idealistic for trying to organize writers through the National Writers Union.

Let me tell you a story. A few years ago I took a leave from teaching at U.C. Berkeley (my *real* job, the one that pays me regularly) to finish the draft of my new novel, *All Good Women*. I went to the Boston area, in order to get far away from home in an amicable environment, and I rented a flat in Somerville. One afternoon as I was leaving the apartment building an old woman stopped me in the lobby. "Don't you work?" she asked, surprised to see a young woman hanging around during the day. "Yes," I said, "I work here. I'm a writer." She seemed baffled and nodded good-bye. The following week she stopped me again. "Don't you work?" she asked. "Yes," I said. "I work upstairs. I write novels." She stared at me. "Oh," she pondered, "I live upstairs, too. But don't you have to work?" I sighed and tried again. "I work at home," I moved my fingers over an imaginary keyboard, "at the typewriter." She regarded me with concern, "Upstairs?" I breathed a sigh of relief. "Yes, upstairs on the third floor." She spoke more loudly now. "Yes, I live upstairs, too. Are you a nurse?" Finally I explained that I was late for an appointment. I dreaded the possibility of seeing her again. Perhaps the reason the woman haunted me was that she echoed those familiar family questions. And I cannot walk away from them. Because of my family I feel as if I have always been late, as if I shall never catch up.

The emotional toll of crossing classes can be enormous. Chances are, by the time you are a published writer in this country, you have moved into the middle class because publishing is largely shut to unschooled people. Thus, because you have gone through college—and even if you're not making a grand salary—you have certain middle-class choices not available to your parents. This process can leave you wrenched by guilt, angry and ashamed by the limitations of your youth yet still disoriented in the middle-class America where you supposedly belong. Your family dismisses the irrevocable changes (after all, they were on their way there too) and the journey is discredited. To the outside world you may look middle-class but you know your birthmarks. Your background plays against you in large and small ways—in friends' incomprehensible references to those early books "everybody read" and to their childhood contacts from "the right schools."

In Marge Piercy's *Braided Lives*, Jill distills her identity during the fourth week of college. "We are poor; we are on scholarships; we are ill dressed; we take the hard courses and come from the wrong cities and addresses; we will not be rushed by sororities" (43). The tangible differences between Jill and her classmates are measured in her sorties to the dorm laundry to steal lingerie, her strategy of eating ravenously on dates to ward off next week's hunger, the brutal abortion she inflicts on herself because she cannot afford safe medical care, the fact that the word "camp" conjures her brother's basic training rather than summer expeditions or idiosyncratic humor. Throughout college Jill and her cousin Donna reassure each other that they are not crazy, that they just came from a "different" background.

Another perspective of cross-class movement in college is offered by Professor Nan Weaver in my novel *Murder in the English Department*. Nan grew up in the cannery town of Hayward and often feels at sea on the elite campus where she teaches.

Perhaps Nan was too conscious of class. She knew she was defensive about being the working-class kid from the cannery. It was something she could never change, no matter who she married or where she worked. Nan, the Buddy Holly fan, and Marjorie, the opera patron.

Nan sometimes worried that Marjorie and the other students could tell she wasn't smart. Oh, maybe she had a knack for common sense, but she wasn't a genuine intellectual. Nan attributed all her academic success to effort rather than intelligence. Although she was a professor at one of the best American universities, although she had published widely, she still didn't feel like a scholar. She felt like a fraud. (27–28)

Those who cross classes like Nan and Jill often remain dissociated for life. Long after they become writers, their nerves pinch—a dialect slips; a social cue is missed. They are gripped by a cultural agoraphobia, paralyzed in "normal" society yet unable to return home.

Still I find that most writers from working-class families are conscious of wanting to make literature accessible. Many choose clear, nonobfuscatory language and colloquial diction.

It's hard to carry the books home. Conventional distribution networks don't accommodate working-class people (the lucky ones who escape the huge pit of American illiteracy). Bookshops—even glitzy chains—can be intimidating. The books these people do encounter—at the supermarket or discount store—are rarely serious fiction or poetry. Singlejack Books gains access to working-class readers by advertising in union journals and conducting a mail-order business. Some authors have found individual solutions. Mary Helen Washington, editor of *Midnight Birds* and *Black Eyed Susans,* reached a large number of black women by taking stacks of the anthologies to her beauty parlor in Detroit. Dorothy Bryant became so disgusted with standard publishing procedures after publishing novels with Lippincott and Random House that she started her own publishing company, Ata Books, through which she has published eight novels and two other books. Some black churches display African-American poetry and novels in their vestibules. "You have to take the books to where the people are," explains Joyce Carol Thomas.

LET'S SWITCH the focus from how working-class writing is treated by American institutions to how the "working-class writing teacher" is treated in our colleges. As someone who has taught for nineteen years, the last eleven of which were at U.C. Berkeley, I can say that the experience is one of being a kind of step-relative. In addition to sharing the same disorientation described by many scholars in this volume, I find class tensions are exacerbated for the novelist teacher as she confronts the university's valuing of the criticism of art over the making of art.

Like many other college teachers from working-class homes, I am amazed when I look around and see myself teaching. Sometimes, like my character Nan, I feel a fraud, fearful that someone will discover I don't belong in front of the classroom. I often find it easier to make friends with clerical workers or low-level administrative staff than with other faculty. I know there is something about my talk, walk, and body language that distinguishes me from my "colleagues." Since most of my teaching has been in elite institutions, these characteristics also often distinguish me from my students. Several times I have had students in my seminar declare, "Of course all of us come from middle-class families," or "I guess everyone's father here is a doctor or lawyer or something like that." Yes, I "come out" at times like this, but the necessity of doing so is disheartening. Why should I be surprised? The university is simply a reflection of a hegemonic culture. Even the affirmative action forms—screening for gender, age, race, and physical ability—don't consider questions about class.

The academy's schizophrenic attitude regarding the labor of art is manifest in its privileging of analysis and the teaching of analytical skills over imagination and the teaching of imaginative skills. Administrators forget the creativity required by good scholarship and the intellectual rigor of serious art. All this explains the equivocal way most universities (especially those without organized creative writing programs) admit writers onto the faculty.

Generally, teaching is more readily perceived as labor than is writing. In fact, some academics see their own writing as a reward for the drudgery of teaching. The rift between writing and teaching deserves an essay of its own. The rift is partially caused by romantic misconceptions about the cloistered pleasures of writing (indeed, I would say that the notion of solitary genesis is itself a misapprehension of the authentic literary process). In American society, the individual enterprise of writing is celebrated over the social service of teaching. The recompense for the former is often supposed to be the experience itself whereas the latter deserves a material wage. Academics perceive the university as a preserve of intellectual analysis in an often hostile, philistine world. Analysis is sometimes artificially juxtaposed with imagination. And novelists or poets who are portrayed as "creative" are taken less seriously than those faculty whose work is "critical" or "theoretical." Likewise, the teaching of intuitive imaginative skills is less highly prized than the development of "serious" scholars.

81

I often think the academic ranking order rivals the military's in stupidity and rigidity. In the University of California faculty system, we have the standard tenure track—professor, associate professor, assistant professor, and, beneath that, lecturer. Lecturers are paid less and teach more than tenure-track faculty. In fact, on the Berkeley campus, lecturers do 50 percent of the undergraduate teaching. Although lecturers are valuable troops, they have little power within the institution and cannot even vote in the faculty senate. Across the country, writers are traditionally hired at this lower level and consequently work for substandard wages and with little job security—an experience that mirrors their treatment by publishers. For the writer from a working-class family, the university class system is all too familiar.

Still, it is virtually impossible to earn a living from writing serious fiction or poetry in this country, so many writers subject themselves to misunderstanding and mistreatment in the academy. The misunderstanding emerges, I think, from that fairy-tale version of writers' lives as well as from an unstated competitiveness between critics and writers.

Six years ago, after being invited to teach creative writing in the English department (my main appointment was in another department), the chair took me out for coffee. I asked why the English department, which had a faculty of over eighty academics, didn't hire fiction writers for tenure-track positions. There was a huge student demand for fiction classes—over one hundred students applied for fifteen places in my class. "Oh," he explained, "We've found that writers like to travel around from school to school. They like the freedom."

"They"? And freedom from what? Freedom from a regular salary? Freedom from health insurance? Freedom from institutional postage, telephone, and duplicating subsidies? Freedom from research assistants? Freedom from university grants and fellowships? Freedom from access to good libraries? Freedom from sabbaticals? I wasn't sure what kind of freedom "they" liked.

Later, I spoke to another department member, someone who had strongly supported my work. She suggested that in order to get a tenure-track job in that department I should go away to another place and then I would be perceived as valuable. But, I said, I lived for four years in Canada and three years in England as a writer. I get invited all over the world to give readings and lectures. "Try living in Massachusetts," she said. Another friendly English department colleague suggested I return to graduate school and get a Ph.D. She knew that I had published widely and had extensive teaching experience. She knew that I had no real interest in teaching literary criticism and that taking five or six years out from my writing might be damaging to my fiction. But she also knew that I would be more acceptable to her colleagues if I passed through the same boot camp. All of these people were generous and thoughtful; all of them liked me and my work. I did not take their responses personally because I knew them to be generic academic attitudes toward writers.

Why don't academics welcome writers into English (and Spanish and French and Italian) departments? Perhaps it's as simple as people understanding what they have experienced—to return to Joyce Carol Thomas's point about publishers. Perhaps it has more of an edge than that. Sometimes I think academics resent writers who want to take a "short cut" to tenure—avoiding the basic training of the Ph.D. programs. Some scholars are jealous of writers—and irritated that they spend so much of their lives writing about writers. Witness the new vogue in literary criticism as veiled autobiography. And some scholars want the "fun" of teaching a creative writing course without doing their own basic training in the writing and publishing scenes. Nonscholar writers not only present the threat of "the other" but they are sometimes more professionally accomplished in fiction or poetry because they have devoted more years to that work.

For the writer from a working-class family, who is constantly battling for her place in the publishing world and suffers reflexive doubts about belonging in the academy, being relegated to the low "class" of lecturer or adjunct exacerbates deep questions about authenticity.

Recently I attended a meeting of a feminist research group at school. Afterward I walked across campus with another lecturer. We both wondered about the identity of a new woman faculty member. Back at the office, we ran into a colleague (a tenured department chair) and asked who X was. She replied, "Oh, I don't know. It doesn't matter. She's just a lecturer." We reminded our colleague that the two of us were "just lecturers." She shrugged off her gaff.

A few months later I was attending a meeting for faculty involved with women's studies. The tenured professor in charge of Title Nine issues was explaining how she worked to support assistant professors in their struggle for tenure, to increase the number of women professors on campus, and to improve their status. Innocently, I asked what her office did for lecturers. "Well," she said, "lecturers? We don't have anything to do with lecturers. We only deal with faculty."

At Berkeley, lecturers do not have access to paid leaves, sabbaticals, fellowships, votes in the academic senate. Most of us have inferior office space, even though we have full-time teaching positions and responsibility for advising many students. In my division, full-time lecturers have to share their offices with one or two other people while some professors who are not even teaching full time have more than one office to themselves. We have one interdisciplinary program, with seven hundred student majors and *no* tenure-track faculty teaching the core courses (students could use existing courses in sociology, political science, or whatever to earn credits for graduation) and no tenure-track faculty advising. All the work falls to lecturers—who do not have access to normal faculty salaries or professional rights on the campus.

By now it's fairly apparent that the situation became unbearable. I finally quit my job at Berkeley after eleven years. At first the dean refused to believe that's what I was doing. Quitting Berkeley? He asked me to take a leave of absence. I turned him down because I knew the situation would not improve and would continue to corrode my sense of self-worth. Finally, when people understood my decision was firm, many of them—clerical workers, professors, students, and other lecturers—came to congratulate me. Several colleagues said they wished they had the courage to do the same thing. Courage? I don't know.

I haven't told my family that I quit. For one thing, I don't want them to worry about me. For another, I know they don't think writing is *real* work and again they will think I'm crazy. My mother always told me I should never quit one job until I had another. She did this once at a restaurant and always regretted it. Luckily I have a little more money saved from my teaching job than she had from her restaurant job. But she's right; I may well regret it.

Recently I had dinner with a well-meaning academic friend. We were eating in one of those nouveaux working-class chic diners. She ordered fish. I ordered ribs and potatoes. After she finished her fish, she helped me eat my ribs and potatoes. Eventually the conversation turned to the job search. I told her about a major university that had offered me another anomalous position with no job security (basically the same position I had at Berkeley). She was very impressed with the university and thought I should take the job. I explained that I didn't want it because it wasn't tenured. It wasn't even tenure track.

"But they'd give you a five-year contract, what do you want?"

"Tenure," I answered.

We talked about other things for a while. Then she said, "But a five-year contract, that isn't bad."

"Why should I move across the country for a contract job that isn't better than the one I had?" Knowing my friend was well meaning, I tried to remain calm.

We changed the topic again. But a little later, she persisted, "Wouldn't you consider it, maybe for a year?"

"Why should I be treated like a peripheral character for the rest of my life?" I asked. "I'm forty-two years old. I've taught for nineteen years. I've probably published more than anyone in the department—five novels. A collection of short stories. Four coauthored books. A collection of essays. Why should I always have to settle for a second-class position?"

We fell silent again.

I asked, "Would you?"

She looked down at the table. We switched the conversation to families and friends and holidays. But my friend was worried about me and she tried once again, "Tell me, what is your bottom line?"

We split the bill equally.

In conclusion, most writers and teachers I talked with for this essay cite vast legacies of insight and strength from their working-class parents. Many also mention a taste for hard work and a consciousness about limited time. Despite their very different work, these people had shared concerns about content, language, audience, and censorship. I am grateful to them for reminding me about the rich gifts of a working-class heritage—including a skepticism about American dream politics; a low tolerance for verbosity and a talent for common sense. I keep remembering something Tillie Olsen told me: "We have something to give literature that's not often there."

Notes

This essay has emerged gradually over the years from presentations I have given at various conferences, including The National Women's Studies Conference, Seattle, June 1985; The International Feminist Bookfair, Oslo, Norway, June 1986; The Marxist Scholars Conference, Berkeley, California, November 1987, and The Modern Language Association, San Francisco, December 1987. Parts of it were published in my article, "Labor Pains," in *The Village Voice*, 5 January 1988.

1. For the sake of being inclusive, I have used the terms "working-class writer" and "working-class teacher" to refer to people who are writers and teachers and who grew up in working-class families. Personally, I prefer to say I grew up in a working-class home than to say I am working-class. Given my current access to privilege, I think it is impertinent for me to now call myself working-class. Many people in my position do continue to call themselves working-class. Hence my use of the inclusive term.

Works Cited

Anzaldúa, Gloria. "Sus plumas el viento." *Borderlands/La Frontera*. San Francisco: Spinsters/Aunt Lute, 1987. 116–19.

Bryant, Dorothy. Personal Interview. 20 November 1985.

Gallagher, Tess. "3 A.M. Kitchen: My Father Talking." *Willingly*. Port Townsend, WA: Graywolf, 1984. 30–31.

——. Personal Interview. 23 November 1985.

Kennedy, William. Personal Interview. 16 July 1986.

Johnson, Diane. "Southern Comfort." *The New York Review of Books* 7 November 1985: 15–16.

Miner, Valerie. *Murder in the English Department*. New York: St. Martin's, 1983.

Olsen, Tillie. Personal Interview. 24 November 1985.

——. *Silences*. New York: Delta-Seymour Lawrence, 1979.

Piercy, Marge. *Braided Lives*. New York: Summit, 1982.

——. Personal Interview. 29 December 1985.

Terkel, Studs. Personal Interview. 28 May 1986.

Thomas, Joyce Carol. Personal Interview. 20 January 1986.

Williams, Sherley Anne. Personal Interview. 28 May 1986.

A Question of Belonging

I SEARCH for words/knowledge that will tell of these things that have happened to me and my community. One piece of the search has to do with oppression. There are many stories that tell of my connection to oppression, some known, some unknown. One unknown story for me is how oppression works inside of us, how it is transferred into bodies, how it feels in the self. I have a burning desire to know about this because one prerequisite for radical change is knowing.

I search for words/knowledge, from within and without, that will tell of these things that have happened to me and my community. From without, because other people's analyses, questions, and thoughts help provide a framework for my experience. And from within, because I believe the most powerful theory derives from personal experience, and I know a great deal about oppression. About racist oppression because I am Arab Canadian, about sexist oppression because I am a woman, about class oppression because I am working class, about heterosexist oppression because I am a lesbian.

Recently this burning desire for knowledge has focused on classism. Because I have finally understood some things. Things like being overcome with feelings of self-hatred and worthlessness while shopping at "smart" clothing stores. Things like an inability to speak in a university classroom.

And so I have attempted to find some answers to explain how class oppression works inside of me, how it was transferred into my body, how it feels in my self. In this article[1] I will examine internalized oppression of working-class people in a capitalist society from my own experience. I do not assume that I am speaking for every working-class person, but I hope there are connections between our experiences and that I may touch on some of these.

Searching for Words

I search for words/knowledge that will tell of these things that have happened to me and my community. The first series of words concern the violence of the capitalist system. Because the word "violence" often has a narrow focus referring to individual acts between two people, systemic acts of violence/violation do not merit attention. Systemic acts of violence/violation that are as much a part of the capitalist system as the profit motive go unnoticed. These include land theft, hungry children, "accidents" that lead to thousands of deaths, poverty, illiteracy, obscurity, crushed spirits, lost dignity. Writer and psychologist Frantz Fanon describes capitalism in this way: "For centuries the capitalists have behaved in the underdeveloped world like nothing more than war criminals. Deportations, massacres, forced labour and slavery have been the main methods used by capitalism to increase its wealth, its gold or diamond reserves, and to establish its power."[2] My addition to Fanon's comment is that such actions also occur in industrialized countries like Canada and the United States. With severe and harmful repercussions for every working-class and working-poor person.

And so I search for words to talk about what happened to me. But they remain elusive. There are words for external oppression, words like "rape" or "poverty." But how to describe the inner acceptance and resignation of a person who has come to believe abusive treatment is her due? Internalized oppression is a catch-all, nonspecific phrase that does not reach the heart of the matter. Frantz Fanon's theory of the colonization of the mind[3] is profound but the focus on the mind makes it seem as if oppression does not happen in the body. Malcom X's "rape of the psyche"[4] is a powerful term but it leaves no hope for change; once you have been raped the act cannot be undone. And so I birthed my own term, a two-part phrase that speaks to internalized oppression and to a hopeful future; the conquered self/the conquest of the self.[5]

The conquered self is, I believe, a term that speaks more directly to the horrendous and violent effects of oppression as it is manifested in its victims. The conquered self accepts oppressive acts and comes to believe she deserves them. I use the term "conquered" because it implies an act of successful domination requiring forethought and intent on the part of the oppressor group, whether that group is male, rich, or white. I use the word "self" because it indicates the mind, body, and spirit of a person is affected. The grammatically passive form of the phrase indicates the passivity of a victim whose being has been defeated.

It is not difficult to see the conquered self; in our society it is all too easy. The conquered self gives itself away in heavy shoulders and downcast eyes, quickness of self-deprecating remarks, silence, slumped body, creeping steps, the refusal to fight, the acceptance of abuse. The conquered self is not hidden. It may be unseen, but that is because the beholder made a choice to render it so.

The term "the conquered self" does not stand alone. I gave it a partner phrase, a hopeful corollary with an active grammatical formation that points to spirited resistance. The conquest of the self describes the successful process of a vigorous, determined struggle to win back what was taken—in this case, one's personhood. It holds out the hope that one can leave oppression behind and move toward liberation, that physical and psychic resistance is possible, that the enemy can be overthrown, that radical change can occur.

I want to examine these concepts in terms of working-class access to university education and my own experience.

The Conquered Self

There are many social institutions and cultural forces one could examine in relation to the conquered self of a working-class person, such as work, church, family, media, culture, health care, education. Education. Specifically university education. It was always clear to me that neither I nor members of my family would attend university. It was not a question of belonging. It was a matter of knowing we did not belong. There was no question, which would presuppose the possibility of an affirmative answer. There was only a definitive statement.

The knowledge surrounding the definitive statement was given to me in grade school and before. As Cy-Thea Sand writes, "[we] were expected to fail within an educational system which systematically limited our choices before we even began to read."[6] This makes sense. Action must be taken early if the self is to be conquered.

And so exclusion was my central lesson from kindergarten on, and the backbone of the lesson was shaped by class divisions that were as sharp as a knife. In our General Motors town in the 1960s, your father worked either on the line or in the office. It was clear where the divisions fell, and it was clear that those of us whose fathers worked the line fell outside the center. A certain group belonged in the center.

That group was chosen to help the teachers. Although some of us waved our hands high and looked beseeching, it was of no consequence.

That group had parents who spoke grammatically correct English without accents. Indeed, some of their parents had *attended* university. That group, repeating their prekindergarten lessons, bragged they were better than us because their father worked in the office, or they picked mercilessly on the group even "lower"—poor children. And there was not much to reply to their assumptions of superiority because we all knew it was true.

Those of us in the other group had different experiences. Several were two or three years older because they failed to advance. The boys in this group were strapped regularly, and they in particular cared little about school. Probably they knew, as other working-class boys did, they were only serving time in an institution that would do little for them.[7] Soon after grade eight, some of the girls in this group became pregnant and others dropped out. We did not celebrate when we no longer had to wear uniforms. As they are everywhere, clothes in our grade school were a dead giveaway of class location.

I graduated from grade school secure in the knowledge that school in general and university in particular belonged to the winners, to that group whose lives seemed smooth and easy and effortless. High school simply reinforced that understanding. Middle-class friends commented on my home "in the sticks," in spite of the fact that my parents were paying a mortgage on a house in a comfortable working-class neighborhood. Teachers discussed university programs with certain students but never with me, regardless of my straight As. These incidents at school were paired with incidents at home in which my parents threatened to withdraw my brother from high school, because of poor marks, and force him to work on the line. This reminded us of our precarious links with the school system.

A paradox existed, because even with all these actions taken to ensure my exclusion from higher education, I wanted it. I wanted it because it was a way out. Perhaps the very way in which we were cut off from university made it seem all the more attractive. Many working-class people know education is a way out and parents hope their children will go to college.[8] I wanted to attend university because I wanted out. Out of my home town, out of an abusive family, and, in my ignorance, out of the working class. I felt panic at the way my life was closing in around me—marriage, some kind of work (probably secretarial), raising children, never leaving town. I wanted out and the only way out I could see was a university education. At the age of ten, I began earning money and saving every penny in the hopes I would be able to put myself through university. I didn't think I had much chance of success, but I had to try. Reflecting on that now, I realize how early working-class children attain class consciousness and identity, and how early we become aware of possible escape routes.[9]

Those exclusions and that paradoxical and seemingly doomed desire went inside of me, shaping self-image, self-worth, self-respect, self. It was a long and slow process, meant to go deep inside of me and anchor there, and it did. Vanquishing will last forever if it is done with enough power and over a long period of time. My conquered self was evident in those grade school and high school years, but it did not emerge full force until I entered Queen's University with some dreams.

Belief Systems

There are many indicators of oppression, many signs and signals. Some of these are self-hatred, body language, depression, hysteria.[10] There are others for which there are no words.

I search for words/knowledge that will tell of these things that have happened to me and my community. I found two words that describe a structure I observed: "belief systems." I define these as internalized justifications for constant oppressive experiences. Mind-sets developed to rationalize day-to-day abuse. Belief systems are sometimes hidden deep within the self, and they are sometimes spoken in casual conversation. I have heard conquered selves speak these bits of wisdom on a daily basis. They are brief, telling statements, signposts of oppression and defeat, that explain the position of the self in relation to oppression. "You are nothing in this world without money," was Cy-Thea Sand's first lesson of life in the working-class neighborhood of Verdun, Quebec.[11] It was a belief system by which her family lived.

I search for words/knowledge that will tell of these things that happened to me and my community. I search for words to describe what happened to me when I set off for university upon graduating from high school, having saved enough money for my first year and a bit beyond. Did I graduate with a bachelor's degree and work as a high school physical education teacher and coach the girls' basketball team and have all of them love me as I loved my coaches? Did I have four wonderful years at one of Canada's oldest and most prestigious universities, years full of interesting classes, friends, pranks, parties, new learnings?

I lasted four months. Depressed, suicidal, and lonely, I feared I was losing my mind. I had no idea why I felt like this, unable to perceive classism as the culprit, not sexism or racism, but classism.

In the end, it all came down to a question of belonging. In the end, it all came down to certain events that had happened many years previous that emerged now in one pithy phrase to conquer my self.

"I don't belong here." The belief system, the few words that summed up in a neat phrase the wisdom of my conquered self. No fighting, no resistance. Just an overwhelming feeling of having a huge array of forces stacked against me, of knowing I did not belong, of knowing the only way out was to leave. Soon. And so I left.

Eight years later, feminist analysis in hand, I approached the women's studies department at University of Toronto. Older, wiser, familiar with many of the concepts and texts we studied. And still. And still. That overwhelming feeling that something was amiss. It was a question of belonging. Or rather, of not belonging, of being a misfit, of being in the wrong place.

I managed to finish my degree and, with the encouragement of one professor, applied to a master's program at a school in Cambridge, Massachusetts. As confused as I was by that professor's encouragement, it was nothing compared to how stunned I was at my acceptance and the offer of financial aid, without which I could not have gone. I would not have been able to propel my self to Massachusetts emotionally or physically had it not been for the active support of my lover, Janet, who moved with me. Once enrolled, I still could not speak in class, still felt "I don't belong here" on a daily basis, still felt I had no right to be there. Finally it became clear what the problem was, mostly because some people took the issue of class oppression seriously. Universities are designed to make working-class people feel like we don't belong. Because we don't. That is the thing about belief systems. They are true. They are not the whole truth, but they are true. When the conquered self reiterates such messages to the oppressed person on a daily basis, it is not because we invented them in a moment of deluded paranoia but because our daily living has taught us their truth. For me to walk around a university campus saying "I don't belong here" was true. Universities are established to keep people like me out, and to keep middle- and upper-class people in. If working-class people suddenly began earning university degrees in large numbers, who would work the lines, scrub the toilets, descend into the mines? Would we remain in the places others have prepared for us?

I do not believe we would. So events much occur that chip away at our selves and that translate into a defeat that expresses itself in a few words whenever necessary. Like "I don't belong here." Only the conquered self would repeat such belief systems. Only someone so beaten down she no longer needs someone standing over her with a gun or whip would set up these internal messages to correspond so beautifully with the oppressors' messages. The oppressors. They, of course, are served by such beliefs, they know these belief systems indicate their victory, they know these belief systems foster not resistance but acquiescence.

The oppressors may not know the potential that lies within each conquered self to make a conquest.

The Conquest of the Self

If it is a question of belonging, then how do you come to belong to an institution intent on keeping you out? Indeed, given the racism, classism, and sexism inherent in academia, does any working-class person want to belong?

I believe that if we do not sell out and we do not allow universities to turn us into parodies of middle-class people, espousing middle-class values and ideologies, it is worth it. If we remember where we come from and give back to our communities, we will gain individually and collectively. For many working-class people, including me, university has opened doors that had appeared forever shut to us.

The question of belonging can only be answered by examining the larger issue about the conquest of the self. How does one achieve a conquest of the self? I am beginning to understand this process and offer my thoughts on it, noting it is an ongoing, fluid process. I move back and forth between the conquered self/the conquest of the self; for a period of time it may be a matter of continuing to experience internal oppression as well as beginning to feel internal freedom, of experiencing both/and, not either/or. One does not change overnight from a defeated person to a victor.

The first thing necessary for the conquest of the self is knowledge. This makes sense. This is a search for words/knowledge that will tell of these things that happened to me and my community. So I need the words and the knowledge. That I am working class. That I am oppressed because of this. That class oppression is a political and not a biological construct. That these facts have a tremendous impact on me. That change is possible. These are difficult pieces of information to discover in our society, which promotes destructive and contradictory ideas around class, such as: class stratification does not exist anymore; class is not an important category; certain types of people are better suited for manual labor (i.e., class is a biological category); class is not one of the major constructs/constraints in a person's life; change is not possible. I need to know all this and I need to be able to analyze these facts and formulate a political analysis with them so the structures of classism are evident.

Along with discovering facts and shaping a political analysis, I must take action. Whether the action is holding a meeting, planning a march, writing a poem, talking to one person, spraypainting political messages in appropriate places and/or fomenting revolution(s), it is vitally important. Because oppression happens to the self and the whole self must be involved in breaking through the oppression. It is not enough that the mind understand the workings of a political construct called capitalism. The body and spirit must take action in order for deep change to occur. In the university classroom, where I sat in silence and fear, I had to open my mouth and speak. It was an incredibly difficult action to take. But it contradicted old messages and began sending different signals to the self. New belief systems emerged. Such as: I do have something to say. I have a right to be here and to speak.

The actions and political analysis must be accompanied by feelings. A layer of numbness encircled the shame and degradation of growing up working class, a wall of amnesia surrounded certain events. I had to let the layers melt, allow forgotten incidents to come hurtling back through defensive walls, feel what I could not feel at the time.

The combination of political awareness, knowledge, action, and feeling led me/is leading me through and toward a conquest of the self.[12] A process that results in a person who feels, who moves from her authentic center, who resists, who believes in her self. A person who has done this work not alone, because no one heals in solitude, but in community. A person who is willing to accept the findings and complete what may be a very painful journey of remembering and realizing the extent of victimization and defeat. A person whose belief systems have changed. No longer do I walk around a university campus hearing the voice in my head say "I don't belong here." A great deal of the time the voice says "I belong wherever I choose to go."

I SEARCH for words/knowledge that will tell of these things that happened to me and my community. The oppressors did their job well. Our conquered selves stayed away from places where we were not welcome, from visions we were not supposed to dream, from hallowed university halls we were meant to walk down only with a mop and pail. But the conquered self can be defeated. The oppressors did not count on our tackling the bitter fruits of their labor with fervor, anger, passion, and love of self. We were never meant to survive.[13] We were never meant to flourish, to rise triumphant from the battlefield of a war we never declared, to live as we desire and to belong in any place we choose. But we are (beginning to) do all those things. I believe such flourishing holds the seeds of true revolution.

Notes

1. This article is one chapter of my master's thesis, "Searching for Words, Searching for Knowledge," Episcopal Divinity School, Cambridge, MA: April 1990.

2. Frantz Fanon, *The Wretched of the Earth* (New York: Grove, 1966), 79.

3. Frantz Fanon, *Black Skin, White Masks* (New York: Grove, 1967). See also Fanon, "Colonial War and Mental Disorders," *The Wretched of the Earth.* Fanon does not use the phrase "colonization of the mind" but I believe it is an accurate representation of his theory.

4. Katie Cannon, associate professor of ethics, Episcopal Divinity School, quoted and discussed this term during a 1989 conversation. She pointed out the hopelessness of this phrase.

5. Katie Cannon encouraged me to create a term to describe the concept of experiencing and resisting internalized oppression, when we both realized an adequate one did not exist. This happened during my time as her student at the Episcopal Divinity School. Without her encouragement, I would not have ventured to attempt such a thing. I want to thank her for all of her support.

6. Cy-Thea Sand, "A Question of Identity." *Class Is the Issue,* special issue of *Fireweed: A Feminist Quarterly* [Toronto] 25 (1987): 8.

7. See, for example, Richard Sennett and Jonathan Cobb, *The Hidden Injuries of Class* (New York: Vintage-Random, 1973), 83.

8. See, for example, Mira Komarovsky, *Blue-Collar Marriage* (New York: Random, 1964), 287.

9. One impressive resource in regard to this is Carolyn Steedman, *Landscape for a Good Woman* (London: Virago, 1986), in which Steedman applies Freudian understandings of identity formation to class.

10. When I use the word "hysteria," I use it in the Freudian sense of a person experiencing symptoms of a physical illness that cannot be traced to a physical cause. See Sigmund Freud, "The Aetiology of Hysteria," *The Freud Reader,* ed. Peter Gay (New York: Norton, 1989), 97–111.

11. Sand, "Question of Identity," 55, 57.

12. I go into more detail about this process in my thesis, where I name and analyze five elements that lead to the conquest of the self. These are: allowing repressed feelings to emerge; remembering and reclaiming personal and collective history; articulating and transforming belief systems; formulating and acting on a political analysis; finding community.

13. Audre Lorde. "The Transformation of Silence into Language and Action," *Sister Outsider* (Trumansburg, NY: Crossing, 1984), 42.

Pockets of Experience

Keeping Close to Home: Class and Education

W E ARE BOTH awake in the almost dark of 5 A.M. Everyone else is
sound asleep. Mama asks the usual questions. Telling me to look
around, make sure I have everything, scolding me because I am uncertain about the actual time the bus arrives. By 5:30 we are waiting outside the closed station. Alone together, we have a chance to really talk.
Mama begins. Angry with her children, especially the ones who whisper
behind her back, she says bitterly, "Your childhood could not have been
that bad. You were fed and clothed. You did not have to do without—
that's more than a lot of folks have and I just can't stand the way y'all go
on." The hurt in her voice saddens me. I have always wanted to protect
Mama from hurt, to ease her burdens. Now I am part of what troubles.
Confronting me, she says accusingly, "It's not just the other children.
You talk too much about the past. You don't just listen." And I do talk.
Worse, I write about it.

Mama has always come to each of her children seeking different
responses. With me she expresses the disappointment, hurt, and anger
of betrayal: anger that her children are so critical, that we can't even
have the sense to like the presents she sends. She says, "From now on
there will be no presents. I'll just stick some money in a little envelope
the way the rest of you do. Nobody wants criticism. Everybody can
criticize me but I am supposed to say nothing." When I try to talk my
voice sounds like a twelve-year-old. When I try to talk, she speaks
louder, interrupting me, even though she has said repeatedly, "Explain
it to me, this talk about the past." I struggle to return to my thirty-five-
year-old self so that she will know by the sound of my voice that we are
two women talking together. It is only when I state firmly in my very
adult voice, "Mama, you are not listening," that she becomes quiet. She
waits. Now that I have her attention, I fear that my explanations will be
lame, inadequate. "Mama," I begin, "people usually go to therapy because they feel hurt inside, because they have pain that will not stop,

like a wound that continually breaks open, that does not heal. And often these hurts, that pain, have to do with things that have happened in the past, sometimes in childhood, often in childhood, or things that we believe happened." She wants to know, "What hurts, what hurts are you talking about?" "Mom, I can't answer that. I can't speak for all of us, the hurts are different for everybody. But the point is you try to make the hurt better, to heal it, by understanding how it came to be. And I know you feel mad or hurt when we say something happened that you don't remember being that way, but the past isn't like that, we don't have the same memory of it. We remember things differently. You know that. And sometimes folk feel hurt about stuff and you just don't know or didn't realize it, and they need to talk about it. Surely you understand the need to talk about it."

Our conversation is interrupted by the sight of my uncle walking across the park toward us. We stop to watch him. He is on his way to work dressed in a familiar blue suit. They look alike, these two who rarely discuss the past. This interruption makes me think about life in a small town. You always see someone you know. Interruptions, intrusions are part of daily life. Privacy is difficult to maintain. We leave our private space in the car to greet him. After the hug and kiss he has given me every year since I was born, the elders talk about the day's funerals. In the distance the bus approaches. My uncle walks away knowing that they will see each other later. Just before I board the bus I turn, staring into my mother's face. I am momentarily back in time, seeing myself eighteen years ago, at this same bus stop, staring into my mother's face, continually turning back, waving farewell as I returned to college— that experience that first took me away from our town, from family. Departing was as painful then as it is now. Each movement away makes return harder. Each separation intensifies distance, both physical and emotional.

To a southern black girl from a working-class background who had never been on a city bus, who had never stepped on an escalator, who had never traveled by plane, leaving the comfortable confines of a small-town Kentucky life to attend Stanford University was not just frightening; it was utterly painful. My parents had not been delighted that I had been accepted and adamantly opposed my going so far from home. At the time, I did not see their opposition as an expression of their fear that they would lose me forever. Like many working-class folks, they feared what college education might do to their children's minds even as they unenthusiastically acknowledged its importance. They did not understand why I could not attend a college nearby, an all-black college. To them, any college would do. I would graduate, become a school teacher, make a decent living and a good marriage. And even though they reluctantly and skeptically supported my educational endeavors, they also subjected them to constant harsh and bitter critique. It is difficult for me to talk about my parents and their impact on me because they have always felt wary, ambivalent, mistrusting of my intellectual aspirations even as they have been caring and supportive. I want to speak about these contradictions because sorting through them, seeking resolution and reconciliation, has been important to me as it affects both my development as a writer, my effort to be fully self-realized, and my longing to remain close to the family and community that provided the groundwork for much of my thinking, writing, and being.

Studying at Stanford, I began to think seriously about class differences. To be materially underprivileged at a university where most folks (with the exception of workers) are materially privileged provokes such thought. Class differences were boundaries no one wanted to face or talk about. It was easier to downplay them, to act as though we were all from privileged backgrounds, to work around them, to confront them privately in the solitude of one's room, or to pretend that just being chosen to study at such an institution meant that those of us who did not come from privilege were already in transition toward privilege. To not long for such transition marked one as rebellious, as unlikely to succeed. It was a kind of treason not to believe that it was better to be identified with the world of material privilege than with the world of the working class, the poor. No wonder our working-class parents from poor backgrounds feared our entry into such a world, intuiting perhaps that we might learn to be ashamed of where we had come from, that we might never return home, or would come back only to lord it over them.

Though I hung with students who were supposedly radical and chic, we did not discuss class. I talked to no one about the sources of my shame, how it hurt me to witness the contempt shown the brown-skinned Filipina maids who cleaned our rooms, or later my concern about the one hundred dollars a month I paid for a room off-campus, which was more than half of what my parents paid for rent. I talked to no one about my efforts to save money, to send a little something home. Yet these class realities separated me from fellow students. We were moving in different directions. I did not intend to forget my class background or alter my class allegiance. And even though I received an education designed to provide me with a bourgeois sensibility, passive acquiescence was not my only option. I knew that I could resist. I could rebel. I could shape the direction and focus of the various forms of knowledge available to me. Even though I sometimes envied and longed for greater material advantages (particularly at vacation times when I would be one of few if any students remaining in the dormitory because there was no money for travel), I did not share the sensibility and values of my peers. That was important—class was not just about money; it was about values that showed and determined behavior. While I often needed more money, I never needed a new set of beliefs and values. For example, I was profoundly shocked and disturbed when peers would talk about their parents without respect, or would even say that they hated their parents. This was especially troubling to me when it seemed that these parents were caring and concerned. It was often explained to me that such hatred was "healthy and normal." To my white middle-class California roommate, I explained the way we were taught to value our parents and their care, to understand that they were not obligated to give us care. She would always shake her head, laughing all the while, and say, "Missy, you will learn that it's different here, that we think differently." She was right. Soon, I lived alone, like the one Mormon student who kept to herself as he made a concentrated effort to remain true to his religious beliefs and values. Later in graduate school I found that classmates believed "lower-class" people had no beliefs and values. I was silent in such discussions, disgusted by their ignorance.

Carol Stack's anthropological study, *All Our Kin*, was one of the first books I read that confirmed my experimental understanding that within black culture (especially among the working class and poor, particularly in southern states), a value system emerged that was counter-hegemonic, that challenged notions of individualism and private property so important to the maintenance of white-supremacist, capitalist patriarchy. Black folk created in marginal spaces a world of community and collectivity where resources were shared. In the preface to *Feminist Theory: From Margin to Center*, I talked about how the point of difference, this marginality, can be the space for the formation of an oppositional worldview. That worldview must be articulated, named, if it is to provide a sustained blueprint for change. Unfortunately, there has existed no consistent framework for such naming. Consequently, both the experience of this difference and documentation of it (when it occurs) gradually loses presence and meaning.

Much of what Stack documented about the "culture of poverty," for example, would not describe interactions among most black poor today irrespective of geographical setting. Since the black people she described did not acknowledge (if they recognized it in theoretical terms) the opposition value of their worldview—apparently seeing it more as a survival strategy determined less by conscious efforts to oppose oppressive race and class biases than by circumstance—they did not attempt to establish a framework to transmit their beliefs and values from generation to generation. When circumstances changed, values altered. Efforts to assimilate the values and beliefs of privileged white people, presented through media like television, undermine and destroy potential structures of opposition.

Increasingly, young black people are encouraged by the dominant culture (and by those black people who internalize the values of this hegemony) to believe that assimilation is the only possible way to survive, to succeed. Without the framework of an organized civil rights or black resistance struggle, individual and collective efforts at black liberation that focus on the primacy of self-definition and self-determination often go unrecognized. It is crucial that those among us who resist and rebel, who survive and succeed, speak openly and honestly about our lives and the nature of our personal struggles, the means by which we resolve and reconcile contradictions. This is no easy task. Within the educational institutions where we learn to develop and strengthen our writing and analytical skills, we also learn to think, write, and talk in a manner that shifts attention away from personal experience. Yet if we are to reach our people and all people, if we are to remain connected (especially those of us whose familial backgrounds are poor and working class), we must understand that the telling of one's personal story provides a meaningful example, a way for folks to identify and connect.

Combining personal with critical analysis and theoretical perspectives can engage listeners who might otherwise feel estranged, alienated. To speak simply with language that is accessible to as many folks as possible is also important. Speaking about one's personal experience or

103

speaking with simple language is often considered by academics and/or intellectuals (irrespective of their political inclinations) to be a sign of intellectual weakness or even anti-intellectualism. Lately, when I speak, I do not stand in place—reading my paper, making little or no eye contact with audiences—but instead make eye contact, talk extemporaneously, digress, and address the audience directly. I have been told that people assume I am not prepared, that I am anti-intellectual, unprofessional (a concept that has everything to do with class as it determines actions and behavior), or that I am reinforcing the stereotype of black people as nontheoretical and gutsy.

Such criticism was raised recently by fellow feminist scholars after a talk I gave at Northwestern University at a conference entitled "Gender, Culture, Politics" to an audience that was mainly students and academics. I deliberately chose to speak in a very basic way, thinking especially about the few community folks who had come to hear me. Weeks later, Kum-Kum Sangari, a fellow participant who shared with me what was said when I was no longer present, and I engaged in quite rigorous critical dialogue about the way my presentation had been perceived primarily by privileged white female academics. She was concerned that I not mask my knowledge of theory, that I not appear anti-intellectual. Her critique compelled me to articulate concerns that I am often silent about with colleagues. I spoke about class allegiance and revolutionary commitments, explaining that it was disturbing to me that intellectual radicals who speak about transforming society, ending the domination of race, sex, class, cannot break with behavior patterns that reinforce and perpetuate domination, or continue to use as their sole reference point how we might be or are perceived by those who dominate, whether or not we gain their acceptance and approval.

This is a primary contradiction, which raises the issue of whether the academic setting is a place where one can be truly radical or subversive. Concurrently, the use of a language and style of presentation that alienates most folks who are not also academically trained reinforces the notion that the academic world is separate from real life, that everyday world where we constantly adjust our language and behavior to meet diverse needs. The academic setting is separate only when we work to make it so. It is a false dichotomy that suggests that academics and/or intellectuals can only speak to one another, that we cannot hope to speak with the masses. What is true is that we make choices, that we choose our audiences, that we choose voices to hear and voices to silence. If I do not speak in a language that can be understood, then there is little chance for dialogue. This issue of language and behavior is a central contradiction all radical intellectuals, particularly those who are members of oppressed groups, must continually confront and work to resolve. One of the clear and present dangers that exists when we move outside our class of origin, our collective ethnic experience, and enter hierarchical institutions that daily reinforce domination by race, sex, and class, is that we gradually assume a mind-set similar to those who dominate and oppress, that we lose critical consciousness because it is not reinforced or affirmed by the environment. We must be ever vigilant. It is important that we know who we are speaking to, who we most want to hear us, who we most long to move, motivate, and touch with our words.

When I first came to New Haven to teach at Yale, I was truly surprised by the marked class divisions between black folks—students and professors—who identify with Yale and those black folks who work at Yale or in surrounding communities. Style of dress and self-presentation are most often the central markers of one's position. I soon learned that the black folks who spoke on the street were likely to be part of the black community and those who carefully shifted their glance were likely to be associated with Yale. Walking with a black female colleague one day, I spoke to practically every black person in sight (a gesture that reflects my upbringing), an action that disturbed my companion. Because I addressed black folk who were clearly not associated with Yale, she wanted to know whether or not I knew them. That was funny to me. "Of course not," I answered. Yet when I thought about it seriously, I realized that in a deep way, I knew them for they, and not my companion or most of my colleagues at Yale, resemble my family. Later that year, in a black women's support group I started for undergraduates, students from poor backgrounds spoke about the shame they sometimes feel when faced with the reality of their connection to working-class and poor black people. One student confessed that her father is a street person, addicted to drugs, someone who begs from passersby. She, like other Yale students, turns away from street people often, sometimes showing anger or contempt; she hasn't wanted anyone to know that she was related to this kind of person. She struggles with this, wanting to find a way to acknowledge and affirm this reality, to claim this connection. The group asked me and one another what we do to remain connected, to honor the bonds we have with working-class and poor people, even as our class experience alters.

Maintaining connections with family and community across class boundaries demands more than just summary recall of where one's roots are, where one comes from. It requires knowing, naming, and being ever-mindful of those aspects of one's past that have enabled and do enable one's self-development in the present, that sustain and support, that enrich. One must also honestly confront barriers that do exist, aspects of that past that do diminish. My parents' ambivalence about my love for reading led to intense conflict. They (especially my mother) would work to ensure that I had access to books, but would threaten to burn the books or throw them away if I did not conform to other expectations. Or they would insist that reading too much would drive me insane. Their ambivalence nurtured in me like uncertainty about the value and significance of intellectual endeavor that took years for me to unlearn. While this aspect of our class reality was one that wounded and diminished, their vigilant insistence that being smart did not make me a "better" or "superior" person (which often got on my nerves because I think I wanted to have that sense that it did indeed set me apart, make me better) made a profound impression. From them I learned to value and respect various skills and talents folk might have, not just to value people who read books and talk about ideas. They and my grandparents might say about somebody, "Now he don't read nor write a lick, but he can tell a story," or as my grandmother would say, "call out the hell in words."

Empty romanticization of poor or working-class backgrounds undermines the possibility of true connection. Such connection is based on understanding difference in experience and perspective and working to mediate and negotiate these terrains. Language is a crucial issue for folk whose movement outside the boundaries of poor and working-class backgrounds changes the nature and direction of their speech. Coming to Stanford with my own version of a Kentucky accent, which I think of always as a strong sound quite different from Tennessee or Georgia speech, I learned to speak differently while maintaining the speech of my region, the sound of my family and community. This was of course much easier to keep up when I returned home often. In recent years, I have endeavored to use various speaking styles in the classroom as a teacher and I find it disconcerts those who feel that the use of a particular patois excludes them as listeners, even if there is translation into the usual, acceptable mode of speech. Learning to listen to different voices, hearing different speech, challenges the notion that we must all assimilate—share a single, similar talk—in educational institutions. Language reflects the culture from which we emerge. To deny ourselves daily use of speech patterns that are common and familiar, that embody the unique and distinctive aspect of our self, is one of the ways we become estranged and alienated from our past. It is important for us to have as many languages on hand as we can know or learn. It is important for those of us who are black, who speak in particular patois as well as standard English, to express ourselves in both ways.

Often I tell students from poor and working-class backgrounds that if you believe what you have learned and are learning in schools and universities separates you from your past, this is precisely what will happen. It is important to stand firm in the conviction that nothing can truly separate us from our pasts when we nurture and cherish that connection. An important strategy for maintaining contact is ongoing acknowledgment of the primacy of one's past, of one's background, affirming the reality that such bonds are not severed automatically solely because one enters a new environment or moves toward a different class experience.

Again, I do not wish to romanticize this effort, to dismiss the reality of conflict and contradiction. During my time at Stanford, I did go through a period of more than a year when I did not return home. That period was one where I felt that it was simply too difficult to mesh my profoundly disparate realities. Critical reflection about the choice I was making, particularly about why I felt a choice had to be made, pulled me through this difficult time. Luckily I recognized that the insistence on choosing between the world of family and community and the new world of privileged white people and privileged ways of knowing was imposed upon me by the outside. It is as though a mythical contract had been signed somewhere which demanded of us black folks that once we entered these spheres we would immediately give up all vestiges of our underprivileged past. It was my responsibility to formulate a way of being that would allow me to participate fully in my new environment while integrating and maintaining aspects of the old.

One of the most tragic manifestations of the pressure black people feel to assimilate is expressed in the internalization of racist perspectives. I was shocked and saddened when I first heard black professors at Stanford downgrade and express contempt for black students, expecting us to do poorly, refusing to establish nurturing bonds. At every university I have attended as a student or worked at as a teacher, I have heard similar attitudes expressed with little or no understanding of factors that might prevent brilliant black students from performing to their full capability. Within universities, there are few educational and social spaces where students who wish to affirm positive ties to ethnicity—to blackness, to working-class backgrounds—can receive affirmation and support. Ideologically, the message is clear—assimilation is the way to gain acceptance and approval from those in power.

Many white people enthusiastically supported Richard Rodriguez's vehement contention in his autobiography, *Hunger of Memory*, that attempts to maintain ties with his Chicano background impeded his progress, that he had to sever ties with community and kin to succeed at Stanford and in the larger world, that family language, in his case Spanish, had to be made secondary or discarded. If the terms of success as defined by the standards of ruling groups within white-supremacist, capitalist patriarchy are the only standards that exist, then assimilation is indeed necessary. But they are not. Even in the face of powerful structures of domination, it remains possible for each of us, especially those of us who are members of oppressed and/or exploited groups as well as those radical visionaries who may have race, class, and sex privilege, to define and determine alternative standards, to decide on the nature and extent of compromise. Standards by which one's success is measured, whether student or professor, are quite different for those of us who wish to resist reinforcing the domination of race, sex, and class, who work to maintain and strengthen our ties with the oppressed, with those who lack material privilege, with our families who are poor and working class.

When I wrote my first book, *Ain't I a Woman? Black Women and Feminism,* the issue of class and its relationship to who one's reading audience might be came up for me around my decision not to use footnotes, for which I have been sharply criticized. I told people that my concern was that footnotes set class boundaries for readers, determining who a book is for. I was shocked that many academic folks scoffed at this idea. I shared that I went into working-class black communities as well as talked with family and friends to survey whether or not they ever read books with footnotes and found that they did not. A few did not know what they were, but most folks saw them as indicating that a book was for college-educated people. These responses influenced my decision. When some of my more radical, college-educated friends freaked out about the absence of footnotes, I seriously questioned how we could ever imagine revolutionary transformation of society if such a small shift in direction could be viewed as threatening. Of course, many folks warned that the absence of footnotes would make the work less credible in academic circles. This information also highlighted the way in which class informs our choices. Certainly I did feel that choosing to use simple language, absence of footnotes, etc. would mean I was jeopardizing the possibility of being taken seriously in academic circles but then this was a political matter and a political decision. It utterly delights me that this has proven not to be the case and that the book is read by many academics as well as by people who are not college educated.

Always our first response when we are motivated to conform or compromise within structures that reinforce domination must be to engage in critical reflection. Only by challenging ourselves to push against oppressive boundaries do we make the radical alternative possible, expanding the realm and scope of critical inquiry. Unless we share radical strategies, ways of rethinking and revisioning with students, with kin and community, with a larger audience, we risk perpetuating the stereotype that we succeed because we are the exception, different from the rest of our people. Since I left home and entered college, I am often asked, usually by white people, if my sisters and brothers are also high achievers. At the root of this question is the longing for reinforcement of the belief in "the exception" which enables race, sex, and class biases to remain intact. I am careful to separate what it means to be an exception from a notion of "the exception."

Frequently I hear smart black folks, from poor and working-class backgrounds, stressing their frustration that at times family and community do not recognize that they are exceptional. Absence of positive affirmation clearly diminishes the longing to excel in academic endeavors. Yet it is important to distinguish between the absence of basic positive affirmation and the longing for continued reinforcement that we are special. Usually liberal white folks will willingly offer continual reinforcement of us as exceptions—as special. This can be both patronizing and very seductive. Since we often work in situations where we are isolated from other black folks, we can easily begin to feel that encouragement from white people is the primary or only source of support and recognition. Given the internalization of racism, it is easy to view this support as more validating and legitimizing than similar support from black people. Still, nothing takes the place of being valued and appreciated by one's own, by one's family and community. We share a mutual and reciprocal responsibility for affirming one another's successes. Sometimes we have to talk to our folks about the fact that we need their ongoing support and affirmation, that it is unique and special to us. In some cases we may never receive desired recognition and acknowledgment of specific achievements from kin. Rather than seeing this as a basis for estrangement, for severing connection, it is useful to explore other sources of nourishment and support.

I do not know that my mother's mother ever acknowledged my college education except to ask me once, "How can you live so far away from your people?" Yet she gave me sources of affirmation and nourishment, sharing the legacy of her quilt making, of family history, of her incredible way with words. Recently, when our father retired after more than thirty years of work as a janitor, I wanted to pay tribute to this experience, to identify links between his work and my own as writer and teacher. Reflecting on our family past, I recalled ways he had been an impressive example of diligence and hard work, approaching tasks with a seriousness of concentration I work to mirror and develop, with a discipline I struggle to maintain. Sharing these thoughts with him keeps us connected, nurtures our respect for each other, maintaining a space, however large or small, where we can talk.

Open, honest communication is the most important way we maintain relationships with kin and community as our class experience and backgrounds change. It is as vital as the sharing of resources. Often financial assistance is given in circumstances where there is no meaningful contact. However helpful, this can also be an expression of estrangement and alienation. Communication between black folks from various experiences of material privilege was much easier when we were all in segregated communities sharing common experiences in relation to social institutions. Without this grounding, we must work to maintain ties, connection. We must assume greater responsibility for making and maintaining contact, connections that can shape our intellectual visions and inform our radical commitments.

The most powerful resource any of us can have as we study and teach in university settings is full understanding and appreciation of the richness, beauty, and primacy of our familial and community backgrounds. Maintaining awareness of class differences, nurturing ties with the poor and working-class people who are our most intimate kin, our comrades in struggle, transforms and enriches our intellectual experience. Education as the practice of freedom becomes not a force that fragments or separates, but one that brings us closer, expanding our definitions of home and community.

A Mennonite "Hard Worker" Moves from the Working Class and the Religious/Ethnic Community to the Academy: A Conflict between Two Definitions of "Work"

"SHE'S (HE'S) A HARD WORKER," is a compliment one Mennonite pays to another Mennonite. And among non-Mennonite employers, Mennonites' hard work, whether blue or white collar, is "legendary" (Cronk, "Work" 5). Among the many legendary accounts is one reported by my cousin, Mary Elizabeth Martin Nolt. As a nineteen-year-old, in 1944, she did housework for Mrs. —— Joseph, a non-Mennonite woman in Allentown, Pennsylvania. After Mary Elizabeth had completed several tasks, Mrs. Joseph asked her to do another: "Would you do this, or are you too tired?" Since a response of being "too tired" would have been unthinkable, Mary Elizabeth replied, "No," and, of course, performed the task. Later she overheard Mrs. Joseph, in a phone conversation, suggest to a friend: "Why don't you get a Mennonite girl to help you? They are good workers, and they don't even get tired!"

A similar Mennonite reputation for hard work (this time, academic) is emphasized in the description beneath my name in my public high school yearbook: "Do you need tickets [for plays, concerts, etc.]? See Laura! You can always depend on Laura to do her share, and more, of work, and to have her lessons prepared too. . . . We know she will be as successful in life as she has been at Manor." My academic hard work is also revealed in these representative yearbook autographs written by my classmates: "to the brain of our class"; "You sure deserve to succeed. You were a wonderful student at Manor"; "Success in all you do. I know it will be yours because you always do." In addition, in the list of seniors and their most outstanding characteristics, the quality listed for both Aaron Souders, a Mennonite boy, and me was "dependability." Finally, in my college yearbook this statement, indicating my respect for hard work, was attributed to me: "Do you mind if I come in or are you too busy right now?"

I have been a Mennonite "hard worker" both inside and outside of the Mennonite group. My movement has had two tracks: from an anomalous, family-crisis-created Mennonite working-class situation to the middle class and from the uniquely Mennonite ethic of hard work to the work ethic of the academy—the "world." Ironically, the Mennonite definition of work, different from that in the dominant culture, helped me to succeed in the academy and thus became an agent in my partial secularization. However, I still retain some Mennonite values concerning work.

The first movement—from working class to middle class—is not typical of Mennonite (female or male) academics. Most Mennonites are not working class. However, my father's desertion of our family—unusual among Mennonites—when I was a child disrupted the scenario for Mennonite family activity and placed us temporarily in the working class. In the ordinary course of events, my father would have taken over his father's farm. His two older brothers had already taken over farms owned by my grandfather, the third son had been killed in an automobile accident, and my father was next in line for a farm—specifically the one that my grandfather himself had farmed before retiring. However, my father and my grandfather disagreed about farming of tobacco, a crop Mennonites raised because it was lucrative and because it involved work for all the family—including children (Cronk, "Work" 10). Grandfather believed in farming tobacco, but my father, who saw an inconsistency in farming it but not allowing its use, did not. My father worried intensely over this conflict and had an emotional breakdown. Later he left us and only periodically came back to the family for short stays. Thus, a disagreement about ethics led to my father's inability to find a "place"—in family and occupation—for the rest of his life, and brought us to our working-class position.

Because my father seldom contributed to our financial support during my childhood, all of us did working-class work. When my father was at home and supported us and when he was gone and did not support us, he was a tenant farmer, a factory worker, and a janitor. My mother did housework and sewing for others and took in boarders. My sister and I did house, lawn, and garden work for others—not to earn spending money for ourselves but to help pay household expenses. The type of work itself was not much different from that done by other conservative rural Mennonites. However, an important distinction existed: the work that land-owning Mennonites did for their own enterprises or, voluntarily, to help relatives or friends, we did for other people for pay. Our jobs and our lack of money made us conspicuous in the several Mennonite communities in which we lived. Our alienation from other Mennonites was intensified by our divided identity: although working-class, we still possessed representative Mennonite values, including those concerning work.

As a working-class family, we were different not only from other Mennonites but also, in one respect, from other people in this class: the lack of formal education in our family was caused not by poverty but by the church's prohibition. The rationale for the prohibition was that formal education would increase contact with the "world" and weaken the connection to the Mennonite family and church. The absence of education, however, did not always mean lack of interest. During my childhood I had several models for my love of education. My parents, although born into conservative Mennonite families, always wished they could have continued their education beyond eighth grade. In fact, Mother did so well in grade school that her teachers let her accelerate and, during seventh and eighth grades, do high school work. However, because the church forbade further formal education, neither parent went to high school or college. Also, I was influenced by two female public school teachers who boarded in our home until I was eight years old. In our home they not only prepared for their classes but also shared library books. From my parents and the teachers, then, I gained a vision of school as an exciting place where I could read and learn—a vision sustained throughout grade school.

For those reasons I did not experience the American equivalent of the division of the British working-class scholarship boy described by Richard Hoggart: "the boy is . . . very much of *both* the worlds of home and school. He is enormously obedient to the dictates of the world of school, but emotionally still strongly wants to continue as part of the family circle" (241). In my enjoyment of school work, I felt not separated from but united with my mother and my absent father.

The working-class position of my family had ramifications that lasted beyond the period of greatest financial difficulty. Although special circumstances had placed us in the working class, we developed empathy for other people in that class. We saw them not as types but as individuals and gained appreciation for their jobs. The cleaning person was not "the girl" or "the woman" because she might have been Margaret Weaver, our mother. The farm laborer was not "the hired man" or "the hired boy" because he might have been Jacob Weaver, our father.

My sister and I also benefited in that a female rather than a male became our role model for income-producing work and manager of family finances. Most Mennonite families have been patriarchal—a situation that Calvin Redekop says is "disturbing and . . . in dire need of correction" for two reasons: first, "Mennonite utopian ideology which has stressed the importance and equality of the person-in-community subordinated to Christ the head," and second, women's "relatively prominent role in the Anabaptist beginnings" (*Mennonite* 104, 169). Of necessity, our family was matriarchal. In our family not my father but my mother fulfilled the conventional male roles described by Kolbenschlag: "worker, maker, producer" (77). Mother, even without a high school education, provided income for us by being a seamstress, a domestic worker (doing cleaning, washing, and ironing), a farm laborer (doing, during one of my father's many absences, the work he had been employed to do), and a manager of the household for the two schoolteachers who boarded in our home. Clearly unlike the women who "fail . . . to see work as a necessary component of identity and autonomy" (Kolbenschlag 77–78), this Mennonite heroine developed an independence unusual in her group and, indeed, in most groups of that time.

Our working-class position was, then, an anomaly in the Mennonite community. However, whether working class, as our family was, or middle class, as most Mennonite families are, Mennonites are united in their unique concept of work. In the dominant culture, a "hard worker" works for his/herself, and hard work leads to individual benefits. Among Mennonites, however, work is done for the community (a term not to be confused with a communal society like the Hutterites), and hard work leads to group well-being. Although most Mennonites do not live communally (except for places such as Reba Place Fellowship, Evanston, Illinois),[1] conservative rural Mennonites usually live in the same geographical area and help each other. Even liberal urban Mennonites have a strong sense of work as service,[2] confirmed, for example, by my interviews of Mennonite women. A thirty-seven-year-old media specialist with an M.A. reported that she "wants to feel [she's] making a difference in someone's life somehow—it's the service element coming out" (Eash). A fifty-six-year-old nurse with a DNS (Doctor of Nursing Science) explained her need to "work hard and help the less privileged" (Janzen).

The motivation for work as community building lies in a key concept of Anabaptism, the basis of Mennonite and Amish groups: *Gelassenheit* (yieldedness and powerlessness). Unlike the medieval mystics' use of the word "to signify internal yielding of the heart and mind to God," the Anabaptists, Sandra Cronk explains, "expanded the concept of yieldedness to structure their social order as well." Mennonites and Amish try "to build a loving community through the ritual use of *Gelassenheit*," for example, in the "rites of hard work" (*"Gelassenheit"* [1978] 183–84). According to this doctrine, work is "a concrete personal gift to others." *Gelassenheit* "curb[s] . . . the . . . selfish desires of the individual" and "create[s] . . . brotherhood [and] . . . mutual interdependence" (*"Gelassenheit"* [1977] 55–56). Consequently, the Mennonite work ethic is distinguished from Max Weber's "Protestant work ethic": "As opposed to the 'Protestant ethic,' which stressed individual effort, the 'Anabaptist ethic' emphasized the collectivity in regard to individual effort, downgraded personal accumulation, and emphasized Christian obligations to the world" (Redekop 359; see also Nafziger; Appling).

Because of this emphasis on community building, in Mennonite groups everyone works. Although gender distinctions in work do exist, both sexes are praised for being hard workers. Therefore, Mennonite communities probably exhibit less than most groups the dominant culture problem described by Kolbenschlag in *Kiss Sleeping Beauty Good-Bye:* "From the earliest years of consciousness the little boy thinks of himself as a potential *worker.* The little girl will more likely think of work as an adjunct to something else, to a *relationship*" (77). Mennonites' philosophy of work as something that builds community and their pervasive complimentary use of the term "hard worker" suggest that both boys and girls in their group are perceived as "potential *worker*[s]." But unlike workers in the dominant culture, Mennonite workers need to submerge their self-will rather than work for individual achievement, which would reflect pride (J. Smucker 274, 286). They are, instead, working for the community.

In my childhood the Mennonite teaching of *Gelassenheit* became very concrete. I remember our sharing in the work of relatives and friends. When we visited other families, the first questions Mother asked, and encouraged us to ask, were "What can I do?" and "What needs to be done?" We were told that "We can visit while we work." And work we did; we helped clean, can food, mend clothes, and iron. When we left after a visit, we felt satisfaction at having contributed to the life of that family. We were taught to take a similar satisfaction about our own work at home. We were expected to fulfill our responsibilities; in our family, as in the Old Order Mennonite families that Sandra Cronk studied, the immediate consequences of laziness were felt by other family or community members who depended on one's work ("*Gelassenheit*" [1977] 55). Not permitted to complain, we were taught to like our work: "If you can't do what you like, like what you do."[3] Whether in other homes or in our family, we subjected our desires to the community. When work needed to be done for others, we were reprimanded if we played, but also if we picked what work we would do.

In addition to *Gelassenheit*, other Mennonite emphases are conducive to effective work: opposition to worldliness (Lemon 19–20), humility (reported in Redekop 99), and practicality (Urry 312). These components of the "Mennonite Personality" (Redekop 90–105), allied with *Gelassenheit*, produce excellent community-building workers. Another Mennonite personality trait, according to D. W. Forsyth's research, in which he used the Thematic Apperception Test (TAT), is "a high need for achievement." Fulfillment of that need could be seen in Mennonites' obtaining high "scholastic achievement scores" and in their being "well respected in their communities for their ability to perform their job in a proficient manner" (reported in Dueck 219). Even this characteristic, an apparent motivation for individual success, could also stem from a desire to serve the community.

These were the ingredients of what I was taught about work. Obeying that instruction, I did both physical and mental work. However, despite the Mennonite doctrine of the community value of work, I found some work, especially gathering eggs and pulling weeds, onerous. From the beginning of first grade, I liked school better than that work; I preferred to read and do my school lessons. School was not only intrinsically interesting, it was also a reprieve from physical work: I wished that we would have school on Saturdays and during summers. School was not play however; I loved school, but I worked there just as hard as

117

at home. The Mennonite "hard worker" had simply found another type of work.

Fortunately, unlike children in most conservative Mennonite families, I was able to go beyond grade school to high school. By the time I completed eighth grade, we were members of a slightly more liberal Mennonite group that allowed high school education. Despite the objections of relatives who thought that my sister and I should quit school to work (especially because my mother was our sole provider), we, working in evenings, on weekends, and in summers, completed high school successfully with good grades and National Honor Society membership.

After graduation from high school, where I had taken the commercial course, because the possibility of college did not occur to me, I worked in an office for two years. Then, encouraged by a lawyer for whom I worked, I enrolled in college. By working part time during the school years and full time during summers and vacations, I financed my college education. After graduation I taught in high school for two years, completed a master's degree, taught in college for eight years, went back to school and completed a Ph.D. I now teach at a small private university. At each stage of my academic career my education was motivated by a love of learning: I liked that kind of "work."

My movements from a family-crisis-induced working-class position to the middle class and from a Mennonite religious/ethnic community to the academy and the "world" have had various effects on my life. However, in all of the changes, I retain some values from the past; tension between opposites is always present. The first movement from my anomalous working-class background to the middle class has affected my attitudes toward educational financing, toward manual work and workers, and toward value judgments regarding social class and education. First, I consider education not a right but a privilege—something "worked for." A degree (even a Ph.D.) gives one only an entry into a type of work. Remembering my childhood and teenage economic deprivations, I am surprised at my students' and my colleagues' children's financial comfort. I have natural empathy for students with working-class backgrounds; I have cultivated empathy for those who have never questioned that their parents will pay for their college education. This cultivated empathy is needed, for example, when (as a teacher of business writing) I read resumés of students who have never done either part-time or full-time work. Second, my attitude toward manual work and workers derives from the experiences other family members and I have had. I value both the tasks and the people who perform them, and I resent the condescending language used for both. Even before contemporary consciousness raising, I was offended by the terms "girl," "boy," or "the help." The third effect is my dislike of snobbishness regarding social class and education. Whenever I see excessive value placed upon family backgrounds and upon degrees from prestigious institutions, I am made more aware of discrimination against people who do not possess these attributes.

Although that transition from the working class to the middle class still affects my view of the world, the movement from a Mennonite religious/ethnic community to the academy and the "world" has had more complex results in my life and has probably created more ambivalence. In many respects I live on a "hyphen," which "provides a marvelous view" (Aycock 2).[4] As I become partially secularized, the focus of my work and the constituency of my community changed. I still am committed, however, to—but also struggle with—Mennonite ideals of work.

One effect of my transition to the "world" is the shift from self-yielding community building to individual achievement, "personal striving" (Cronk, "*Gelassenheit*" [1977] 57). Although I did not go to college or graduate school to garner prestige, my teaching and research do bring academic recognition, a certain type of prestige. This recognition, given also, of course, to my university, is primarily individual. To obtain and retain a position, I need to call attention to my achievements in a manner that contradicts my Mennonite teaching. In constructing resumés, doing self-evaluation for tenure and promotion and yearly self-evaluations for merit raises, I have to use strategies resembling the self-aggrandizement that I had been warned against and that had not been my motivation for going to school and choosing teaching as a profession. Although rewards—consisting of compliments for hard work—are also given within the Mennonite community, the strategies used to attain recognition in the academy seem like expressions of *Hochmut* (pride) (Redekop 118).

As a consequence of my secular academic success, the Mennonite community has been at least partially replaced for me by a professional community. Other people in the academy, and especially in my discipline, now support and judge me—in both my teaching and my research. This change is probably an inevitable result of specialization. "The profession often becomes the source of beliefs, values, and attitudes of the individual, and the satisfier of emotional and relational needs" and may even "become the surrogate church" (Redekop and Bender 137). Some Christian scholars have detected dangers in this changed allegiance. For example, Calvin Redekop and Urie Bender, writing from a combined perspective of Christianity and the social sciences in *Who Am I? What Am I?* warn, "Professionalism can thus become one of the most insidious forms of idolatry" (137). My background in Mennonite community building enables me to recognize that danger, but because the profession provides stimulation for me, I continue to give much of my energy to that community of teachers and researchers.

Despite those changes, I still retain Mennonite values and try to practice them—but, because I discovered their potentially destructive professional consequences in the academy, I do so with anguished ambivalence. Although Mennonite standards of work have helped produce my academic success, the Mennonite idea of work as service is not really valued in the academy. Unlike the Mennonite emphasis, in which selfless service to the department and the university would have the highest priority, service in the academy is often perceived as negative—as weakness, as something that subordinate classes, including women, do. The "service ethic," a " 'supportive' mind-set" with which women have been "brainwashed" (Kolbenschlag 97, 95–96) in society as a whole, is considered just as demeaning in the university. For example, composition taught as a "service course" still often has second-class status in a hierarchy that places upper-level literature courses at the top. Consequently, the person who performs "service" is often exploited. Even the term "hard work" itself—whether done for others or for oneself—has negative connotations in academia. The image of a hard worker often suggests a drudge or an unimaginative, passive, conforming person— someone who will serve on routine committees and organize conferences. This person, too, is often exploited.

Another Mennonite concept about which I am ambivalent is finding joy in one's work. Joy, as taught by Mennonites, means more than just not complaining about the work one does; it means volunteering to do extra work. Work is celebrated as "an expenditure of energy that has real meaning either intrinsic in terms of a task well-done, or having relevance to the good of the larger community" (Redekop and Bender 40). In the past I felt as did the older Old Order Mennonite children whom Cronk questioned about "what they liked to do best": they were "quite uniform in responding that they like to work" ("Work" 10). Cronk found that for Mennonites, work is not drudgery. It is not necessarily a "task . . . to be finished to achieve a goal" but, instead, "the fabric of life" ("*Gelassenheit*" [1977] 56). Because of that genuine joy in work, I, like Redekop, have always resisted the charge of workaholism (Redekop and Bender 287).

However, I sometimes question the authenticity of my celebration of work. We were taught not to "get tired," but now the absence of fatigue or of complaining may be a mask that I assume. That mask is worn because I do not have permission to be tired; I feel guilt for my complaining and for my not experiencing joy in work. And my protest or my attempt to change my working situation may also lead to guilt. Then burnout may result.

For example, during a recent semester, in which I had an especially heavy teaching load (four courses, including one new literature course, one new literature-composition course, and two composition courses), I complained more than ever before. I counted the number of papers: in addition to numerous smaller papers, I graded rough drafts and final versions of thirty-eight ten-page research papers in a research and report writing class (total—760 pages); rough drafts and final versions of nineteen ten-page research papers in a world cultures class (total—380 pages); and sixty-four three-page papers in a world literature class (total—192 pages). Also, during the same semester in my regular conferences with approximately sixty students I needed to cultivate a smile and a strategy for expressing interest in each student's work. And, in my rush to finish reading new material shortly before I was scheduled to teach it, I regularly counted available hours before my class met. In fact, in this factorylike atmosphere, I found myself counting hours until the end of the day, days until the end of the week, and weeks until the end of the semester. Then this Mennonite woman did become tired!

However, as soon as I feel that my protest is valid, I wonder whether my raising the possibility of burnout itself indicates my secularization and whether assuming a mask of joy might be not an inauthentic act but an appropriately disciplined act. Somehow even in a horrendous semester some joy persists. Perhaps I can wear not a conditioned-reflex mask but an informed mask of joy in work.

As I reflect on my hyphenated existence (partial secularization and simultaneous affirming, wrestling with, and rejecting of Mennonite work values), I wonder whether the Mennonite concept of work can operate outside the Mennonite community. What happens to hard work divorced from a sense of community? If that sense is lost, for whom is work done? In a milieu of individual achievement, is work done only for oneself? Or, for others like oneself in a professional community?

I would like to belong to both the Mennonite community and the university community. I clearly find intellectual and emotional satisfaction when I succeed. But my success is also rewarding to the Mennonite community. When I read (for example, in *The Mennonite Weekly Review*) of a Mennonite's success anywhere, but specifically in the academy, I am happy for her/him as for a family member. Likewise, my success will be appreciated by another Mennonite. Therefore, it is not only Laura Weaver but the Mennonites who succeed as well. Such interaction can also occur in the university community as I envision it. There one would genuinely work for others as well as for oneself in a community that authenticates joy in hard work. Colleagues in the department and in the university would benefit from one's teaching and scholarly activity.

MY PERSISTENT celebration of work, despite its sometimes oppressive features, has been generated by two main components of my past experience: the deprivations in the working class and the rigorous work training in the Mennonite religious/ethnic community. The working-class deprivations, intensified by my being in a working-class position when my Mennonite friends were not, were of money and the certainty or even the possibility of going to high school and college. But disadvantaged as we were, my sister and I gained more education than observers would have expected. Therefore, some of my delight in obtaining an education derived from its being unexpected, and that delight persists. My joy in education translates now into joy in work. The second component of my past consists of my Mennonite training in work. That training in discipline, self-denial, and humility in the presence of the unknown is admirable preparation for scholarly work. In addition, those qualities can engender creativity. Hard work is not opposed to but can precede or operate simultaneously with creativity. What might have appeared to be the Mennonite community's training in asceticism was actually training for scholarly and creative activities. Again, joy comes through my continuing practice of these work habits.

Whether authentically or temporarily inauthentically joyful, my work will always be influenced by my having lived in the working class and in the Mennonite religious/ethnic community. I will always be a "hard worker," and I will continue to claim my Mennonite identity—even in the academy and the "world." I will, however, also claim my right to be tired and to try to change my working situation. My dilemma now, as a Mennonite academic woman, is whether I can combine worldly individualistic work with self-yielding, community-building work. I need to discover whether the university can also become a true community!

Notes

I am writing from the perspective of someone reared in a conservative Mennonite family and community. Although all Mennonites share some basic beliefs, they are not a monolithic group.

1. For a discussion of various Mennonite socioeconomic models, see Donovan E. Smucker. For descriptions of Reba Place Fellowship, see Dave Jackson and Neta Jackson, *Glimpses* and *Living*.

2. An effective example is Joseph Smucker's interviews of twenty-nine Mennonites, "members of a small, recently established Mennonite church in a metropolitan area with a population of approximately 400,000 . . . in southern Ontario" (279).

3. This statement was quoted by an urban Mennonite interviewed by Joseph Smucker in Ontario (285).

4. Aycock, in a poem "Hyphen-nation," refers to Japanese-American, Mexican-American, and Italian-American as people living on a "hyphen." However, whereas he finds incompleteness and a lack of direction in the hyphen, I find it a satisfying place to live.

Works Cited

Appling, Gregory B. "Amish Protestantism and the Spirit of Capitalism." *Cornell Journal of Social Relations* 10 (1975): 239–50.

Aycock, Wendell. "Hyphen-nation." *MELUS* 7 (Spring 1980): 2.

Cronk, Sandra. "*Gelassenheit:* The Rites of the Redemptive Process in Old Order Amish and Old Order Mennonite Communities." Diss. U of Chicago Divinity School, 1977.

———. "*Gelassenheit:* The Rites of the Redemptive Process in Old Order Amish and Old Order Mennonite Communities." *Mennonite Quarterly Review* 52 (1978): 183–85 [abstract of U of Chicago Divinity School diss.].

———. "Work in Anabaptist/Mennonite Thought and Experience." Paper presented at Colloquium on Theology of Work. Winnipeg. June 1988.

Dueck, Al. "Psychology and Mennonite Self-Understanding." *Mennonite Identity: Historical and Contemporary Perspectives.* Ed. Calvin Wall Redekop and Samuel J. Steiner. New York: UP of America, 1988. 203–24.

Eash, Esther Kreider. Media Specialist. Lodge Elementary School, Evansville, IN. Personal interview. 2 June 1989.

Hoggart, Richard. *The Uses of Literacy: Changing Patterns in English Mass Culture.* Boston: Beacon, 1957.

Jackson, Dave, and Neta Jackson. *Glimpses of Glory.* Elgin, IL: Brethren Press, 1987.

———. *Living Together in a World Falling Apart.* Carol Stream, IL: Creation House, 1974.

Janzen, Erica. Associate Professor. Dept. of Nursing, Bethel College, Newton, KS. Personal interview. 2 August 1989.

Kolbenschlag, Madonna. *Kiss Sleeping Beauty Good-Bye: Breaking the Spell of Feminine Myths and Models.* New York: Doubleday, 1979.

Lemon, James T. *A Geographical Study of Southeastern Pennsylvania.* Baltimore: Johns Hopkins UP, 1972.

Nafziger, Estel. "The Mennonite Ethic in the Weberian Framework." *Explorations in Entrepreneurial History* 2 (1965): 187–204.

Nolt, Mary Elizabeth Martin. Personal conversation. 1 August 1989.

Redekop, Calvin. *Mennonite Society.* Baltimore: Johns Hopkins UP, 1989.

Redekop, Calvin, and Urie A. Bender. *Who Am I? What Am I?* Grand Rapids, MI: Academie Books-Zondervan, 1988.

Smucker, Donovan E. "Gelassenheit, Entrepreneurs, and Remnants: Socioeconomic Models among the Mennonites." *Kingdom, Cross, and Community: Essays on Mennonite Themes in Honor of Guy F. Hershberger.* Ed. John Richard Burkholder and Calvin Redekop. Scottdale, PA: Herald Press, 1976. 219–41.

Smucker, Joseph. "Religious Community and Individualism: Conceptual Adaptations by One Group of Mennonites." *Journal for the Scientific Study of Religion* 25.3 (1986): 273–91.

Urry, James. "'The Snares of Reason'—Changing Mennonite Attitudes to

'Knowledge' in Nineteenth-Century Russia." *Comparative Studies in Society and History* 25 (1983): 306–22.

Weaver, Laura H. "Margaret A. Weaver: A Mennonite Heroine: From Lonely Coping to Valiant Creation of Community." *The Ethnic American Woman: Problems, Protests, Lifestyle.* Ed. Edith Blicksilver. Expanded ed. Dubuque: Kendall/Hunt, 1989. 373–76.

Grandma Went to Smith, All Right, but She Went from Nine to Five: A Memoir

For Nana, for Sandy and the Heights Kids

T HE AREA marked "Property of Smith College" on Northampton town plats comprises the nearest sizable green space to the house where my family lived until I turned seven, in the same upstairs apartment where my mother was born.* That house, 53 Old South Street, was torn down in the mid-1950s, but I like knowing that my mother and I came to consciousness in the same set of rooms, that our eyes first learned to distinguish squares of sunlight shifting across the same kitchen floor, the same tree shadows on the wall.

The Smith campus, too, my mother and I both knew early in our lives. But here there is a difference between my mother's experience and my own, for she explored that place only after she was big enough to go there with her gang of neighborhood kids. Her mother, the grandmother I called Nana, seldom took her there. Smith land and Smith events have traditionally been open to townspeople, but Nana was Quebec-born, with a few years of grade school education, not the sort of Northampton resident likely to assume the college was accessible to her. Besides, even though my mother was her only child, Nana had little leisure for long walks with a toddler. Walks were what Nana took on her way upstreet from our house on the flats to go shopping, to go to Mass, or to go to work; walks were what she took to the bus stop, en route to visit relatives or to nurse them. She and my grandfather, who died when my mother was in her late teens, both came from sprawling and often hapless families, hers French Canadian and Micmac, his Irish. Both sides were riddled with tuberculosis, alcoholism, infant failure-to-thrive—the classic diseases of the poor. The stunning exception, the one success in my mother's family, was one of my grandfather's brothers, who made his way upward through ward politics to a term as mayor of

---

*"Plats" are maps of sections of cities; "green space" is the city planning term for undeveloped open land. "Upstreet" and "slate sink" are colloquial to western Massachusetts.

Northampton in the thirties; his success was short, and apparently, unlike T.B., it was not catching within families.

For Nana, Smith College was primarily the place where she worked intermittently throughout her life cleaning dormitory bathrooms and hallways. It is easy to see why she did not think of the Smith campus as an arena for leisure or pleasure, as a place to take a baby. My mother was the first in our family to see the grounds of Smith as in some way a part of her turf. She played there as a child; as a grown woman, she ventured into the art gallery, attended public lectures and foreign films, though always with a sense that Smith was special, its delights not her birthright, but privileges graciously extended to her.

As for me, her daughter, I cannot remember a time before the Smith campus was a familiar presence to me. I knew it first through my body, through bare feet and skinned knees, by way of the dirt lodged in the creases of my palms and caked beneath my fingernails, dirt Nana scrubbed off with gritty Boraxo in our slate sink. I learned to walk, and later to ice skate, on the campus; my first bullfrogs hunkered on the margin of the lily pool by Lyman Plant House.

And Smith was where I first understood metaphor, not in any freshman English class, but in the woods at the western edge of the campus heavy in early spring with the rich smell of leaf mold, soaked through by melting snow, where I hunkered down to inspect a jack-in-the pulpit. On walks there, my parents taught me the wonderfully satisfying names of things: rose-breasted grosbeak, Solomon's seal, nuthatch, dogtooth violet, lady's slipper.

Within the boundaries of the campus, the Mill River widened out and briefly changed its name to Paradise Pond, though Nana said it was really still the same old Mill River. The Paradise Pond skating rink was kept glossy and clear of snow by the Kingsmen, Smith patois for the male groundskeepers and maintenance men. No question of Kingspersons in those days. There were cooks and chambermaids, all women. And then there were Kingsmen. *Kingsman* is said to derive from Franklin King, an early president of Smith, whose name at full length was also given to the colonnaded neo-Georgian dormitory where Nana worked as a maid. A *chambermaid*.

For me and other Northampton kids whose relatives did service work at the college, *Kingsman* and *chambermaid* were words of double meaning. They meant the ordinary jobs held down by familiar adults.

But the words also evoked the quaintly dressed people in the illustrations of Mother Goose books, the world of Humpty Dumpty and Old King Cole and the four-and-twenty blackbirds. When I entered Smith, the information booklet for freshmen commented upon the nice aptness of calling gardeners and janitors *Kingsmen,* for "they help put Smith back together again," no matter what maintenance problems might arise. I don't remember any mention in that booklet of chambermaids, only an oral explanation during some orientation session that those women were not to be tipped and were to be treated with courtesy. There was little danger of anyone tipping them, of course; as for the courtesy, I came to Smith knowing Nana's stories. And I had done some time by then as a waitress myself.

I grew up in a politically progressive family, where unions and strikes were common table talk. But as a little kid, I like most of my friends had no notion of the class assumptions evident in cutely calling working people Kingsmen. It seemed only one more odd conjunction of language, one I might some day figure out—and there were so many of those adult puns and euphemisms to puzzle over. My dad's stepfather, the only grown man I saw regularly during the war years, would chuck me under the chin and pinch my nose, and ask if I wanted to hear the story of Goldilocks and the Three Beers; when my brother Mike was born, and I asked my mother why Pop Noffke called Mike's tiny penis an "erector set," she said it was because the first erector sets were made at the Gilbert factory where Pop worked as a janitor (no "Kingsmen" in the Holyoke mills, to be sure), and Pop loved erector sets, and he loved baby Mike. . . . She trailed off. *Kingsmen* was probably that sort of mystery.

The adult world was full of such secrets, of mysterious imports and double meanings. I took for granted the significance of names, words, multiple identities, even if often I could not guess what the significance might be, whether the doubling of meaning were portentous or playful.

But I knew one thing from an early age: there was some acute difference between being a chambermaid in the way Nana was and the apple-cheeked girls dressed in ruffled aprons and mob caps in the Mother Goose book. In a folklore course at Smith, I discovered the Opies' *Oxford Dictionary of Nursery Rhymes,* where I read avidly about the politics, sex, and class wars secreted in those texts. At four, at seven, I knew only that the chambermaids in the bright pictures seemed spunky, healthy, young, and largely cheerful, even when threatened by blackbirds and crosspatch mistresses. But then, as Nana once remarked when I asked her about the connection between her job and the pictures, those maids didn't have to scrub toilets. In the pastoral vision of the illustrators, maids milked bonny cows; they hung out clothes, they stood prettily all-in-a-row. It was different with Nana.

It is a soft spring evening in 1948. I come upon Nana sitting in her rocker in the darkened kitchen, rubbing her thick ankles. She is crying. I am five: I am terrified. In all the world, she is my steadiest point, steady and beautiful, like her name: Julia Larock Dunn.

What, Nana, what? I ask.

Oh, those girls, she says, and I know she means the students who live at Franklin King House. But what have those girls done?

They called me a bitch, she says, *right to my face!*

She sees I don't know the word, and now she's sorry she's used it, but I press her: *They called you what?*

A bitch, she says. *A she-dog. Like Lady.* And she names the mongrel next door, a very doggy-smelling dog with dangling teats.

I cannot believe this. I am sobbing, and now she is holding me, rocking me, singing to me in her gravelly Quebecois: *Allouette, je te plumerais.* Little skylark, I will pluck your wings. Don't cry; everything is all right.

Two kinds of bitch, two kinds of chambermaids, and the Mill and Paradise the same flowing water; many of my first confusions of language centered around Smith.

In the April after I turned seven, Nana felt poorly one evening, but not yet so poorly that I could not go in to kiss her goodnight. In her room I whispered to her the prayer she taught me, one she perhaps picked up from the Irish in-laws, a prayer I now know is called "The White Paternoster," and is recited in the British Isles as a charm against ghosts:

> Four posts round my bed,
> Four angles o'er my head.
> Matthew, Mark, Luke, and John,
> Bless the bed I lie upon.

And I spoke the names of all whom I wished to bless. By the time my father waked me in the morning, the ambulance had come and gone with Nana. I ran home from school breathlessly that noon, willing myself to hear from the backstairs landing the sounds of her stumping about the kitchen, singing along with the radio tuned to "The Franco-American Hour." I prayed now not for Evangelists to guard me, but to smell tomato soup, baking apples, a chicken roasting, to find everything somehow in place.

Instead, there was only Aunt Anna, trembling, telling me with a terrible false smile that Nana was all gone, that Nana was with the angels now.

For a few years after, I would sometimes wake in the darkness of my room, after an evening when I had gone to bed sad or afraid, to feel a rough hand gripping my thumb beneath the covers. In time, these tactile visitations frightened and disturbed me more than they comforted me, and one night I asked Nana aloud to go away. She did.

I never told anyone of those experiences, and never heard from anyone a comparable story until I read Chapter four of *Moby Dick*, with Ishmael's (and Melville's, I'd bet) memory of the ghostly hand. I was at Smith by then, and I cried after reading that passage, looking out my dormitory window across the darkened quadrangle toward Franklin King House.

The day after Nana's funeral, the gas company property manager called on us to serve an eviction notice. The company owned the house, and they had allowed Nana to continue her lease on grudging sufferance, as she was the widow of a gas inspector; we were only a gas-company widow's survivors. And so Aunt Anna moved to Florence to share a tiny house with three cheerful maiden ladies, as they called themselves, who worked beside her at Pro Brush, and we moved, my father, my pregnant mother, my baby brother, and I, to Hampshire Heights, a low-income veterans' housing project newly built at the edge of Northampton on land carved out of woodlots and farms. In the space of a few weeks, we had become a nuclear family.

The Heights spilled over with 1950s energy, alive, raw-edged, very hopeful, a little dangerous. Many of the fathers, five years after the war's end, were still shaken, given to fits of depression or sudden explosive rage. We kids accepted anger as an adult male norm, the way fathers were. When I think back on our mothers, I remember them pregnant. Kids were everywhere at the Heights; you could not be granted a lease unless you had at least two. The oldest tier was all my age, seven and eight. Most of us had come to the project from wartime homes like mine, homes shared with grandparents, aunts, uncles. Families composed only of parents and children seemed to many of us small, unripe, ingrown, scarily lacking in extra sources of support and comfort, and we older kids bonded fiercely in a large nomadic tribe that transcended gender and ethnicity. We roamed parking bays and clothesline yards, playing hide and seek among wet flapping sheets; we explored woods and fields, each of us in charge of at least one younger sibling. They trailed behind us on foot, or we pulled them in wagons or sleds. We coached them on how to slide under barbed-wire fences, while one of us stood guard to make sure the lethargic bull was preoccupied in a far corner of his pasture; we carried them across the stepping stones of the brook to the Piney Woods, where we built forts of resinous boughs: we took them to the free Christmas production of Humperdinck's *Hansel and Gretel* at Smith, hissing them silent, holding them when they cried at the witch; we warned them away from the construction constantly underway around the project: *Billy Ouimet, Tony Perfito, Mikey Clark. I see you, get over here right now or you'll get a licking!*

Our bond was the stronger because by moving to Hampshire Heights we had become suddenly identifiably lumped together as low-income working-class kids. We older Heights kids rejoiced out loud at how brave, how smart, how strong we were; as it turns out, we seem to have been all those things. Those of us now in our mid-forties who belonged to that first generation of Heights children keep splendid oral histories, and I know of few stories of failure among us.

In our grade school classrooms, it would have been hard for an outsider to pick out us Heights kids. But kids themselves unfailingly know who is who, and on the walks home we needed to band together, fighting, flailing against taunts: *Heights kids: Project kids!* After school it was simply easier not to try to venture beyond our own group, however welcoming other kids who lived outside the project might initially seem.

Joanie lived in a pretty ranch house in the Gleason Road addition just across Jackson Street from the Heights. Joanie said her mom would let us come over until more ranch houses got built on Gleason Road, when Joanie would have more playmates of her own sort. We knew well enough not to report these remarks to our own proud families. And it was tempting to play over at Joanie's house. The best climbing tree in the neighborhood grew there, left over from the time when it was all farmland, a venerable apple tree with sturdy perches we gave names to: The Baby Seat (a foot off the ground); the Lookout (the topmost fork).

I lay stretched out on a middle limb, dreaming, my whole body banked by sweet apple blossoms. That afternoon I was the last Heights kid left over at Joanie's. Suddenly from up in the Lookout, Joanie began her soft chant: *Every* kid on this *Apple* tree is *coming* to my *BIRTH*day party *except pat clark* . . . and YOU KNOW WHY. And from various nooks around the tree, out of the massed blossoms and sticky new leaves, the refrain came from the mouths of hidden children: *yah, yah. hah hah, you* live at *hampshire Heights!*

I dropped ten feet to the ground and landed running, yelling up at the whole beautiful tree, *Who cares? Who cares? Who cares about you and your stinking party?* As I ran through the front yard, I glimpsed Joanie's mom and her gentle, Polish-speaking grandma at the big picture window. Her mother's face was set; her grandma waved at me, looking sad. I did not wave back.

Well, who cared, indeed? I cared. Since then, the parties I have attended stretch in a long line from that party I was not invited to, right to the present: high school proms, college mixers, graduate school sherry hours, faculty receptions, museum trustees' dinners in honor of scholarly books to which I've contributed. And I never have, I never will, attend one such function without looking surreptitiously around, checking it out, figuring out who's here, who's here who's like me, trying to spot my kind: *who's here who wasn't born knowing how to do this?*

Always, I am looking around for the Heights kids.

When I was ten, my father was transferred, and we moved straight from Hampshire Heights to an old farmhouse on the outskirts of Portland, Maine, where I lived until I graduated from high school. Those years don't need chronicling here, except for the last summer before I entered Smith, the college I chose because it was the one I knew. And because, though now I cannot recall her ever saying she hoped I would grow up to go to Smith, I wanted to give Nana a Smith girl who knew what Julia Larock was worth. My parents were pleased, but they were also fearful, afraid I might not succeed, afraid I would and alter into some unknowable stranger. I remember two stories from that summer, one told by my mother, the other by my father.

The quote under my mother's Northampton High School yearbook picture, from Thomas Hood, reads "And she had a face like a blessing." And so she did; high-cheekboned and radiant, she smiles shyly there on the page. Other old snapshots show her slender and graceful, even in a shapeless 1930s tanktop swim suit; she is dressed for a dance with an orchid in her hair, à la Rita Hayworth.

One afternoon that last summer while we were shelling peas she told me a story about herself newly out of high school and enrolled at McCarthy's Business School in downtown Northampton, thrilled one October Saturday because she had a date with a college man, a student at Amherst. At the last moment she tucked into the picnic basket one of her favorite books, *The Poetical Works of John Greenleaf Whittier.*

I know that book well, and I love it still, uncritically, not just "Snowbound," but the ballads of shipwreck, heroism, love gone astray. Sweet Maude Muller among her hayricks, whom the wimpy judge rejects as a possible wife, and Kathleen's wonderfully wicked stepmother, getting in her licks in the class wars:

> There was a lord of Galway
> A mighty lord was he,
> And he did wed a second wife,
> A maid of low degree.
> But he was old, and she was young,
> And so in evil spite,
> She baked the black bread for his kin
> And fed her own with white.

No worse than batches of Keats or Yeats, or whatever my mom's date was reading—D. H. Lawrence, I bet. On the grass by Paradise Pond, that boy pounced not on my mom but on her book; *What's this? Oh, my god, Whittier!* And he read snatches of it out loud, roaring with laughter, his hands greasy from the fried chicken, laughing at Maude and Kathleen, at Mom. When she cried and the picnic was ruined, he called her a bad sport.

My mother told this story without pointing any moral, just as a sad little tale about how things don't always pan out. But by the time I heard this story, I had some idea myself why they might not: college man from Boston suburb, business school townie. I carried the story with me to Smith; I can still hear the cold water running in the sink, the shelled peas pinging down into the colander, as my mother imitated that boy's voice, the way he held the book out of her reach. I think of him every

133

time a college bookstore announces the readers for a poetry series that devalues the lyrical, the narrative, and awards the avant-garde; I think of him every time I hear a teacher criticize a student's taste: "You mean you *like* 'O Captain, My Captain'?"; eyebrow raised, faint smile.

My father also had a story for me that summer of 1960, and his are never told as anything *but* moral exempla.

Late August on the beach of Prout's Neck. I am holding so much joy and fear and expectancy inside this summer, my whole self feels like a brimming cup I am trying not to spill. But now in a voice heavy with import my father commands me to walk with him down the shimmery waterline toward the private beaches of the big Victorian resort inns. It is low tide, and the beach is very wide, strewn with wavey parallel lines of kelp and shells, pebbles and bones, plastic bleach-bottle floats, bits of glass buffed to opalescence, all the old garbage the sea keeps trying to refine.

My mother winces, mutters, "Just get away as soon as you can," and I realize she is guessing better than I can what's coming. And indeed I could not have guessed. What my father wishes to tell me is not about the burden on me as the first to go to college, or even his usual sermon about how though I must certainly *go* to college, I will lose family and soul if I turn into "one of those girls too proud to wipe her own arse." Instead he relates a twisted picaresque epic of the easy sexual conquests he and his buddies made at Smith and Mount Holyoke; about how many girls he knew in high school ended up seduced and abandoned by callous college boys. (Underneath his picture in *his* Holyoke High yearbook they wrote "The girls really fall for the charm of Joe 'Clicker' Clark and the sweet strains of his Hawaiian guitar.") He explains earnestly that (1) college girls are loose, and all townie men know that; (2) college boys believe that all townie girls are loose, and they may well be right; (3) it will be easy for anyone to spot me for what I am, and so therefore (4). . . .

But I don't stay for (4). I run back along the beach, crying *please, Dad, no*, rubbing at my ears as if that could erase the sounds I have heard, but it is too late. His words reinforce my deepest fears: I am overreaching by going to Smith, condemning myself to a life of being neither duck nor swan, with no true allies, infinitely vulnerable to the worst each "sort" can say about or do to one another in these class wars I've been witness to my whole life.

I gained much from Smith, eventually. But my first years were bewildering, marked more often than they might have been by shame and despair. I lost my freshman scholarship in a dismal welter of C's and D's, though my adviser kept pointing out that I'd entered with soaring College Board scores, hoping perhaps that I'd suddenly say, Oh yeah, now I remember, I'm a good student.

But too many other things compelled my attention. Spellbound, I wandered the campus and the streets I had known as a child, not a college town to me but a landscape of myth whose significance I found it impossible to impart even to the classmates closest to me. I hung out around Franklin King House, too shy to ask the people now working there if they had known Nana. I saw my Heights friends when I could, but they were working, getting ready to be married; I'd met the man I would marry myself. And I was supposed to be studying.

The great gift that first year came through the accident of being placed in a dormitory with a recent reputation as "debutante house" with a lowering scholastic average which the housing office tried to stack with freshmen on scholarship. My classmates tended to be politically left, socially dim, good at friendship, spirited debate, and high nonsense. The seniors caucused about us; we were so hopeless, there would be little point staging freshman mixers on our behalf. We grinned at each other. It was like the Heights. We had each other. We still do.

Those women got me through. What one of us didn't know, someone else was sure to. In the house dining room set with linen and candles, I learned from them how to manage a knife and fork, how to approach soup. Someone's Canadian graduate student fiancée smuggled Enovid down to blue-lawed Massachusetts; someone else could make thrift-shop hems hang well; all of us shared the stories of where we'd come from, told one another how good we were, supported one another through and beyond the time when we found, as we almost all did, the classes and teachers who mattered, the work we really wanted to do. For me, that took the better part of three years.

As a freshman, I would stay awake all night talking, or devouring books that weren't assigned, while forgetting to study for a biology exam on mitosis. I memorized great swatches of poetry, and yet the trick of the five-part essay eluded me, and I could not seem to avoid the marginal comment of *overly personal response* on papers for my English professors. The first teacher to grant me a B at Smith remarked to another student that he thought it remarkable I was so perceptive, given that I came of "poor stock." And for those first two years, given that background, I was a listless language student. My dad forced me to take Spanish instead of the French I loved because Spanish was the "language of the future," and because, as he put it, French was spoken only by "fancy diplomats" and "your own relatives who still don't have a pot to piss in." *Aren't you glad?* he asks me, now that I have lived in New Mexico for nearly twenty years. *No,* I say. I'd have learned Spanish here, where I need it. But in that time, in Northampton, at once so strange and so familiar, so haunted with my ghosts, what I required most was to reaffirm my own roots.

My sophomore year, allowed to return on loans, I resolved to dig in and do well. In a creative writing class, I tried to write about my family, my life, not Northampton, not Old South Street or Hampshire Heights, not yet, but about Maine, about summers waitressing or working at Sebago-Moc, hand-stitching the uppers for pricey moccasins such as no Algonquian ever wore; about practicing with my .22 on chunks of paper pulp floating down the Presumpscott River below our house; about my brother coming home bloodied, proud of decking the drunk who tried to mug him at the Riverside Roller Rink.

My British teacher, pale and anorexically thin, wears huge geometric earrings, nail polish in odd shades of green and fuchsia. My stories come back with C+'s and B−'s, sparse comments in her minuscule handwriting—"inappropriate diction." When I describe Richard Widmark's wiping out a machine gun nest with three grenades, she notes "one would be sufficient surely." She reads to us from D. H. Lawrence, Mary McCarthy, never talking about our own stories, and I never get to say it took three grenades because the Japanese kicked the first two out of their foxhole. When I showed up timidly at her office hour one day, she asks sharply, "Are you fishing for a change of grade?"

I say no, stuttering, I just want to do better next time. "Give that here, then," she sighs, and she takes from me the story about my brother's fight, the one that contains the description of the Widmark movie. Her fingers are almost translucent in the light through the gothic window of her office. The silence is very long.

"This, here," she says at last, and her blue fingernail taps a sentence where a father is ranting about a "nefarious sod who couldn't find his own arse with both hands." This character, she says, would not use this language.

"How come?" I ask. I truly do not know what she means; is it the profanity? Does she think someone who says "arse" wouldn't use a word like "nefarious?" But she thinks I am being insolent. Or just dumb, hopelessly dumb. She sighs again. If I don't see the point, she says, she doesn't see how she can very well convey it to me. So I don't try to explain about the grenades, about the rolling silver and vulgar eloquence of working-class Irish. I leave her office diffusely ashamed and angry, still not sure of how I've failed. But whatever that failing is, I think, it will surely keep me from being a writer.

My friends kept me together. And there came at last the meaningful classes, Daniel Aaron's American literature, most dramatically, with a syllabus miraculously advanced for 1962; not just Thoreau and Melville, but Chopin, Norris, Harold Frederick's Irish immigrants, Cather's and Jewett's country people, Dreiser's working men and women. And there was Aaron himself, assuring me that I could write: Aaron, upon my shyly mentioning Nana, displaying interest and pleasure: *That's really wonderful, you know: tell me about it. What dorm . . . ?* I cried after I left his office that day from sheer relief, the relief of validation.

When I read the autobiographical accounts in Ryan and Sackrey's *Strangers in Paradice: Academics from the Working Class,* what surprises me is how little they speak of what that experience has meant for them as teachers of their own working-class students. Most of us, I think, carry a sense of not fully belonging, of being pretenders to a kingdom not ours by birthright. In the year I came up for tenure at UNM, I dreamed of leaving the university before I could be asked to leave, taking a job as a waitress in what I call in a poem "my sad downtown that was always waiting." Some teachers bury their sad downtowns deep inside them; they strive to be more punctilious, academic, "objective," more "Ivy League" than most of the professors who actually taught me at Smith or Yale.

But for most of us, I think, our pasts are a strength, a means of connecting with our own students' lives, with literature itself, a talisman to carry into any classroom to remind us of the multiplicity of histories, of the stories we study in that room in addition to the printed ones, the stories that together with the books make up the real text of our class. At a state university in the southwest, those stories are especially multiple.

D has been my problem child in my Whitman and Dickinson course—a body builder, often late, annoyingly macho. A good month into our work on Whitman, after much talk of gender, sexuality, biography, he suddenly exclaims, "Hey, wait a minute: Was Whitman queer?" He cannot, he claims, "seem to feel all this emotion you guys feel when you read poetry." In desperation, trying to help him find a paper topic, I suggest he try *Specimen Days* instead of the poems. I steel myself to read his paper.

But D's paper is a stark account of his childhood as an MIA's son, a fatherless kid trying to figure out how to be a man, manly. It is about using his high school graduation gift money on a fruitless trip to Saigon to look for clues about his father, and his determination now to get on with his own life. And his paper is about the reawakening of all his old questions in reading Whitman's descriptions of released Union prisoners-of war. D's paper ends by saying, *I love Walt now, but I hate him too. Because he has made me remember. And he wants to be my father.*

C is in the same class, a Pueblo Indian, a shy, attentive single mother living too far from the close-knit community where she was raised. We're on Emily now—my home-girl, from Amherst, Hampshire County, in the state of Massachusetts. I've told the class how I didn't even know she was dead until I was eight or so, because every time we drove down Amherst's main street, my folks would point and say, "There's Miss Dickinson's house."

Last Friday was a beautiful October day when we were all getting a little overdosed on death kindly stopping and looks of agony, and I suggested we just read together the nature poems that often don't get taught because they don't require much teacherly help or comment. It was a wonderful hour of hummingbirds like revolving wheels, leaves unhooking themselves from trees, and the frog who wears mittens at his feet. I smile to myself, remembering the bullfrogs of Smith. C nodded and nodded as we read.

Today, Monday, C comes up after class, and asks, "Did you know I'm Frog Clan?"

No, I didn't. But I do now.

She tells me she brought Dickinson's frog poems home with her over the weekend to show her clan elders back at the pueblo. "They liked them," she says, and adds, grinning, "Frog people are supposed to be good talkers."

I say I think Dickinson would have loved knowing that.

Yeah, she agrees. She's been having trouble writing her paper, but she got the draft done this weekend at home. It felt good, she says: "It was kind of like taking Emily home to meet my folks, you know what I mean?"

Yeah, I do. I do.

A Farmer's Daughter in Academia

B EING oppressed because of one's marginal status of race, gender, and social class creates defensive skills that evolve as part of a strategy for social mobility. As my career illustrates, all three variables, though present, are not equally relevant in any single situation, and one or two alone can assert a primary potency. A person with marginal status can maintain a reserve of skills for cultural self-defense and justice.

Five generations ago in north central Alabama, the men and women of my family were farming the plantation lands owned by their white masters. From Emancipation in the mid-1860s to the early 1900s, the majority of my ancestors still lived on or near their homelands, continuing their farming tradition mostly under a debt-peonage system known as tenant farming or sharecropping. It was some white landowners' unscrupulous manipulation of this farming system, made possible by the institutionalized racism of the justice system and widespread illiteracy among black farm families, that made it nearly impossible for black farmers to buy land.

These "push" factors, combined with the attraction of economic opportunity in urban areas, served to create an exodus of more than 400,000 blacks from the rural South to northern cities between 1910 and 1930 (Ploski and Williams 587). Many members of my family were among these migrants, including several clusters of great-aunts, uncles, and cousins. Not all the migrants remained in their adopted cities. A few returned home after their sojourn, lured back by the call of the land. My mother was one who returned. She decided she would rather live in the country than in the city; she preferred to till the soil as a farmer than toil in a hotel as a waitress or in a laundry as a clothes presser. The man she later married shared her feelings about farming and her ambitions for her family.

As parents in the post–World War II era, my mother and father tried to pass on a legacy by teaching their children the work ethic of a family farm, by accumulating enough money to buy their own land, and by providing access to higher education. In terms of profits from crop sales and as loan collateral, owning our farm was essential for the sustenance and education of six children.

The economic instability of agriculture usually requires small farmers to seek additional incomes with second, nonfarming jobs. Thus, the operation of our family farm, where we grew cotton, sugar cane, and corn, had to be supplemented by income from my father's civil service job as a tool clerk on a military base and from my mother's career as a hospital maid. Otherwise, our farm could have suffered the same fate as that recorded by census figures, which show a continual decline in the number of small farms, especially black family farms. For instance, the rate of decline of black family farms during the 1970s was nearly three times that of white family farms, 65 percent compared to 22 percent (Ploski and Williams 587). After my father's death in 1978, my mother continued to operate the farm, albeit on a smaller scale. Recent figures for Alabama show that in doing this she was one of a rapidly dwindling number of female operators of farms. In 1978, there were 2,894 white women and 362 women of color (blacks and other races) who ran farms; by 1987, there were 2,779 white women but only 178 women of color (*1987 Census of Agriculture* 20).

Owning their own farm was essential to my parents' dream of providing all their children with a high level of education. They understood the value of education and their dream was influenced by their experiences with southern school systems built on the "separate but [un]equal" practice of public education. The school year for blacks was shorter than for whites, and smaller per capita expenditures meant there was always a lack of good equipment, too few books, and not enough teachers.

My father often shared stories about the way he was deprived of all but an elementary education because his father sent the children to work in the white man's fields instead of sending them to school. My father thought his father had been wrong in keeping him and his brothers out of school, but as a sharecropper his father had to get along with the white landowner by using his children's labor, and this need prevented his seeing the value of education. In our family, higher education became a paramount goal, one that was greatly affected by the civil rights movement.

Although the Civil Rights Act of 1965 eliminated numerous segregation laws and practices, some things were not changed. For instance, our town's library retained its policy of restricting blacks from checking out books. My mother responded to this by subscribing to a variety of magazines (*Ebony, U.S. News & World Report, Life*) in order to provide us with more reading materials; and for reference sources, we had the *Encyclopaedia Britannica.*

Although it met with foot dragging, the most momentous change wrought by the Civil Rights Act of 1965 was the creation of "freedom of choice" in the selection of schools. In the black school system, some parents and teachers decided to exercise this freedom lest it be taken away. My parents volunteered their children to help integrate the town's public schools. Suddenly my blissful years in our all-black schools came to an end.

There were so few blacks attending the city school that there was just *one* black in each grade, seventh to twelfth. We rarely saw each other except in passing as we changed classes. We were mostly silent, seemingly at a loss for words to describe the lonely experiences. Then one day, not long into the fall term, I saw a glimmer of color as I passed the mirror in the girls' restroom and I stepped backward to look again. My brown face, reflected in a pool of white faces, posed a startling contrast in the mirror. I studied that image, not certain how I felt. Later I described the incident to my brothers. For me that conversation marked a turning point, for my brothers and I discovered that each of us had a story to tell. Those stories helped us educate ourselves about surviving the oppressive status of racial minority.

In the 1960s styles of school integration, our social status as outsiders was evident not only in the numerical ratio but also in the cultural bias in our curriculum. History texts scarcely recognized the existence of blacks except as slaves, so there was rarely mention of black inventors and scientists unless we students spoke up. In literature, Mark Twain's runaway slave Jim in *Huckleberry Finn* was the closest my tenth-grade class ever came to studying a black presence. Becoming aware that it was necessary that I take an active, not a passive, role in the educational process, I began to supplement my classwork with literature, history, and political philosophies that spoke to my experiences as a member of America's oppressed classes. I subscribed to *Negro World* (later *Black Digest*) and as each of my brothers went off to college, I enlisted him to send home books by and about blacks. I wanted education to be a liberating opportunity, a chance to change the traditions of white supremacy over women and men of color and of gender supremacy of males over females.

When we graduated from high school, our parents allowed us to select the college of our choice. Expense was to be a secondary consideration for they would remortgage the farm if need be. My oldest brother chose Fisk University (Nashville, Tennessee), but two years after his graduation, our parents were still repaying his tuition loans. My second brother and I chose Berea College (Berea, Kentucky), a less-expensive college with free tuition and a work-study program. Although three of us were in college at the same time, the two of us at Berea could pay most of our own expenses, a situation that lessened the financial strain for the next college-bound child.

We had been farm laborers since childhood and my brother and I were no strangers to the work ethic; having spent several years integrating a white school, we were also well socialized to academic competition and collaboration with whites. Among our black classmates, there were several who had similar school integration experiences but of these, more were from urban than rural backgrounds. I was particularly attracted to a fellow student leader from the latter group, and by graduation, had married this activist (and poet).

By staging protest demonstrations, marches to Berea's city hall, and sit-ins at the college president's office, we challenged injustices from the city's and college's administrations, the local police, and merchants. Despite being predominately white, Berea College had emphasized interracial education since its founding by abolitionists in the mid-1800s. State law had forced it into racial segregation from 1904 to 1950, but the college was at the height of its reintegration efforts by 1971 when black students had become nearly 10 percent (130) of the total student body. The black student body was large enough to sustain a sense of community and a reassurance of self-worth that I had not encountered since grade school. On several occasions, our numbers swelled with the presence of white cohorts who were committed to civil rights. Our interracial coalitions succeeded on many fronts, and we won such "victories" as greater inclusion of black scholarship in the curriculum, increased hiring of blacks as faculty and staff, improved liaisons between police and students, and reinstatement of a popular residence hall director.

As other activists and I progressed through college, the euphoria of the civil rights activities subsided. Embarking on new careers, we had ideals about self-dignity and justice being an integral part of one's work. However, the reality of job hunting after graduation was a shock because the country was entering a recession.

In Kentucky, the recession caused a temporary hiring freeze on state employment, which aborted my chance to get a social work position. To obtain such a position might have placed me on a career track deemed nontraditional for a black woman because traditional jobs for us are in agricultural work and domestic service, as mill and factory operatives and teachers (Newman 10). Instead, I got a job as a clerk-typist in a local factory, a traditional job for white, but not black, women. I was hired for the beauty of my skin, not for my degree in sociology! Being a racial token did not make me as unhappy as the routine nature of the work and the minimal salary. Within a year, I resumed my search for a meaningful job with an equitable paycheck.

Although my husband's job as a counselor/teacher in a comprehensive educational training program (CETA) seemed meaningful, the pay—because it was subject to annual grant renewals—was tenuous. When my search led me to a very nontraditional job as an enlisted member of the military, we discussed the potential limitations for his career but decided to take the risk. I joined the army, received electronic communications training, and worked as an internal management consultant with an infantry brigade in the Panama Canal Zone. Due to my top performance in the electronics school and my college degree, I was promoted to sergeant's rank after six months. This unprecedented mobility prompted the school commandant to ask, as he pinned on my new stripes, "Are you really that smart?" I saluted and said, "Yes sir."

The commandant's question probably stemmed from his surprise at seeing a black woman at the head of the class. In 1976 women of any color were still the exception rather than the rule in the army, especially in a nontraditional field like electronics. As for me, I felt I was being treated justly for the first time, receiving promotions commensurate with my abilities.

One tour of duty was enough to quench my wanderlust and it enabled me to discover my abiding interest in academics. While stationed in Panama, I earned a master's degree in human relations, and after my honorable discharge, I planned to pursue a graduate degree in sociology. My husband was eager to resume his career, freed from the strain that came with the role of being a military "dependent." He accepted a job as college admissions counselor for our alma mater and we resettled in Berea.

In retrospect, my transition from a soldier stationed in Central America to a graduate student in a North American Ivy League university, Yale, seems as incredible to me as it did to my graduate school peers. I felt as though I spent the first six months answering the question: "How did you get *here?*" My best (and most truthful) response was that my husband had sent me. After all, it was his idea that I apply to a school in the East when we lived in the South. Those long-distanced miles symbolized a cultural gap between my working-class heritage and that of my upper-middle-class white schoolmates.

My class consciousness was raised, but not by the Rolls Royces double-parked outside the residence halls on family visits or the elegant furs my classmates wore about campus after the first snowfall. Rather, it happened in a casual conversation with classmates about our families' education. While I had assumed (rightly) that their parents had college degrees, even doctorates, I was amazed to hear that several of their *grandparents* also possessed higher education degrees. In contrast, my grandparents had obtained basic literacy skills, albeit no small achievement given the educational conditions for blacks and other poor southerners. I had never been more aware than at that moment of the vastness between society's haves and its have-nots.

Being part of a sexual minority in the military enabled me to hone survival skills I had learned during school integration. However, the prevalence of class distinctions was a new overlay for my perceptions and social interactions. I became extremely cognizant of how extraordinary an opportunity it was for anyone, other than members of America's elite families—let alone a southern black farmer's daughter—to attend Yale. My school expenses were being met by university and government fellowships, loans, and veterans' benefits, and I was determined to finish what I started, or, in a mystical sense, to finish my part of a generational relay, a motion started by all those relatives who scrubbed floors and hoed fields. This one was for *us*.

Aside from the academic rights, there were out-of-classroom learning opportunities such as study groups and teaching and research assistantships, where race and gender politics were subtle but crucial. I joined with other peers to form a community of outsiders working together across disciplines, across racial, gender, and (some) social class distinctions. After three years in residence and four more in researching and writing my dissertation, I obtained a doctorate in sociology. I was job hunting once again.

Entering the specialized job market of academia was a reassuring experience compared to my earlier ones in the general market. This time employers were seeking me as much as I was seeking them. Before I finished my dissertation, I had begun teaching as a part-time sabbatical replacement in the sociology department at Berea, my alma mater. This had been so mutually beneficial that the college retained my services. After a national search, I was hired, with promotion, as a full-time replacement for a retiring colleague.

At Berea College, the general campus culture is concerned about the presence and retention of black students, faculty, staff, and administrators in numbers above the level of tokenism. Keeping college decision makers aware of the college's historic commitments (i.e., to educate women and men regardless of race), provides a strong rationale for special strategies to combat oppression. For instance, a task force on gender issues presented its proposal for women's studies on the premise that the college's historic admission of women serves as a precedent for curriculum revisions to integrate feminist scholarship.

I enjoy congenial and supportive relations with my colleagues, and we often talk candidly about gender, race, and class concerns and related topics. Across campus, however, some of my black colleagues (students and faculty) are not so ideally situated. For them, the campus climate appears as "chilly" as those reported in a recent study of many colleges and universities (Moses 18–20).

To keep myself abreast of the chilling conditions that some of us encounter, I try to touch base with each black colleague on a frequent basis. For instance, we have established a standing date for a weekly lunch meeting. This is on an informal basis and any single meeting includes as many of us who can make it that day. Besides the "small talk," we discuss teaching concerns, upcoming organizational developments, and tips on faculty committee assignments. We supplement the orientation of the relatively new faculty and staff to our college and town. Because our group represents a variety of disciplines, we can give

146

information ranging from health and nutrition to literary critiques and financial advice.

In addition to being part of our black support group, I (along with most of the rest of that group) also participate in our campuswide women's issues group and in an interdisciplinary professional development group. These experiences allow us to exchange influences through an interracial, coeducational network. Maintaining this network does require time and effort, but I shall continue to participate not only because of the vast encouragement that I get by being in the company of friends, but also because our network enables us to draw upon each other's strengths in order to stay vigilant against the subtle injustices aimed at "outsiders." The presence of injustice anywhere threatens justice everywhere, even for the "insiders."

Works Cited

Moses, Yolanda T. *Black Women in Academe: Issues and Strategies.* Project on the Status and Education of Women, Association of American Colleges. Washington, August 1989.

Newman, Debra Lynn. "Black Women Workers in the Twentieth Century." *Sage* 3.1 (1986): 10–15.

Ploski, Harry A. and James Williams, ed. *The Negro Almanac.* 5th ed. Detroit: Gale, 1989.

U.S. Department of Commerce. Bureau of the Census. *1987 Census of Agriculture.* Washington, DC, 1987.

Yer Own Motha Wouldna Reckanized Ya: Surviving an Apprenticeship in the "Knowledge Factory"

And I? I will do everything and anything until the end of my days to stop anyone ever talking to me like that woman talked to my mother. It is in this place, this bare, curtainless bedroom that lies my secret and shameful defiance. I read a woman's book, meet such a woman at a party (a woman now, like me) and think quite deliberately as we talk: we are divided: a hundred years ago I'd have been cleaning your shoes. I know this and you don't.

Carolyn Kay Steedman, *Landscape for a Good Woman*

Everyone knows that a "woman of letters," which is what it seems, as a graduate student in an English department, I am in training to become, is not someone who grew up in "the projects," a trailer court, a split-level exactly like all the rest on the block, in subsidized housing, or otherwise on the "wrong side of the tracks." Rather, the image of the female scholar, whose "job" is to pass her cultural knowledge of literary texts from one generation of students to the next, is one of refinement: she exudes an elegance of manners and intellect particular to that class of well-educated women to which she belongs. She is Virginia Woolf, arguing passionately for a "room of one's own"; she is Gertrude Stein, reinventing language—she is not Emma Goldman who, among her more newsworthy activities, lectured and wrote extensively about literature, nor is she Anzia Yezierska, who imagined a way to "authentically" represent the Russian and Jewish immigrant culture which was part of her verbal landscape as a child.

Although many English departments have become relatively comfortable with a critical agenda that asserts that the writers we study come from a multitude of race, class, and gender positions, the backgrounds of those of us who study those writers is not generally given much thought at all. The actual life experience of a female scholar is

148

rarely discussed and generally her ascension through the ranks of academia is assumed to be an unproblematic acquisition of the written, verbal, and cultural skills needed to perform well in a university setting. The participation of most poor and working-class women in academia, however, is frequently not easy or comfortable and is often attended by chronic interruptions while we seek outside avenues of cultural validation, financial support, or whatever else is necessary in order for us to continue. Yet there are many of us who are successful in obtaining jobs inside academic institutions. We often stick out because we do not choose to adopt the largely middle-class (and, of course, white) discourse in which most academic institutions conduct their business. We rankle the various ranks of academia to which we belong. We demand texts that describe our concerns when we study, speak to a different audience when we teach, prescribe to different critical agendas when we argue, and write about different subjects when we write.

We also write theory and find ourselves resisting theoretical models that refuse to include descriptions of the reality of working-class life. We participate in the activity of theory making even though theory can represent the very sort of abstract thought that has traditionally marked unfamiliar ground in our socially constructed experiences of working-class culture. If we are to accept, for example, current theoretical trends, which posit a notion of the "subject" secured by its "position" within "discourse" (and not by reference to some sort of transcendent essentialism), we accept both a limiting paradigm and a way of saying what we mean that linguistically alienates most of those "subjects" we intend to describe. In short, discourse theory with its formulation of passive subjects tends to overlook the ways that any symbolic system is subject to notions of "experience," the realm where class relations are understood, felt, and actually lived. The experiences of working-class women with the specific forms of knowledge gained from those experiences are never simply coded in one discourse but woven in between, through, and around a multitude of discourses. Forms of knowledge are ultimately discovered in what the fabric created by these often disparate discourses says or shows.

To begin to describe ways in which working-class "subjects" might be construed as active agents rather than as passive subjects necessitates a discussion of the role of experience in social relationships which is often missing from theories that focus on a concept of subjectivity as merely a function of the structure of discourse. To describe experience allows an opportunity to see how social relations can be appropriated, resisted, and undermined; it can also provide the basis for action.[1] I will accordingly try to focus my comments here on experiences, beginning with my own and later discussing some of those related to me by other poor and working-class women who have struggled with their apprenticeships as academics. What is the role of women working-class intellectuals (if that's what our training in academia makes us) in reproducing class society? How do our experiences of being working class shape our relationships to academia?

When I was about twelve, a girl from one of my classes invited me to her house. Her mother wished to encourage a friendship between the two of us because we had the highest scores on that year's academic achievement tests. Her father was a neurosurgeon and her mother a part-time nurse. My father worked in a factory and my mother worked part time in a department store. The Murphys had a house in the country, about two miles outside of the town where our school was. My family's house was about one mile on the other side of town in what were referred to as "the developments." My friendship with the daughter didn't last too long. I was allowed to visit at her house but there was always an excuse as to why she couldn't come to mine. But her mother and I became mutually fascinated with one another. Mrs. Murphy (Audrey, she insisted but I never felt quite entitled to say) seemed to want to know everything about me and about my family. How long had my father been in this country? What about my mother? How was it that I had such a large vocabulary and could use such sophisticated phrases? Why did I think it was that the rest of my family wasn't as smart as me? No adult had ever had time to take such an interest in me before, and I wanted very much to be listened to.

In my best twelve-year-old reasoning I explained to my friend's mother that my sophistication had come from reading, that my mother read between four and six books a week, and that I had picked up "reading" from her. She told me that it was an admirable thing that my mother kept herself up through reading, especially with all my brothers and sisters, and became embarrassed when I attempted a defense by asking her how many books a week she read. With her response and a trip to the room that housed their family library, I acquired my first definition of what literature was: what Audrey read were called novels, my mother read paperbacks. From that day on my reading practices changed. I became determined to know whatever it was that Audrey got from reading novels that my mother didn't get from reading what she read. Along with coveting the books she owned, I coveted Audrey's confidence, graciousness, and apparent wisdom and I tried desperately to find it at our town's tiny branch of the public library. And, although I occasionally slipped back into reading a gothic novel or two, after that most of my time was spent reading what my sister and I (and most university English departments) referred to as "classics."

What I was unable to understand until many years later was exactly how much the barely discernible note of disdain in Audrey's voice, as she differentiated my mother's reading habits from her own, was able to change totally the arrangement of one small part of my world and cause me to negotiate an adjustment to what I privately began to think of as more accepted or normal. I was, of course, making similar negotiations in other parts of my life. The older I grew the more familiar it became to keep making adjustments on many different levels. Without understanding what I was doing or why I was doing it, I began to feel ashamed of who I was, who my family was, what they thought about, where they came from, and I began to alter myself and my appearance in an attempt to escape association with what they seemed to represent to others.

By providing me with a range of choices and an advanced vocabulary, the novels I read began to help me satisfy my desire to get free from what I then perceived as the constraints of the social class in which I was being raised. The seemingly better worlds and richer landscapes each individual narrative offered provided me with a fantasy of escape and helped me to see how it was possible to make up for whatever social sophistication I lacked through language. More and more I began to live in two very separate worlds, the one that I was born into and the one I was constructing out of various fictions of what I thought normal, intelligent, educated people were really like. Today, I've learned to label these self-limiting activities as attempting to "pass" for middle class, but for a long time, including all of my undergraduate years, I lived in a confused state of preconsciousness where I often, although not always, felt an urgent need to mask my working-class origins. Nowhere did I feel a greater need for disguise than inside academic institutions where the heightened level of discourse both fascinated and intimidated me and put me in situations where I most feared that someone would discover that I was only pretending to be "educated" and force me to leave. Although I felt a great deal of tension, confusion, and discomfort, I was not able to articulate these feelings as linked to class oppression. The mechanisms of a dominant discourse were fully in operation: I internalized my feelings as somehow related to something out of place or missing in me rather than as indicative of a system of oppression carefully masked by myths of equal access and opportunity.

A deep passion for reading, which is intricately connected to notions of escape, survival, and passing, is part of the reality of almost all the poor and working-class women in academia that I know. To pass means to attempt to disguise working-class origins by outwardly adopting codes of behavior that come from outside working-class experience. Academic institutions present ideal situations for successful passing as they ostensibly operate under the premise that intelligence rather than background determines ability. Yet passing should also be seen positively as a skill that women from working-class backgrounds have developed in order to survive in academic environments. When used consciously, the ability to pass can become a valuable tool, capable of causing internal disruptions and potential manipulations of the institutions it operates within. But I'm jumping ahead of my argument here. Before I talk about how such experiences can be used for political ends, I must first describe their origins in class oppression.

For me, to be at college and to be able to read and interpret texts meant a freedom to experience words and worlds way beyond the grasp of what I had once considered to be available to me, but it also meant leaving behind the familiar validations of experience and community offered by my family and friends. My own passing included, among its other manifestations, altering my speech, changing the way I dressed, remaining silent during conversations about family, pretending to have enough money when I didn't, claiming I wasn't hungry when I was. I also developed a tendency toward automatic lying, filling in what I perceived as gaps in my background, telling people what I thought they wanted to hear, inventing, creating, making up stories. At that time in my life, these parts of me that I was giving up seemed unimportant, and I felt them as necessary sacrifices in order for me to be seen as legitimate. Nor did I think too much about the extra energy I was expending in my attempts to fit in: the trade-off was to become "educated," which would bring liberation.

Before I had developed any sense of class consciousness or a way to articulate class-based experience, I had learned to successfully negotiate my behavior away from the working-class culture I had been raised in to match that of the middle-class culture I had become immersed in. From this notion that there was a different set of cultural codes to adjust to eventually would come the recognition that the frames of reference for both sets of codes were illusory. At that time I was not concerned in any conscious or intentional way with identifying the nature of class relations as they operate within academic institutions. Nevertheless, through my experiences of difference eventually came the knowledge that exposed the central fallacy under which all educational systems operate: that success is determined by effort or ability rather than by class background. This was not an outside knowledge brought to me through a theory of class relations but something that arose out of my experience of class-based oppression.

Just as passing presents an aspect of experience that is unique to poor and working-class women in training to become academics, there are other social and intellectual survival strategies we use in attempts to continue to gain access to the cultural expertise offered by a university education. Where there are no family resources to provide us with the necessary financial or cultural prerequisites for our educations, we learn to do just about anything to be able to keep reading books. Economic survival is often the most basic of our concerns, and I will accordingly recount here some of the strategies other working-class women in academia have used in order to remain in school. I have one friend, for example, who described a period of about six weeks where she would take three or four books per night to sell at a used-book store on her way to the supermarket so she could have money to buy food. She was a Victorianist and, after being unable to part with Jane Austen, was alphabetically up to Dickens before her student-loan check finally arrived. This was after having sold off her classics, seventeenth-, eighteenth-, and twentieth-century texts and her copy of the abridged OED (which she was overjoyed to get thirty dollars for, describing the money as almost enough to feed her for two weeks).

Another friend had developed techniques for reading books without breaking their spines so she could return them a few days later claiming she was no longer enrolled in the course. Another shoplifted books but kept a record of every time she did, hoping to pay the money

153

back in some future time when she had more cash. She knew that if she were caught she would have to agree never to "shop" at the university bookstore again, but she was hoping to make it through all her course work before that happened. She later acquired a stamp marked "used book" and began to change prices.

Another friend found a way to successfully hide her enrollment at a local university from the state so she could receive food stamps, which she then traded with others for money so she could buy books. Another worked every Monday night, the "single women and children" shift, at a local food bank. She told others that it was her way to help homeless women but privately confessed to me that it not only guaranteed her a meal but usually provided her with extra food she could take home. Another woman forged her father's name on a new income tax return when he refused to stop declaring her as his dependent.

One particularly desperate friend described how she frequently signed herself up as a paid participant for psychological and medical experiments conducted at the medical school of the university she was attending. She particularly liked the ones that involved only a few hours of her active participation but included two or three weeks of isolation and felt that she got some of her best studying done in hospital rooms. She stopped participating, however, after having agreed (for $460) to be part of an experiment comparing the spinal fluid of anorexics with that of "normal volunteers." Something went wrong with the spinal tap that her doctor-in-training performed on her; she spent two weeks in bed recovering from the botched procedure.

Another strategy common to women students from working-class backgrounds when faced with a lack of funding to continue their education is to seek employment within universities as clerical workers. There are a large number of working-class women in academia who have worked as secretaries, receptionists, filing clerks, word processors, or administrative assistants in universities, often in the very departments that will eventually grant them their degrees. In the English department where I am currently enrolled as an advanced graduate student, there has been a steady stream of fellow graduate students who also work as secretaries in our department. Many of them are relieved to find employment in such a familiar environment even though their jobs frequently put them in uncomfortable situations with both their professors and other students.

154

Of course, all students at one time or another find themselves in financially difficult situations. What makes the situation of poor and working-class women so unique is the way in which economic survival strategies are intimately connected to our self-esteem and collective notions of fear, shame, and defiance that make up our individual family or neighborhood landscapes. For the women I described above to have to "go on welfare" in order to stay in school meant she had to carry around a great deal of shame and a sense of having betrayed her familial and cultural values. In addition, her eventual employment as a secretary in a university left her feeling as though that was where she belonged: her proper place in the overall scheme of things was as a worker rather than as a thinker.

Much of what students from middle- or upper-class backgrounds take for granted and expect to be a part of college life is quite outside the experience of those of us who were the first in our families to attend college. I can imagine that most students from middle-class backgrounds have not had the experience of enjoying dining hall food (because it is like "eating out" every night) nor do they delight in the privacy offered by a dormitory room shared with only one other person. Furthermore, they probably don't feel as though their delight and excitement at their new surroundings needs to be hidden. These feelings were all part of my first few days at college.

If I had remained only within university environments, I may never have discovered that I was raised working class. Although three generations on my mother's side and two generations on my father's side of my family had been laborers, they all thought of themselves as equal players in a mainly middle-class America, the land of opportunity for all. The members of the Polish side of my family, my grandmother, aunts, uncles, and cousins, had a concept of themselves as culturally distinct, but there were no class distinctions made even though a general mood of inferiority and lack of a sense of entitlement pervaded almost all their interactions outside their immediate neighborhood. Their struggle was so entirely defined as an attempt to rid themselves of the markers of their status as immigrants that the fact that some of those markers were class based did not occur to them as that important. It must have seemed to them that to stop sounding, acting, and looking Polish would unquestionably mean one had obtained the status of sounding, acting, and looking like middle-class Americans.

Having been "born and raised in America," both my parents had achieved their parents' goals of cultural proficiency, but the class-based markers remained. In terms of their dealings with the world, these translated into very little confidence, pride, or conviction in their own right to exist, and what I learned from them was that in most cases it was best to submit to those in positions of greater authority, power, and knowledge. Clichéd messages like "Don't rock the boat"; "It's best to just let a sleeping dog lie"; and "It doesn't do any good to try and buck the system," which had been passed to them from their parents, informed their personal vocabularies of self-debasement and shame, which they then passed on to me. This discourse of subjugation and deference to others had become so naturalized in them that they were unable to imagine any other, let alone begin to touch on the causes or reasons for the differences they must have felt.

Education was devalued in the white working-class culture in which I was raised.[2] My parents actively tried to discourage me from attending college. Prophesies of failure from my mother abounded; she was sure that I wouldn't finish my first year, let alone graduate. Although they could afford to, they provided no financial support; they did not want to participate in my separation from them. They did not want me to go outside their world, to become unfamiliar, to become a part of any of the institutions that they vaguely sensed were responsible for their manipulation and oppression. They were, it seems, at least somewhat correct in their fears: my college education made me no longer completely one of them. Not only did my vocabulary change by the time I had finished college, but I also had begun to dress differently, was eating different foods, and, among countless other small changes, insisted on fresh ground rather than instant coffee. I also began to notice a change in my family's responses to me. My mother occasionally now used the tone of humility and deference with me that she usually reserved for authority figures like police, bank officials, and bureaucrats while privately asserting her dismay to my brothers and sisters at how much better than the rest of the family I thought I had become.

My understanding of feminism, which had become much more grounded in the four years of relatively uninterrupted "reading" that college had provided, also helped to alienate me from my family and cultural roots. I had become an activist, organizing demonstrations, participating in acts of civil disobedience, attending conferences, and helping to publish a feminist newspaper. The feminist agenda to which I had committed myself, however, failed to include a class analysis. Nevertheless, my participation in feminist and radical communities did provide me with the tools of self-discovery that I needed to begin to analyze the sense of difference of which I had always been acutely aware.

Coming out as a lesbian was the main event that prepared me for the much more difficult ordeal of coming out as working class. As part of the powerful discourse of positive self-esteem and discovery present in most lesbian and gay communities, the experience of coming out taught me to turn shame and fear into anger and action. For me, a critique of power relations first came from the oppression I felt as a member of a sexual minority. The process of growing to understand myself as working class was very similar to the process of growing to understand myself as lesbian. Because of my early proclivities for "reading," I went to the library. When I began to think of myself as a lesbian, I took out every lesbian novel I could find. A whole new world and language was opened to me. When I began to think of myself as working class, I searched the library again. I wanted retellings of experience, not theory, yet this time I had a harder time knowing quite what headings in the card catalog to look under to find novels told from the perspective of working-class women.

My discoveries in the library gave me the beginnings of a class analysis, a reason to begin graduate school, and a subject to study once I got there. Talking with other women graduate students who also identified as being from poor or working-class backgrounds became the only way to ensure my sanity in graduate school and to validate my own class-based experience. Once I began to share the strategies I had used for survival with these women and began to listen to their experiences, my own no longer seemed so strange or even so extreme. Together we began to unravel the layers of shame, fear, and insecurity that represented our legacies as working-class scholars. We also began to imagine the beginnings of an analysis of class and gender relations that would not only describe our experience but also help us develop pedagogical approaches to use with other women students.

The lived experience of class-based oppression is what forces many working-class women academics from a cultural understanding of the operation of difference to a political recognition of the way in which social relations are ordered. We eventually learn to create rearticulations of our experience in order to discover a sense of identity. Leaving behind what is familiar to us in exchange for unfamiliar intellectual and economic survival strategies often provides a catalyst for critique and a desire to understand new terms in the subject/subjugated argument, allowing for the possibility of agency and real movement. The way that we exist as working class forms an identity not automatically written into the internal power relations of any particular context or discourse. What began as survival strategies have changed, for many of us, into powerful instruments we use to manipulate our environment. We have learned to reclaim the weapons of fear and shame once used against us, appropriating them for acts of defiance and creative undermining.[3]

There are, after all, advantages to our position. One fellow scholar argues that women from working-class backgrounds have nothing at stake in the middle-class ideologies that often pass for knowledge in academic institutions. She feels that her lack of complicity with the cultural values advanced by universities has put her in a better position than others to ask questions, "for bourgeois scholars, deconstruction is the latest critical theory, for working-class scholars it has always been a way of life."[4] The ability to see from at least two viewpoints at once, which the experience of passing provides, often makes it easier for working-class women to form alliances with members of other oppressed groups who experience similar disjunctions. We are also usually very adept at translating between individuals and institutions, exposing and demystifying self-perpetuating systems of authority. We tend to place the emphasis on individuals rather than on a set of invisible rules of conduct, trying to recognize and validate those students who seem to have a hard time adjusting to academic life.

The experience of feeling like an outsider in academic environments allows many of us access to a better understanding of the ideological function of the institutions we work within. One friend described to me how her position as working class gave her a clear understanding that the role of the state college she attended was to churn out teachers and low-level managers. She subsequently felt more knowledgeable and less pressured than those around her to adopt the façade of success that was being proffered by the institution. Another woman described how she used her ability to pass to gain access to classrooms. She knew what cultural knowledge she was supposed to be passing on to her students but instead chose to use her role as teacher differently. Common assignments for her included initiating discussions that, among other goals, would help students begin to deconstruct their experiences of difference and their complicity with the power relations at work within their immediate surroundings.

In general, we women graduate students from working-class backgrounds have an understanding of the nature of "work" that differs from those around us. On the one hand, our experience of work as physically difficult and labor intensive makes academic work seem easy, hardly like work at all. On the other hand, it is easy for us to see how institutions often disguise work as something other than work: where being nominated to serve on an undergraduate curriculum committee, for example, is presented as a helpful addition to a curriculum vitae instead of as the additional two hours per week work time that it is. Many working-class women academics also have more of a notion of work as separate from life: being an academic is what you do for a living as opposed to who you are the rest of the time.[5]

Working-class women academics who have also worked as secretaries in educational settings are quick to understand exactly where decision-making power lies within their departments. One friend describes using her sense of camaraderie with other secretaries to cut through much of the bureaucratic red tape experienced by her fellow graduate students. She was able to secure office and classroom assignments, keys to rooms, parking permits, and other everyday survival needs through her ability to interact with secretaries as peers. There is also no better way that I can think of for deconstructing the intellectual and cultural mystique of the ivory tower than being "on staff," where it becomes very clear that undergraduate acceptances, graduate appointments, faculty appointments, and tenure decisions are based on politics rather than merit.

Through the experience of living within the particular social relation of being both female and a working-class scholar comes the knowledge of how both articulations of dominant forms of discourse and resources against them are carried in permanent conflict. This recognition punctures and deflates the persistent myth of both working-class and female passivity just as our position as "educated" destroys the fiction of working-class ignorance and subordination. Although these comments should not be seen as an attempt to valorize the survival strategies used by working-class women in academia, they do recognize those strategies as forms of resistance being cultivated within the very system that has produced our subordination. It is equally important to note that the danger of our potential incorporation into the middle class is great and that we must learn new ways to resist the temptation to abandon our cultures and families of origin for the promised land of middle-class respectability. "The master's tools will never dismantle the master's house," but perhaps we apprentices will begin to see ways that the internal form of a particular discourse can be used to control the master.[6]

Even today I am sometimes haunted by echoes of the shame I once felt but had no words for. I feel a great deal of sadness for the young scholar who carried that shame around and at the same time I am embarrassed by the "simple beliefs" I once had. My newly gained sense of entitlement often seems too fragile to sustain me, and if I'm not careful I can still become too paralyzed to use the privilege of my education to speak. But at last, after a long struggle, I have not needed to discard my family or cultural values. I live instead in a strangely ambiguous middle ground, insisting on the validity of my working-class roots and experiences yet also feeling outside of them, transported by means of education and political awareness to another place I can't quite call home.

My mother occasionally sends me what she calls "survival packages" to help me get by at school. They contain food, never money. In fact it always amazes me that she spends more money mailing the package to me than it would cost to send me a check and let me buy the food myself. But I'm glad she doesn't. Along with the canned beef stew that I no longer eat and always end up giving to a food bank, she inevitably includes a package or two of "International Coffees." These instant coffee drinks have pretentious packaging and names: Orange Cappuccino, Irish Creme, Suisse Mocha, Double Dutch Chocolate, and Cafe Vienna. She never drinks what the box proclaims are "elegant drinks" herself; she only buys them because they match her perception of what I like now that I live and work in such a "classy" environment. Her gifts never fail to bring a smile. Her attempts to understand me almost seem an ironic recognition of the in-between space in which I am always finding myself. I guess these are the coffee spoons with which I get to measure out my life.

Notes

1. See Paul Willis and Philip Corrigan, "Orders of Experience: the Differences of Working Class Cultural Forms" in *Social Text* 7 (Spring-Summer 1983) for an extensive discussion of the positioning of working-class "subjects" within discourse theory and the importance of "experience" in formations of meaning and knowledge.

2. My experience may be more typical of white working-class culture. In many experiences of working-class culture, education is valued as a tool for upward mobility. For example, in a workshop on classism I attended at the 1989 NWSA Conference, many of the black and Jewish working-class women reported having had a great deal of pressure from their families to attend college. In cases where family resources were limited, however, preference was given to support the education of male members of the family.

3. I am especially indebted to my conversations with Helen Boscoe, Pamela Fox, Beth Hutchison, Barbara Schulman, and Rachel Stevens for their thoughts on both the subjugation and the resistances of working-class women in academia.

4. From a conversation with Rachel Stevens, November 1989.

5. For an in-depth study of the ideological role of the academic institution as workplace, see Evan Watkins, *Work Time: English Departments and the Circulation of Cultural Values* (Stanford UP, 1989).

6. Audre Lorde, "The Master's Tools Will Never Dismantle the Master's House," in *This Bridge Called My Back*, ed. Cherríe Moraga and Gloria Anzaldúa (Watertown, Mass.: Persephone, 1981).

Going to Class

Pass the Cake: The Politics of Gender, Class, and Text in the Academic Workplace

IN HER 1925 NOVEL, *Bread Givers*, Anzia Yezierska's protagonist, Sara Smolinsky, reflects: "Whenever I passed a restaurant or a delicatessen store, I couldn't tear my eyes away from the food in the window. Something wild in me wanted to break through the glass, snatch some of the sausage and corned-beef, and gorge myself just once." *Bread Givers* is based on Yezierska's own experience of growing up female, immigrant, Jewish, ambitious, and working class on New York's Lower East Side. She goes on to say: "Nothing had ever come to me without my going out after it. I had to fight for my living, fight for every bit of my education."

Cherríe Moraga writes, in "La Guera": "It was through my mother's desire to protect her children from poverty and illiteracy that we became 'anglocized'; the more effectively we could pass in the white world, the better guaranteed our future."

A student in my course, "Working-Class Literature," wrote in her journal: "I know from my own family history that my grandmother worked and fed her family on cabbage soup, and vegetables from a neighbor's garden on occasion. . . . However much or little money there was, which was never enough, it was stretched to fit the needs of the family."

Mike Lefevre, a steelworker interviewed for Studs Terkel's *Working*, says: "I would like to see a building, say, the Empire State, I would like to see on one side of it a foot-wide strip from top to bottom with the name of every bricklayer, the name of every electrician, with all the names. So when a guy walked by, he could take his son and say, 'see, that's me over there on the forty-fifth floor. I put the steel beam in.' Picasso can point to a painting. What can I point to? A writer can point to a book. Everybody should have something to point to."

This talk was given in a Modern Language Association Forum on women and social class, in December 1989.

In *Silences,* Tillie Olsen writes: "In the twenty years I bore and reared my children, usually had to work on a paid job as well, the simplest circumstances for creation did not exist. . . . It is no accident that the first work I considered publishable began: 'I stand here ironing, and what you asked me moves tormented back and forth with the iron.'"

Langston Hughes, in his poem "Passing," writes:

the ones who've crossed the line
to live downtown
miss you,
Harlem of the bitter dream,
since their dream has
come true.

And in *Brown Girl, Brownstones,* one of Paule Marshall's Barbadian-American characters remarks to her friends: "In this white-man world you got to take yuh mouth and make a gun."

Finally, a quote from the journal of a student in my course, "Working-Class Literature," in the aftermath of a humiliating experience she had, as a defined "hardship case," applying for financial aid to take the law school boards prep course.

"This experience tells me that my class background is with me not only in the fact that I still am in need of financial assistance to achieve my education goals, but that my internalized shame and inferiority complex is raging just below the surface of my self-assurance and confidence. . . . I understand now that it does affect me and will continue to do so for the rest of my life. I think of the Morrison passage (in *The Bluest Eye*) when Pecola is buying candy. And although I am not black and therefore the situation is not exactly the same, I can identify. During the interview, my 'inexplicable shame' was, too, replaced by anger. 'Anger is better. There is a sense of being in anger. A reality and presence. An awareness of worth. It is a lovely surging.' However, for me too 'the anger will not hold . . . the shame wells up again, its muddy rivulets seeping into her eyes. What to do before the tears come.'" And she goes on to discuss *The Bluest Eye* in more detail, asking "Am I forcing a parallel between a race confrontation and a class confrontation? I hope not."

I want to speak here of my own experience as a woman from a working-class background crossing over into the land of academe, and

166

of my work with students from similar backgrounds who are also making that journey, or some part of it.

To repeat Yezierska's Sara Smolinsky: "Nothing had ever come to me without my going out after it. I had to fight for my living, fight for every bit of my education." This statement captures very well the experience of marginalized students. The majority of my students at the University of Massachusetts/Boston are from groups traditionally underrepresented in the academy; they have not had the launch pad of a middle-class upbringing. They represent a range of race and ethnic background; they range in age from seventeen to seventy, many of them work full time and are raising families while they go to school. They have made tough life choices to be in school. They have chosen an education and their education means a lot to them. Consequently, they work hard, they work us hard, and they are a joy to teach.

Working with these students keeps my own educational experience fresh—both the struggles and the occasional feeling of achievement. Like many of my students, I was the first in the history of my family to go to college. Certainly there was never any expectation that I would do so. I grew up the oldest of four children. My parents had both finished high school. My father was an enlisted man in the navy; my mother went out to work as a clerk in a bank as soon as her kids were all in school. One of my brothers has his B.A.; my sister and my youngest brother dropped out of high school, though they did later take and pass their GEDs. One of my brothers works in the oil fields of Texas (when there's work), the other is a construction worker in Boston. He moved to Boston because there wasn't any work in Texas. My sister works in a state office in Texas, has been raising a child, and cannot get any more wage increases or promotions unless she goes to college, which she is understandably apprehensive about doing. It seems like an alien world to her, even though her big sister immigrated to that foreign country some years ago.

The expectation for me, as the oldest girl, was that I would work in an office for a while and then get married and start having children. My mother had made sure that I took every business course the high schools I was in offered—so I would "have something to fall back on" if my marriage didn't work out. In fact, I did work as a clerk-typist for a year after high school. Then I got married, right on schedule. However, I also enrolled at a community college in Poughkeepsie, New York.

Evenings and weekends I held down a job at the information booth at nearby Vassar College, an experience that kept the concept of class stratification alive for me. After a year, I transferred to a state university. I went to school full time and worked from 5 P.M. to midnight five nights a week typing loading manifests at a trucking company. On weekends I cleaned the house and wrote term papers. The marriage didn't last but I did get a fellowship to graduate school. I was so used to working that the semester I started graduate school the first thing I did after finding a place to live was to get a job—and it took four months for it before it sunk in that I'd been given the fellowship so I wouldn't have to work and could study full time.

Because I had worked almost full time as a undergraduate, I had had little social/intellectual life outside the classroom. As a graduate student, once I stopped working and started hanging out in the library cafeteria like everyone else, I found that I often didn't know how to talk to people who had had Shakespeare or T. S. Eliot read to them when they were children, who spent their winter vacation in New York seeing the latest plays (I hadn't even seen a play until I was twenty-two), and whose parents were paying for their education. Perhaps there were other people also hanging out in the library cafeteria who had working-class backgrounds, but if so, they were keeping as quiet about it as I was. Time passed and I was trying to live on a teaching assistant's salary (which some of you will nostalgically remember was about $2700 a year in the early 1970s), and not making it stretch to cover the rent and groceries, so I took an extra weekend job as a security guard.

Lest this sound unremittingly grim, I want to say that I loved school. I was daily astonished and delighted that I actually got to spend my time reading (even though almost all of what I was reading at that time was written by economically privileged white men and Virginia Woolf) and I began to realize that if I could get a job in an increasingly difficult job market, and if I could then hold on to that job and get tenure, I would be able to spend my working life continuing to read literature and write about it and talk about it with students. That sounded really wonderful. There was nothing in the context in which I grew up that had even suggested this as a possibility.

Meanwhile, back in Texas, my family didn't understand much of this (how could they, they weren't living it), but they could see that what I was doing was better than working in a factory or an office, so they were happy for me. They did worry about whether I would become someone they didn't know. And every time I come home to visit, at some point my mother says with relief, "Pam, you haven't changed at all." She means this as, and I take it as, a compliment—though, of course, it's not entirely true. I have changed.

How ONE comes to some kind of personal and political consciousness, some sense of identity as a member of a group, is an odd underground kind of process. I had to work through to my own sense of class identity obliquely, by taking the first two courses in black literature (all texts by male writers) offered at my school in the late sixties, then by getting involved, however tentatively, in attempts to establish a women's studies program. (In my entire college career, only one book by a woman writer had been assigned in any of my courses—Virginia Woolf's *To the Lighthouse* in a seminar on modern British fiction. When I was studying for my Ph.D. qualifying exam, I came across this sentence about Marianne Moore in the then current edition of *Literary History of the United States:* "She is feminine in a very rewarding sense, in that she makes no attempt to be major." But by now all this is an old story to feminists of whatever social class.) I had encountered Marxist literary criticism by this time, but all that theoretical language didn't seem to have much to do with my own living experience both of nonprivilege and of feeling like an outsider.

Getting a job at UMass/Boston, where for the first five years I was alternately on part-time and one-year appointments, brought me into daily contact with working-class students, who reminded me vividly of myself a few years earlier. Then the leftist faculty group on my campus organized a retreat to talk about the relationship between our family backgrounds and our politics. As I listened to one person after another talk about their upbringing in middle- to upper-middle-class homes, their parents lawyers, doctors, and college professors, I realized with dismay that when my time came to talk, I was going to be highly visible, I was going to be revealed as an alien, someone different. And although I was not in the least ashamed of my background, it was going to be very uncomfortable to be the one working-class specimen in the group. The response to my story was mainly surprise—"we had no idea you were from a working-class background"—which let me see that I had been drifting along, passing as middle class, in something that was not quite a fog of denial but more like W.E.B. DuBois's concept of dual consciousness. Though not quite like that either—for relative visibility or invisibility affects the way one's marginalization is experienced. Class, like sexual preference and some forms of disability, is less immediately visible than race or gender. One can choose not to pass, to claim one's identity and heritage and the recognition of complexity that goes along with that or one can choose to deny all this.

Shortly after that experience, I decided to teach a course on working-class literature (and in the process I hoped to educate myself about the culture of my own people). I discovered that Tillie Olsen had taught a special topics course on working-class literature when she was a visiting professor at UMass/Boston in the early 1970s. So, feeling rather like the person who waters the young tree that Johnny Appleseed planted, I revived that course and have been teaching it for ten years. I taught that course the first year I had a regular tenure-track job. Two years later, I added another fairly controversial course, "Writing as Women," an intermediate-level writing course that studies women writers as models, considers recent work in feminist linguistics, and attempts to give students a space to discover their own powerful female writing voices. Though these two courses are not the sum of the teaching and writing I do, they are the two clearest forums where I've worked out my personal solution to the awkward situation of being an immigrant into the land of academe: that is, they have allowed me to identify myself clearly as an outsider—as (1) a woman and (2) from a working-class background—and to teach about class and gender from that perspective, trying to provide a context, a space, and a set of literary texts where students can engage the combination of personal, political, and literary issues that emerge. I think the outsider perspective is pedagogically and politically useful as well as honest. As one student remarked in his journal for working-class literature: "We live in a culture where something as forceful as [the film] *Salt of the Earth,* or [Harriet Arnow's novel] *The Dollmaker,* or [Alice Walker's short story] 'Everyday Use,' can only be made by outsiders."

Anzia Yezierska calls the part of her novel when her protagonist is in college "Between Two Worlds." And though she primarily means that in terms of the Americanization of her Eastern European immigrant heroine, it is clear that for her, Americanization is practically synonymous with upward mobility into middle-class status, as she says, with becoming a "person." And I think that sense of being an immigrant is a common experience for working-class students who go to college and are suddenly confronted with a culture in which people dress differently, eat differently, use language differently, express anger differently, perhaps don't even use their hands when they talk, have different notions about money, privacy, creativity, family, work, play, security. As Valerie Miner has written, we sometimes experience "cultural agoraphobia"; the landscape seems dotted with land mines that might blow up in our faces at any time.

What makes the experience even more complex is the peculiarly American denial of social class and the fervent belief in social mobility. I'm pretty sure, for example, that my family doesn't think of itself as working class and I therefore feel a certain amount of guilt and a sense of betrayal talking about us in those terms. Americans don't like to think of themselves as working class; at the same time we think of the working class as something to get out of. My favorite definition of the working class is Paul Lauter's; they are those who, "to advance their conditions of life, must move in *solidarity* with their class or must leave it." This is the actual lived experience and conscious dilemma of most working-class people in college. Class identity is so connected to our two-pronged national ideology of the Protestant ethic and the American dream—our vision of individualism, self-reliance, and "you can make it if you try"—that we tend, for example, to blame ourselves if we can't find a job, instead of seeing ourselves as part of "the reserve army of labor," which in times of capitalist economic recession is the first fired and last hired. In fact, as Harry Braverman points out in *Labor and Monopoly Capital: The Degradation of Work in the Twentieth Century*, more and more of what used to be seen as the middle class has been proletarianized in the degree of control it has over its work and in its ability to make ends meet.

Because of these complex attitudes about class, fairly early in "Working-Class Literature" we read *Ragged Dick*, an 1867 popular novel by Horatio Alger, whose title character is a ragged young shoeshine boy who, through luck, pluck, honesty, industry, good looks, a quick mind, and a sense of humor, finds benefactor after benefactor and ultimately crosses the class line to become Richard Hunter, Esquire, an educated young clerk on his way to fame and fortune—or at least to middle-class respectability. Not exactly what I'd call "literature,"

Ragged Dick is nevertheless a beautifully pure and unselfconscious expression of American dream ideology, a fantasy against which we place more realistic accounts of working-class characters who might be immigrant, female, African American, Native American, and/or angry (and therefore often lacking in a ready sense of humor), whose struggles to achieve a reasonably secure and satisfying life don't necessarily meet with the instant success of Alger's white, male, handsome, and lucky hero.

In addition to the works I've quoted from or titles I've mentioned already, the course has included Ann Petry's *The Street*, Tillie Olsen's *Yonnondio*, Richard Wright's "The Man Who Went to Chicago," Meridel LeSueur's "Women on the Breadlines," Mary Wilkins Freeman's "A Mistaken Charity," Maxine Hong Kingston's *The Woman Warrior*, Sharon Riis's *The True Story of Ida Johnson*, Langston Hughes' *Montage of a Dream Deferred*, Judy Grahn's *The Common Woman Poems*, Dorothy Richardson's *The Long Day: The Story of a New York Working Girl*, Thomas Hardy's *Jude the Obscure*, Alan Sillitoe's *The Loneliness of the Long Distance Runner*, Carolyn Chute's *The Beans of Egypt, Maine*, poems published by a group of Colorado miners in their union magazine during a 1903 strike, blues songs, films like *Modern Times*, *Union Maids*, *Our Daily Bread*, *Salt of the Earth*, and deSica's *A Brief Vacation*. With a few exceptions for purposes of contrast, we mainly focus on twentieth century American writing; the literary texts are supplemented by materials from economics, like Braverman's book, history like *The Jewish Woman in America* and *If All We Did Was to Weep at Home*, cultural criticism like Hazel Carby's article on the sexual politics of women's blues singing, excerpts from *Cheap Amusements*, a study of working-class leisure activities at the turn of the century.

It is not enough, however, simply to provide a "nontraditional" course content and then teach it in the traditional way—with a lecture format, exams, and standard explication-of-the-text papers. If the course is to serve as a bridge for working-class students between their lived experience and the academic world, then the pedagogy needs to be changed too. In the class, pairs of students take responsibility for preparing and leading discussion for part of a class on the assigned reading. In terms of written work, I have gradually phased traditional papers out of the course and replaced them with a critical reading journal. With the journal, I ask students to analyze individual works and

discuss them in the context of the secondary reading; respond personally, politically, intellectually to the course materials; make connections
between the texts as the semester goes on; make connections between
the literature and their own lives; argue or explore points brought up in
class discussion; bring in any other reading they are doing that seems
useful; and experiment with creative writing a bit, perhaps in the mode
of a writer we're studying. The reading journal fosters a continuity of
relationship to the course and encourages various types and levels of
connection. The point of both the student led discussions and the journals is to develop in students a sense of active ownership of the material.
Another way of saying this is that I, the designated teacher, have to
share ownership of it with them. This is especially important in literary
studies because culture and the canon have been the property and the
province of the privileged classes. In fact, one of the continual and
irritating problems in teaching working-class literature is the way much
of the literature has been kept out of print or keeps going out of print.
As with feminist, African-American, gay and lesbian, and ethnic literature, much archaeological work has had to be done to recover obscured
and buried texts—and much credit goes to the diggers as well as to the
publishers, often small presses, who have put the work back into print.

Since social class in the United States is so pluralistic, I've made a
conscious effort in all my courses to include as much cultural, racial,
gender, and other diversity as I can. In "Working-Class Literature," for
example, we don't look just at the male urban factory worker of proletarian novel fame (which is what some people think of as synonymous with working-class literature). There are, obviously, working-
class women as well, in factories, offices, and homes. Some of these
women are Italian, or Vietnamese or Native American, some are African
American, some are Anglo and some are lesbians. There are also people
from poor and working-class backgrounds who are old. There are rural
as well as urban varieties of the working class. There are class divisions
in the black community and in ethnic communities. And the ways in
which class is experienced have changed throughout the twentieth century. Further though, I think focusing on any aspect of diversity and
nonprivilege can be a first step to sensitizing people to other forms of
oppression. After all, when you add up all the marginalized groups in
this country alone, you find that we make up the vast majority of the
population.

Having dismantled the myths of neutrality and universality, that is, that the traditional white, male privileged canon of literature is *the* embodiment of LITERATURE, we should try not to stop, as we reconstruct our courses, with the compensatory approach, what Charlotte Bunch has called "add women and stir" and what I have criticized as the "teaching-a-unit-on" approach—teaching a unit on women writers, on African-American writers, on working-class writers—which ghettoizes such writers into a week or two of the course. The message that format gives to the students is that working-class literature or gay and lesbian literature, for example, do exist, but that they live in a separate room, which we can leave and shut the door, going about our business in the real world. Both specialized courses and fully integrated, "mainstreamed" courses should be available to students. And we need as well to change our ideas about genre to include "private" and "nontraditional" literary forms like letters, journals, slave narratives, songs.

There is perhaps an even more pressing need to transform the way we teach writing, because in required writing courses we reach all students and not just English majors. We need to redefine what we mean by an expository essay, since our present definition of a good essay—linear, hierarchical, and pointed—is not necessarily amenable to the way, for example, many women think, as Gilligan and Clichy have pointed out. I would speculate that that form is also not necessarily the best one for men from marginalized groups. Writing issues that come up around class and race as well as gender include an articulateness in speaking that students can learn to transfer and translate into their writing and an interest in and ease with particularity, detail, and vivid sense-based language, which can be encouraged and can serve as models for the middle-class students, who are more often mired in vagueness and abstract language. Students from marginalized groups often are suspicious or have a struck-dumb response to "high" language and they often quite rightly have a sense that the classroom itself and the reading and writing they're supposed to be doing is alien and uncomfortable. Insofar as students feel powerless, dispossessed or unpossessed of a tradition in language and literature, the literature or writing classroom may be uncomfortable for them and may silence or mute them. Such students have a different, more ambivalent, more problematic relation to middle-class academic language. I'd like to suggest that we look closely and critically at the land of academic discourse for which we serve as customs officials.

Questions we need to ask ourselves as we organize writing classes: What models of essay writing do we provide students with? Do we allow students to write about topics that passionately interest them and are grounded in who they are, in all their multifaceted variety? Do we let them "play" with free writing, journals, and papers written in the first person but retain as our end of semester goal mastery of the standard objective research paper in the standard format? How do we handle grading? Do we expect in student essays the usual power dynamics of syntax in every sentence—the subordination of some ideas to others, for example, so that a hierarchy is created in the paragraph that mirrors and supports inequality and hierarchy in the culture as a whole? Do we value linear writing that muscles its way straight toward its goal more than writing that, say, enfolds a subject and radiates toward a conclusion? How can we invite each student to write out of how and who she or he is while at the same time equipping each one with the survival skills she or he will need? Do we provide a classroom that is cooperative, a writing community where students learn in part by teaching each other, or do we hang on to authority and the keys to what the right way is? Can we study directly the sexist, racist, classist, heterosexist biases in language, making that a specific topic in the writing course? There is a substantial body of work in feminist linguistics done in the past fifteen years and, in the past five years or so, in approaches to teaching writing that take into account the diversity of students in the classroom.

A point needs to be made about our own work as writers and teachers. Those of you whose work has also been on literature in its social context, on revising the canon, and on teaching writing in a way that you hope reaches students from marginalized and nontraditional groups will know that your choice to work this way doesn't always make your case a piece of cake at hiring, tenure, and promotion time. The content of one's work, if it seems to rock the canonical boat, is often labeled "soft" or "trivial" or, to bring up the most potentially dangerous word in our profession, as not "excellent" enough.

BUT I'D LIKE to suggest that an even more problematic use of the standards of excellence has to do with judgments about the *way* one

175

writes. There has somehow gotten to be the notion that the difficult, the inaccessible, the erudite, and the highly theoretical is more excellent than language that is clear, accessible, experientially based, practical, and useful. To overstate the case a little, it is as if depth is measured by the degree of obscurity and the eliteness of the audience; clarity raises the immediate suspicion of superficiality and (god help us) a popular audience.

So I think there has been a temptation for feminist scholars to write about controversial subjects in language that is dense, very scholarly, and inaccessible to the great majority of people who might benefit from the insights. I think many of us come up against difficult questions of expediency vs. integrity when our job security is at stake, but I think these choices are much more painful if we are members of a marginalized group in the academic world; for me (I wouldn't want to speak for anyone else) the choices then became whether to betray my identity and my background. I would very much like my family to be able to read what I write. Also my working-class students. Also the people I'm writing about. As well as my academic colleagues.

Finally, a footnote about "excellence" in teaching—I'm pretty sure the teacher-centered classroom is seen by most people who have the power to grant tenure and promotions as more admirable and "excellent" than a classroom based on cooperative learning models. And yet, I have watched with pleasure over the years my courses become more cooperative and correspondingly tougher, more effective, and more useful for the students. A student taking a graduate-level version of the course last summer—a high school English teacher—wrote in his journal: "The reading and the writing for this course have caused me considerable pain. . . . It has . . . made me feel angry about the fact that these voices were missing from my own education. . . . It has caused me to think deeply about the choices we as English teachers make for students and how we unwittingly contribute to the conspiracy of silence about so much of this material. Most of all, it has forced me to confront the memory of my working-class father." The course was useful in several ways for this student. I have come to realize that "useful" is a more important concept for me than "excellent" (though equally subjective)—and I have no doubt that usefulness as a priority comes right out of my working-class background. It seems to me that one of the more useful things I can do is to provide courses that help students, especially women students and students from working-class backgrounds, validate and respect, read and write, their own experience. Such courses can be a bridge over which they can cross into the rest of the academic world, if they want to, without having to leave a good bit of their identity behind at the border.

Works Cited

Alger, Horatio. *Ragged Dick*. New York: Macmillan, 1962.

Arnow, Harriet. *The Dollmaker*. New York: Avon, 1954.

Baum, Charlotte, Paula Hyman, Sonya Michel. *The Jewish Woman in America*. New York: New American, 1975.

Belenky, Mary, Blythe Clinchy, Nancy Goldberger, Jill Tarule. *Women's Ways of Knowing*. New York: Basic, 1986.

Braverman, Harry. *Labor and Monopoly Capital: The Degradation of Work in the Twentieth Century*. New York: Monthly Review, 1974.

Carby, Hazel. "It Jus Be's Dat Way Sometime: The Sexual Politics of Women's Blues." *Radical America* 20, no. 4 (1986).

Chute, Carolyn. *The Beans of Egypt, Maine*. New York: Ticknor and Fields, 1985.

Gilligan, Carol. *In a Different Voice: Psychological Theory and Women's Development*. Cambridge: Harvard UP, 1982.

Grahn, Judy. *The Work of a Common Woman*. Trumansburg, N.Y.: Crossing, 1978.

Hardy, Thomas. *Jude the Obscure*. New York: St Martin's, 1977.

Hughes, Langston. *Selected Poems*. New York: Vintage, 1959.

Kennedy, Susan Estabrook. *If All We Did Was to Weep at Home: A History of White Working-Class Women in America*. Bloomington: Indiana UP, 1979.

Kingston, Maxine Hong. *The Woman Warrior*. New York: Vintage, 1975.

Lauter, Paul. "Working-Class Women's Literature: An Introduction to Study." *The Radical Teacher*, no. 15 (March 1980).

Le Sueur, Meridel. "Women on the Breadlines." *Ripening: Selected Work, 1927–1980*. Old Westbury, N.Y.: Feminist P, 1959.

Miner, Valerie. "Labor Pains: The Loneliness of the Working-Class Writer." In *Rumors from the Cauldron: Selected Essays, Reviews, and Reportage*. Ann Arbor: University of Michigan Press, 1992.

Moraga, Cherrie. "La Guera." In *This Bridge Called My Back: Writings by Radical Women of Color*. Latham, N.Y.: Kitchen Table/Women of Color Press, 1984.

Morrison, Toni. *The Bluest Eye*. New York: Washington Square P, 1970.

Olsen, Tillie. *Silences.* New York: Delacorte/Seymour Lawrence, 1978.

——. *Yonnondio.* New York: Dell, 1974.

Peiss, Kathy. *Cheap Amusements: Working Women and Leisure in Turn of the Century New York.* Philadelphia: Temple UP, 1986.

Petry, Ann. *The Street.* Boston: Houghton, 1992.

Richardson, Dorothy. *The Long Day: The Story of a New York Working Girl.* In William L. O'Neill, *Women at Work.* New York: Quadrangle, 1972.

Riis, Sharon. *The True Story of Ida Johnson.* Toronto: Women's P, 1976.

Sillitoe, Alan. *The Loneliness of the Long Distance Runner.* New York: Random, 1959.

Terkel, Studs. *Working.* New York: Pantheon, 1972.

Walker, Alice. "Everyday Use." *In Love and Trouble.* New York: Harcourt, 1973.

Wright, Richard. "The Man Who Went to Chicago." *Eight Men.* New York: Pyramid, 1969.

Yezierska, Anzia. *Bread Givers.* New York: Persea, 1975.

"Someone to Watch Over Me": Politics and Paradoxes in Academic Mentoring

W HEN I TELL friends and colleagues that I am writing on the subject of mentoring within the academy, they ask me to clarify what
I mean by mentoring. Despite my attempts to define a mentor as a
"guide," "role model," "expert," "surrogate parent," or even "guardian
angel," mentoring remains a slippery concept, often encompassing a
rather conditional and paradoxical set of unspoken rules. It is a process
that takes place both consciously and unconsciously, at many times and
under various circumstances. In its most generic sense, mentoring, as
defined by James E. Blackwell, is "a process by which persons of superior rank, special achievement and prestige, instruct, counsel, guide,
and facilitate the intellectual and/or career development of persons
identified as protégés." Laurent A. Daloz presents a more spiritual and
idealized definition—mentors are "designed to fill a psychic space somewhere between lover and parent—they embody our hopes, cast light on
the way ahead, interpret arcane signs, warn us of lurking dangers, and
point out unexpected delights along the way."[1] His model harkens back
to Mentor in *The Odyssey*, one of Athena's incarnations, who guides
young Telemachus in his search for his missing father.

Mentoring within the academy is more complex than either of
these definitions can account for. For mentoring feels necessary (and
takes place) in formal as well as informal settings; it ranges from asking
for help in getting a paper published to raising impulsive or naive
questions from time to time. One kind of "aboveboard" or clearly recognized form of academic mentoring happens when, in graduate school, a
student is required to have an adviser, who directs and guides in choosing, refining, and completing a dissertation, thus paving the way for the
end of the graduate career.[2]

In examining this or any other hierarchical relationship within the
academy, we need to underscore and raise questions that are part of the
dynamic. Some pertinent questions: How do you recognize and choose

this person who might help to "shape" or "promote" your work, and will he or she also choose you? What kind of relationship can you expect, given different experiences and styles? Will there be a willingness to acknowledge or ignore the politics of the mentor-mentée interaction? What are the boundaries and terms, both explicit and implicit, of such highly charged connections?[3]

, In my attempt to situate these questions, I posit mentoring as part of the overall challenge we face in the inseparable worlds of life and education. It is a process and subject, but one that often goes unrecognized or is confronted only when there's a perceived need to initiate or ease one group into the (more established) practices of another. Although it seems important that mentoring is finally being recognized as a politicized practice, the power structure itself is not always incorporated into the analysis. As mentoring becomes less informal and more institutionalized, partly as an effort to help eradicate injustices against women and nonwhites in the academy,[4] what will it take for these efforts to be able to produce or work toward implementing the results they set out to achieve? Will they be able to work within existing institutional confines and hierarchies?

My project is to explore and clarify some factors and stakes pertaining to mentoring within academe, especially as they intersect with concerns about class, gender, and race. I will be focusing on graduate students who teach freshman writing, and are therefore in the position of seeking mentors at the same time we are potential mentors to other students—undergraduates as well as peers.[5]

For many of the people I interviewed for this project, searching for a mentor within academe is or has been a dreaded process, although the possibility of making significant connections helped dispel some of the terror. There was skepticism, a sense of "not knowing how a particular professor really feels about me, if he or she thinks I am exceptional," or of "receiving mixed messages," and it was hard to know what the professor was really thinking. The necessity for years of approval from these authority figures was both frustrating and exhilarating, depending on the moment. Most of the students I interviewed felt the burden of locating a mentor rested with them, since they clearly were the more dependent party. But there is shopping around on both sides that can feel like a high-stakes hunt.[6] Professors often get release time from teaching if they supervise enough dissertations, and their power in a department is based in part on popularity among prestigious students. The selection process goes beyond specialization or field and involves transference and subjectivity on both sides; what we call "personality" or "chemistry" comprises numerous facets, desires, and specificities.

Some graduate students I spoke to were comfortable with and even looked forward to locating mentors in their departments. One woman who recently entered a Ph.D. program in English stated:

I would be nowhere without my mentors. They are the reason I am in graduate school. One of the things that drew me to this profession is my drive for knowledge and learning—and I can absorb a lot from those who are willing to share what they know. I make it my business to find role models. I have no reason to think that I won't continue to find mentors who will help me to publish and also become my friends.

As the youngest in a family of much older siblings, this woman admitted that she was used to looking to older, more experienced role models for knowledge and guidance and that she had no problem pursuing and asking for help; however, many of the women and some of the men I interviewed were not as comfortable in assuming they could work out a reasonably acceptable relationship with an authority figure. They found the traditional "master-apprentice" or "expert-novice" dichotomies problematic and difficult for a number of reasons; many had to do with issues of power and boundaries.

Those who labeled themselves as working class[7] or class conscious seemed to have the greatest problem with the "master-apprentice" model, but some working-class students also found comfort in it. These contradictions suggest mentoring might present a potential but partial solution for those with a strong need to find models that enable them to separate or distance themselves from their working-class backgrounds; moreover, those who consider themselves working class are often particularly aware of and sensitive to making the transition from outside to inside academe without becoming totally alienated or suffering distinct cultural loss. Part of the problem might also stem from what bell hooks recognizes as an ambivalence "about the rewards promised": "Many of us [graduate students from underprivileged class backgrounds] were not seeking to be in a position of power over others. Though we wished to teach, we did not want to exert coercive authoritarian rule over others" (*Talking Back* 59).

For students from working-class families, locating mentors within the academy might reinforce a sense of belonging that is hard to find elsewhere. In my case, as the first in my family to finish college and pursue a Ph.D., I am viewed as bright but impractical. As I become more critical of the status quo in many aspects of culture, my parents see me as running the risk of painful alienation. They have emphasized practicality and security, but have also taught me to be leery of elitism. Education was seen as the key to self-actualization and upward mobility, but not as an end unto itself. Although my parents have always been supportive of my choices, I can't turn to them when I want to discuss Nathaniel Hawthorne or Kate Chopin or Charlotte Brontë (their books were not in the house when I was growing up). There was no one to tell me which schools to apply to and to point out how the choice of school can pigeonhole a person for life. Private institutions were financially unfeasible, but that didn't seem to matter—hard work and common sense would bring payoffs. This was our embrace of "The American Dream." Is the resulting "defense mechanism" brought on by the sense of being something of an "outsider" a burden and a hindrance to my chances for success? Perhaps; but it can also fuel a need for more analysis and accountability, which takes material circumstances into consideration, whether in reading literature and applying theory, or in interactions with colleagues and students.

Other working-class students I interviewed, especially those who immigrated to the United States, expressed a conflict between the need to find work that offered security and high income and the desire to explore their creative or intellectual goals. For instance, Marie, an undergraduate who has lived in the United States for ten years, said her parents wanted her to succeed in college, but not get "too big for her britches," or forget her obligations to them, which include agreeing to an arranged marriage and returning to her native country. This student is deeply conflicted. Her American education prepared her to become independent and express herself through work; her parents value education but not at the expense of tradition.

A common question of working- or middle-class women I spoke with was "Where and how do I fit into academe?" They might be considered elitist or overly critical or too feminist by family standards, and yet within the academy, they have to learn new jargons, roles, and modes of behavior that others already know or more readily accept. In one sense, they feel they will never be able to compete with students from private schools or with those whose parents were well educated and/or white-collar professionals. The students with more "privileged" backgrounds were more likely to have already internalized the ideology of what it takes to make it in the system and to have the advantage of positioning themselves accordingly in academia. However, anxieties exist for students from any number of backgrounds, and "privilege" needs to be examined in its particular context. Everyone brings her or his own unarticulated needs and expectations, opinions, emotions, and relationships to school.[8]

Since many of us feel estranged from our family when we choose careers, it seems natural that mentors are appealing as figures who will at least theoretically nurture us as our surrogate family. You might say we have a hunger for recognition in this world of new possibilities.

Let me return to Marie, the undergraduate I mentioned. She found a teacher who came from a similar class and ethnic background; this teacher had successfully challenged her own family's restrictions and was willing to confront Marie's parents, to try to convince them to let Marie continue her education. For Marie, it was essential that her mentor had roots in a similar culture but had found a way to subvert traditional restraints. In Marie's situation, the teacher's power and authority seemed necessary if change was to be effected and her parents persuaded.

In my view, Marie's struggle is admirable; however, her classwork suffered from what seemed like a lack of concentration and effort. At midsemester, she requested that I give her a grade that would require her to repeat the class. I wondered if, in asking for the "repeat" grade, in telling me that she knew she needed another semester's worth of freshman English, Marie was allowing herself to "play safe" or even safely fail. I didn't give her a definite answer, but told her to try to do her best and offered to work closely with her. In the end I did give her the "R" grade, but I felt in some way I hadn't measured up as a teacher. Despite my efforts, I hadn't been able to motivate her to work harder. Marie was positioning herself, I suspected, without really thinking through the consequences. If she didn't work on improving her basic writing skills she might not pass composition next semester; this might make her more vulnerable to her parents' attempts to ease her out of college. I was angry with Marie for fighting too passively, for not taking full advantage of my offer of special attention.

This story illustrates dynamics that do not fit into a clear-cut category of student-teacher relating or mentoring. In cases like this, teachers' powers and mediating positions can be perceived as part of the possible solution as well as part of the problem in a complex maze of cultural and social pressures. Teachers, are, after all, authority figures who represent the hegemony not only of the school system, but of the family and the state. As Elizabeth Fay puts it, "in academic institutions, we operate within a complex model of feudal, oedipal, and capitalistic power formations played out in faculty, teacher-student and administrative groups."[9] Yet we are individuals.

Those of us who are graduate students and teachers may feel unsure of how to behave in either role. We have authority and responsibility but are considered trainees; we must make the shift from teacher to student and back again, with little support, all the while conscious of the buzzing in our ears that repeats the same story: to become too "caught up" with teaching interferes with scholarly credentials and reputation. Which side of the fence are we really on? We are warned not to relate or identify with other adjuncts, encouraged to see ourselves as upwardly mobile, temporarily exploited on the road to something better. This of course emphasizes the hierarchies among adjuncts, and may keep us from working together to demand better conditions. It adds another stratification onto the many within academe.

As a teacher, I find myself at times secure, and at other times, totally suspicious of and at odds with my authority in the classroom; this is also true of my feelings as a participant in graduate seminars. I suspect some of my teachers find authority just as problematic. This complex dialectic both in and outside the classroom almost certainly overwhelms any expectation of or need for real stability; what is called for, I think, is more support that valorizes and transforms the relations of instability.

Nadya Aisenberg and Mona Harrington in *Women of Academe* point out that women teachers "want more than men to be liked by their students and fear simultaneously that their students will not accept their authority" (75). This factor complicates the mentoring question. If being liked and accepted is one of the heavily emphasized equations of the mentor-mentée dyad, it becomes clearer that these desires should be embodied in an open-ended and self-consciously critical manner, with reciprocity, exchange, and reinvention as possible goals. Acknowledging the anxiety and discomfort surrounding conflicting feelings needs to become part of the discourse, not hidden beneath the surface. And it should not be assumed that the mentée, or person with less power, is the only one who needs to be liked or validated. Mentors and teachers can feel threatened by students; they, of course, also have their own insecurities and battle scars. If totally unacknowledged or ignored, these insecurities become a significant distancing device, which is bound to discourage rather than encourage meaningful relations. We should not easily dismiss the tension and conflict inherent when one needs approval or feels threatened at the same time one is in a position of authority. For that authority, especially in the case of women in academe, is often not as stable as it might appear to a student. Again, the particular situation or stake must be considered.

As Culley and her collaborators write in "The Politics of Nurturance," part of the problem for women in academe is that the roles of nurturer and intellectual have been separated in our culture, not just by gender, but by function, and such separation creates confusion in the way we deal with our students and, I would add, with our mentors. "It may be that as women academics we have become the fathers, entered into the realm of history which men have always controlled. Yet, in a more profound sense, feminism repudiates the law and order of the father and transforms history by bringing to it what we know about being mothers and being mothered" (18). The context of academic nurturing takes place within a competitive, patriarchal institution.

I handled Marie's case in what I call an attempt at nonhierarchical mentoring, which takes into account an individual student's needs and yet acknowledges the investment and point of view of the mentor. It also emphasizes the inherent difficulties and the awkward positions we may find ourselves in. What happens when, having expressed a willingness to relate to our students and develop a certain level of trust and camaraderie, one of them confesses a serious problem or lets us know he or she wants to test the resiliency of the bond?

Another case illustrates this point. One of my brightest and most articulate students often expressed anger and great frustration with conventional gender roles in classroom discussions on cultural stereotypes. Although Carmen's passionate outbursts made other students flinch, I felt no need to try to silence or "check" her intensity. Her anger struck a chord. She came to my office to talk about her writing and confessed she worked as a prostitute. She said prostitution allowed her the freedom to live on her own, away from her domineering father. I encouraged her to find other work, emphasizing the capabilities she had clearly demonstrated, and even told her about fellowships she could qualify for if she raised her grade-point average. I also allowed her to make prostitution the topic of her research paper. She continued to defend her choice of work while also admitting its demoralizing effect on her life and schoolwork. Although I offered myself as someone she could confide in and as someone who recognized her intelligence, I felt that there was a limit to what I could or would be willing to say or do; moreover, I was uncomfortable because I wasn't sure what kind of response or feedback she wanted or hoped for. After spending some time with her, I suggested she seek counseling and urged her to work on her writing skills with a tutor.

A few weeks before the end of the semester, Carmen stopped attending class without contacting me. I wondered what had happened and was upset that she hadn't even made an attempt to communicate after confiding something so personal; had she read some of my signals as coercive, judgmental, and ultimately rejecting? Was she in danger? What could be done? In the end, I felt my position as an authority figure was both comforting and threatening; perceived cultural and racial differences may have also come into play.[10] Carmen may have decided that I would never be able to understand the dilemma in which she found herself, and perhaps she was right. On the other hand, Carmen's decision might have had nothing to do with me—as I really knew little about the specifics of her situation—but I wasn't about to make that assumption automatically.

These two examples represent a kind of mentoring that had no obvious or clear-cut goal; they were extensions of the student-teacher relationship, and both involved personal problems as well as work-related ones.[11] Marie and Carmen were undergraduates who had difficulty balancing the demands and pressures of their lives with those of college, partly because they were attempting to challenge their parents' values. In these cases, my position as the authority figure did not result in immediate solutions or in helping the students "make it" or secure a comfortable position within the system, perhaps because I myself am not yet secure in the system. It is possible that my interactions with and faith in these students helped in some immeasurable way; as teachers, we realize that what we give our students may manifest itself at a later date when we cannot observe it. I do know, however, that some students have benefited from my style of mentoring, which relies on flexibility and individualized attention, spontaneity, and some risk.

We graduate students, with our greater investment in academic life, sometimes require tangible evidence of our mentors' faith in us. That might mean being invited to a dinner, included on a panel, or treated with seriousness and respect; a woman I interviewed recalled how, when she was in graduate school and going through severe financial difficulties, one of her professors handed her a twenty-dollar bill. Although it was awkward to take the cash, it became a token of faith that she indeed would pull through. This professor was not her official adviser, but became what she considers an important ally.

In the examples I have presented so far, the way one mentors or aligns with potential mentors is an informal process. After all, there is virtually no way one can train or learn to mentor or be mentored; there is no absolute sense of what *could* or *should* be done, because of course that would vary with personality as well as with field and school. At the graduate level, students and faculty are usually more aware of mentoring; there are clear-cut tasks that need to take place, such as forming orals committees, deciding on a dissertation topic, applying for fellowships.

There are different ways one can go about finding sponsors and advisers. Some students already know their specialty and look for mentors among those best known in the field; others choose their field because a teacher suddenly makes it seem vital; still others go by criteria of their own devising; others let it fall to chance. One professor I interviewed said a mentor should be "the person you would most want to become." He was able to find someone who fit that description, although that person discouraged him from working on his original dissertation idea because it was considered outside the established canon, and therefore, less marketable. A graduate student in English said "I chose someone in my field who seemed available. But I chose badly. He condescends to me." This person felt it was too late, however, to make a change—it would look bad and could embarrass them both. But, I wondered, isn't it worse to stay in such an awkward and unequal relationship?

A sociology student said she had two potential mentors and they interpreted her research differently and had divergent sets of plans and expectations for her work. She chose the one who was less well known but who had actually helped her to secure an award for her project.

These examples illustrate the randomness of the mentoring experience and how much can depend on circumstances as well as on a willingness to clarify or reassess goals, plans, and ways of relating in light of available resources. As I pointed out earlier, some students are just not comfortable, and they have a tough time assuming it is their right to make demands or ask for attention from an authority figure; some mentors seem distant and unavailable much of the time. Furthermore, if there are few women, "minority," and gay and lesbian faculty members to chose from, students might have to vie for the attention of those who *are* available and receptive; issues of competition and scarcity also need to be acknowledged and confronted, by students and faculty, as do generational differences and the increasingly tougher requirements that a tightened job market has created.[12]

Recent research has shown that female students paired with female role models and mentors report higher satisfaction with their student role than male or female students paired with a man; there is also evidence that females who have male mentors might be exploited in the relationship, because of sexism in protégé selection and the attributions made for female protégées' success (luck rather than ability). As John W. Kronik has written of the relationship between male mentors and female students: "Whenever a man serves as a mentor, the discourse and institutions of power are in his hands. . . . the greatest danger of abuse of the male mentor's power over the woman lies in their sexuality. . . . For the male mentor to open the issue of sexuality is confusing and damaging to the woman, who must then fall into everything that society has negatively programmed her for."[13]

The question of what behaviors constitute the "opening" of sexuality are not detailed by Kronik; nor are the varying responses that a woman might have for different types of innuendo. What constitutes appropriate and inappropriate behaviors between faculty and students deserves much more attention, especially since sexual harassment takes many forms that have not been recognized or legitimized. Research suggests that sexual harassment might be a factor in many faculty-student interactions.[14]

One favor our mentors and sponsors can do is to help us demystify and face the politics of the profession early in our graduate careers. We need to be "let in" on the real stratification that exists in the system before we're on the job market. In her essay "A Map of the World and Instructions on How to Use It," Joan E. Hartman points out that when students are "introduced to dossiers and interviews and teaching and tenure and promotion, they must be introduced to stratification, which affects all these matters. Often they are not . . . because we are reluctant to acknowledge the seamy side of the institutionalization of English."[15] Once we acknowledge the "seamy side," we can try to find ways to openly address it and perhaps even call attention to and change it, rather than merely duplicating what is taken as a given.

Mentoring is emerging as a practice that needs to be formally recognized and come to terms with;[16] at the same time I believe it should continue to undergo evaluations and adjustments if necessary, for it can become just another empty term. When mentoring becomes institutionalized, it is usually part of an initiation process and ideally seen as a strategy to help bridge a gap, but this role might not be clearly communicated or realistically defined. One of the CUNY colleges recently asked professors to mentor incoming undergraduates (not necessarily those from their own departments), but never gathered the students and teachers in one place to find out what each side thought was going to happen. One of the professors who participated in this program said it was developed in part to compensate for the lack of counselors available because of CUNY budget cuts; she also said she felt the program generally failed.

Perhaps one of the problems in mentoring incoming students is that the students don't know enough about the institution and haven't yet defined their own position in relation to their department. The relationship at this point is bound to be one-sided, with the authority figure telling the new student the most basic information about requirements or policies. This can be useful in that it helps to orient the student, but it seems as though a commitment to progress and development should be part of any mentoring initiative. Perhaps peer mentors could better handle the "rope learning" stage, with faculty getting involved a little later in the process.

Tracking student progress is one of the components of a recent Mellon Fellowship project for minority students at Hunter College and other CUNY campuses. These students will go on to do graduate work in the humanities, funded by a Mellon grant that aims to encourage more African-American, Latino, and Native American students to become college professors. Each adviser will follow a student's advancement, make contact with that student's mentor on the graduate level, and remain closely involved. The students and their advisers will also meet together for roundtable discussions that include topics related to race, gender, and class analysis. Such a stipulation would seem to indicate that the administrators of this program recognize that these concerns need to be articulated, rather than assumed or silenced.[17] Because multiculturalism and its stakes within academe have come under siege, often in a reductive and reactionary manner by the general press, more talks, discussions, and open forums need to take place at all our institutions, and the most varied participation needs to be encouraged.

Other institutionalized mentoring programs try to help women build support networks by pairing graduate students, adjuncts, and nontenured faculty women with tenured-faculty mentors. I recently received a letter from the CUNY Women's Mentoring Bank, inviting me to apply. The bank is an outgrowth of CUNY's Women's Research and Development Fund, formed by consent decree in 1984 as the result of a sexual discrimination suit. It states its intention as supporting "women faculty, staff and administrators in their professional development. Mentors, out of their own experience, will coach mentées in career strengthening, which may include promotion and tenure, or completing a degree program." While only nontenured women are eligible to apply to the program, mentors will be both tenured men and women. I was accepted into the bank, and am now waiting to be assigned a mentor.

I wonder if such concerted efforts will make any difference in the long run. Although I was asked why I wanted a mentor, the focus of my research was not considered a factor, which makes me wonder on what basis the pairing will take place. Will mentors who hope to foster "professional development" be prepared to deal with issues that relate to racism, classism, sexism, and heterosexism? Will we get to meet each other before we are matched? It seems safe to say that mentoring banks or other similar support systems cannot ensure that women and non-whites receive promotions and tenure and finish degrees; achieving these goals will take a much broader effort across institutional, professional, and departmental lines. The work will have to be carried out on many levels, using a variety of strategies from within and without, because institutionalized mentoring is bound to reflect many of the values of its institution.[18]

One way to reinvent the meaning and value of mentoring is to try to incorporate it into the infrastructure of policy at the planning stage. Graduate students who are working to establish a Cultural Studies Ph.D. program at the CUNY Graduate School and University Center want mentoring to be as central as curriculum. The students are asking for an equal share of power in all decisions, including admissions; they see mentoring as less a one-on-one proposition than a place for multiplicity—students must support and mentor other students. At this time, they are working with faculty and administration and it is not clear what will emerge. But at least mentoring is not being ignored or seen as a peripheral practice, separable from disciplinary subjects.

This example also highlights what I see as one of the most pertinent revisionings of the mentoring configuration. That is the idea of collaborating, or creating dyads, triads, and multiple combinations where power and positioning of the mentor-mentée dynamic are constantly shifting and regrouping. Feminist theory has advocated and often exemplified the benefits of plurality and collaboration. Projects within and across disciplines influenced by feminist practice reflect the fruits of shared authorship and work. I will close with a few examples of what I see as attempts at pluralistic or collaborative or joint mentoring, and I will offer my concerns about the feasibility of such efforts.

Recently, the Eugene Lang Student-Faculty Research fellowships at Hunter College have been designed to stimulate interest in scholarly research and accomplishment among undergraduate students. The goal, according to the letter demonstrated by the office of the provost, is to "produce joint research by students and faculty of such high quality that it will lead to the publication of its results." By funding such collaborative projects, it seems as though the risk of ignoring or downplaying student research will be minimized, and that the student will see some tangible rewards and recognition, which might encourage her to take her work more seriously and even rethink career goals. But since students and faculty must team up for this project, those students who are known to their professors and seem most qualified or willing to collaborate ultimately will benefit most. I would hope that the definition of what is considered "research of high quality" is broad based.

191

On the student-student level, informal reading groups, salons, and student conferences, where works-in-progress are presented, can encourage mutual mentoring, with response and feedback part of the process of developing one's work and community. Different leaders and organizers can shift and help diffuse the power that students are not immune from seeking. Critiquing and building upon each other's viewpoints has helped many of the graduate students I spoke with define and refine their own positions; such interactions enable us to recognize and minimize and/or maximize perceived differences such as academic field or discipline, or even our racial, economic and gendered positions. For some, these relationships were at least as satisfying and influential as relationships with professors, and students felt they could be more relaxed, maybe more honest too. After all, these peers and colleagues might be seen as part of an elaborate web, not as outside, or inferior to, an "inner" circle, but in a position subject to change.

In concluding, let me say again that mentoring is a slippery and provocative process that has preoccupied and will continue to preoccupy me for some time. The constant reinvention and investment in relationships between mentors and mentées hold great potential and multiple challenges for us to experience, analyze, critique, and subvert. Since I first conceived this chapter, several years have passed, and in that time I have been fortunate in having found mentors who have been supportive of my work and of me in general. It is to those mentors and also to my friends and students that I feel indebted, not only for providing me with the impetus and inspiration to develop more completely and deeply, but also for making me conscious of and even thankful for rich and difficult complexities that contribute to where we are.

Notes

1. James E. Blackwell, "Mentoring: An Action Strategy for Increasing Minority Faculty," *Academe*, Sept/Oct 1989; published by the American Academy of University Professors, Washington, DC. Laurent A. Daloz, *Effective Teaching and Mentoring* (San Francisco: Jossey-Bass, 1986), 17.

For a general discussion of the term mentoring and the methodological approaches to mentoring research, see Cheryl N. Camin, "Issues in Research Mentoring: Definitional and Methodological," *International Journal of Mentoring* (International Centre for Mentoring, Vancouver, BC) 2. 2 (1988).

2. In the handbook *Winning the Ph.D. Game* (New York: Dodd, 1985), Richard W. Moore details methods for finding mentors in academe and describes the different stages and some of the conflicts involved in mentor-protégé relationships; he bases many of the interactions on the notion of task-based reciprocity within the dyad. Moore draws from the business model provided by Linda Phillips-Jones in her book *Mentors and Protégés: How to Establish, Strengthen and Get the Most Out of a Mentor-Protégé Relationship* (New York: Arbor, 1982).

3. The Milan Women's Bookstore Collective has coined a phrase for a practice that takes disparities in mentoring relations into account. They call it entrustment (*affidamento*). In entrustment, one woman gives her trust, or entrusts herself symbolically, to another woman, who becomes her mentor. Because of recognition of the difference in class, social position, age, professional status, etc., the illusion of neutral, genderless justice is minimized, as are "guilt feelings and resentment" connected with that "neutral" authority. Teresa de Lauretis, "The Practice of Sexual Difference and Feminist Thought in Italy: An Introductory Essay," in The Milan Women's Bookstore Collective, *Sexual Difference: A Theory of Social-Symbolic Practice* (Bloomington: Indiana UP, 1990), 8–10.

4. According to studies cited by Nadya Aisenberg and Mona Harrington in *Women of Academe: Outsiders in the Sacred Grove* (Amherst: U of Massachusetts P, 1988), in 1983, women made up about 26 percent of the full-time faculty at four-year colleges and universities, but only about 10 percent of the full professors. At universities alone, only 6 percent of full professors were women (5). According to James E. Blackwell, in 1985, the percentage of full-time faculty positions held by minorities in American institutions were represented as follows: North Americans, 0.3; Hispanic, 1.7; Asian, 3.9; African Americans, 4.0. ("Mentoring" 8). For a fuller discussion of the question of injustices that minorities and women face in the academy, see Mary L. Spenser, Monika Kehoe, and Karen Speece, *Handbook of Women Scholars, Strategies for Success* (San Francisco: Americas Behavioral Research, 1982). This book contains names of organizations, caucuses, committees, and research centers. In *Academic Women: Working Towards Equality* (South Hadley, MA.: Bergin, 1987) Angela Simeone provides statistics and case studies that trace the patterns of women's networks and strategies for integration; bell hooks specifically reflects on being a black female graduate student in Chapter 9 of her book, *Talking Back: Thinking Feminist, Thinking Black* (Boston: South End, 1989).

5. This essay is based on my experiences and those of students and faculty members I interviewed informally. When it seems important, I will distinguish between interviews with undergraduates and those who are pursuing or have received doctorates. Names of my students have been changed to pro-

tect their privacy. I wish to thank Sandy Flitterman-Lewis, Michelle Tokarczyk, Michele Paludi, and Electa Arenal for their generosity in helping me frame the issues.

6. According to Blackwell, "those who teach are often guilty of subconscious (though sometimes conscious and deliberate) efforts to reproduce themselves through students they come to respect, admire, and hope to mentor. As a result, mentors tend to select as protégés persons who are of the same gender and who share with them a number of social and cultural attributes or background characteristics, such as race, ethnicity, religion and social class" ("Mentoring" 11).

7. Whether one uses the term "working class" to define his or her identity/background is fraught with different meanings and subtexts that cannot be explored in depth here.

8. In "The Politics of Nurturance," Margo Culley, Arlyn Diamond, Lee Edwards, Sara Lennox, and Catherine Portuges discuss the feminist classroom as the site of transference for many conscious and unconscious "texts" of students and teachers, which can include outbursts of temper, tears, denunciation, and divisiveness. In *Gendered Subjects: The Dynamics of Feminist Teaching*, ed. Margo Culley and Catherine Portuges (Boston: Routledge, 1985).

9. Elizabeth Fay, "Dissent in the Field; or, a New Type of Intellectual?" in this volume.

10. bell hooks points out that different cultural codes need to be taken into account in the development of support networks, and I would add that they obviously come into play in one-on-one mentoring situations. Black students and other nonwhite students, says hooks, "may learn that it is important not to accept coercive authoritarian rule from someone who is not a family elder— hence we may have difficulties accepting strangers assuming such a role" (*Talking Back* 59).

11. Angela Simeone suggests that women may perceive and implement the role of sponsor differently than men: "It seems that they may have a more personal relationship with their students, but a less productive, work-oriented one. This was supported by anecdotes of the women interviewed for this study, who reported that students were more likely to come to them than their male colleagues for personal problems or moral support. If indeed this is true, it seems both men and women could benefit from some borrowing from each other's style" (*Academic Women* 118).

12. For an in-depth discussion of the problem of competition among academic women, see Evelyn Fox Keller and Helene Moglen, "Competition: A Problem for Academic Women," in *Competition: A Feminist Taboo?* ed. Valerie Miner and Helen E. Longino (New York: Feminist Press at CUNY, 1987). For analyses of crucial debates that feminist theory has raised and of the impact of

feminism in various institutional settings, including academe, see *Conflicts in Feminism*, ed. Marianne Hirsch and Evelyn Fox Keller (New York: Routledge, 1990).

A panel at the 1991 Modern Language Association conference in San Francisco was devoted to the subject of generational differences within an academic feminist context.

13. John W. Kronik, "On Men Mentoring Women: Then and Now," *Profession 90* (Modern Language Association, 1990), 56.

14. Michele Paludi, Lisa Goldstein, Pam Schneider and Elizabeth Wilson-Anstey, "Mentoring & Being Mentored: Issues of Power and Politics," manuscript in preparation. Paludi et al. cite studies by Gilbert, Gallessich, and Evans, "Sex of Faculty Role Model and Students' Self-Perceptions of Competency," *Sex Roles*, 9, 597–607. Research on sexual harassment suggests "30 percent of undergraduate women experience sexual harassment by at least one of their professors during their four years at college. When definitions of sexual harassment include sexist remarks and other forms of gender harassment, the incidence rate in undergraduate populations reaches close to 70 percent. The incidence rate for women graduate students and faculty is even higher" (M. Paludi and R. Barickman, "Sexual Harassment of Students: Victims of the College Experience," in *Victimology: An International Perspective*, ed. E. Viano [New York: Springer, forthcoming). On sexual harassment, see also Paludi and Barickman, *Academic and Workplace Harassment: A Resource Manual* (Albany: State U of New York P, 1991), and Paludi, *Ivory Power: Sexual Harassment on Campus* (Albany: State U of New York P, 1991).

15. Joan E. Hartman, "A Map of the World and Instructions on How to Use It," *ADE Bulletin* (Association of Departments of English, subsidiary of the Modern Language Association), no. 89 (Spring 1988). Hartman adds that stratification (among institutions, positions, tenure requirements, etc.) is both morally and emotionally troubling, and that it ought to be, "for like parents, we are complicit in the unbeautiful world we initiate our children into. But that is no reason for graduate faculty members, by definition winners, to avoid mapping the profession. Their most difficult task is deciding what instructions to issue along with the maps, how to value efficacy in getting ahead without devaluing equity for all" (65).

16. My discussion of institutionalized mentoring programs and projects is basically limited to those going on within the City University of New York, although such programs appear to be on the upswing all over.

17. Mentoring programs are part of an effort to try to increase the retention rates of minority students in colleges across the country, for example, Prince George Community College in Maryland (see David P. James, "Increasing Retention Rates of Black and Minority Students," *Mentoring International*

3, no. 2 [Spring 1989]) and Western Michigan University (see Griselda Daniel, "Western Michigan University's Minority Mentor-Protege Program," ibid.). However, because of drastic cuts in state and federal financial aid and inadequate support at poor urban high schools, black and Latino enrollments at some universities are declining ("Changing Composition of Students," *Radical Teacher* 32 [April 1987]: 21).

18. According to Angela Simeone, increasing the number of women faculty members, "while helpful, will not change attitude, erase stereotypes and revise practices which have prevailed for three centuries in American higher education, particularly if power continues to rest in the hands of men" (*Academic Women* 118). For a provocative discussion of the problems and politics faced by women in philosophy, including master-disciple and institutionalized relationships, see Michele Le Doeuff, "Women and Philosophy," in *French Feminist Thought: A Reader,* ed. Toril Moi (Oxford: Blackwell, 1987).

Working-Class Women As Students
and Teachers

L EARN to write!" Tillie Olsen told a group of working-class students
at the University of Massachusetts/Boston. Olsen was a visiting
professor in the mid 1970s. Her presence was of great interest to students and faculty because she writes about working-class life. She
argued that the story of Western experience is biased because it was
written by white men of privilege who thought that their history was
important and should be documented. They had the education and
skills, as well as the leisure, to record their ideas and activities. The
majority of living humans were women, working class, poor, slaves, or
some combination of these, but despite their numbers their lives were
deemed unimportant and, therefore, mostly ignored. If the lives of the
lower classes were mentioned it was usually in connection with an
important event and the story was told from the perspective of a privileged white male. In the last decade of the twentieth century the same
situation still usually exists. Many technological advances have, however, led to social changes that were undreamt of even fifty years ago.
These changes have meant that average people have been exposed to
information and ideas that they would not have had access to in the
days before TV and the mass media, computers, and low-cost travel. As
a result, women, blacks, the poor, and members of other oppressed
groups have found their voices and are able to express their needs and
desires. Many of their desires have to do with improving the quality of
life and obtaining relief from oppression and exploitation. People seeking basic changes often have focused their demands on the need for
higher education. This paper will look at the experiences of working-
class and minority women who come as students and teachers to an
urban public university.

I am a black older woman who went back to school at forty-seven
to get a B.A., having worked as a nurse since I was twenty-one. I went on

to get a Ph.D. in social psychology and then returned to my alma mater to teach students who were very like myself. It is from these perspectives, as a student and faculty member, that I write.

History of the College of Public and Community Service, University of Massachusetts/Boston

Before I discuss my particular case, I will give a brief description of the college. The College of Public and Community Service (CPCS) at the University of Massachusetts/Boston was opened in 1973. Its mission was to train students to work in the public sectors of human services, housing and community, and law. The expectation was that its graduates would be able to work at professional jobs at reasonable wages without having to go on to graduate school. The potential students were inner-city residents already in the work force, many at public agencies. They were older than the typical college student, many were women from minority backgrounds, and most were from the working class. Not a few were ex-addicts or felons working in rehabilitation programs. These students came to school for a variety of reasons but most had to do with being stuck at the bottom of the career ladder because they lacked education credentials. Many of the students who were ex-offenders, especially those employed in substance abuse programs, had been the original founders of the programs they worked in. In the early years of such programs, the professional community was not interested in treating addictions, but when grant money became available from the federal government, professionals became interested. It was these professionals who, because of their expertise, were able to get larger grants, which meant that the original programs had to hire doctors, psychologists, and social workers at much higher salaries or lose their funding. This caused resentment and motivated many to come to CPCS to learn the skills needed to compete in the new professionalized world of treatment. One Hispanic student, the director of a grass-roots multiservice program, told me that he had to get a degree because his program now required all new administrative personnel to have master's degrees and that he could not presently be hired for his own job. Other students started in their jobs as assistants in schools, mental health facilities, court systems, day care centers, and housing facilities when professional help was scarce or hadn't been developed. These people found them-

selves stuck at the bottom, unable to be promoted as more professionally educated people took the higher-level positions.

The faculty of CPCS were traditionally educated scholars from
appropriate disciplines such as social work, psychology, sociology, housing management, law, community planning, and architecture. Many of
these teachers were idealists who had been activists in the 1960s, working in voter registration drives in the South, antiwar campaigns, union
organizing, and all the other social causes of the times. These men and
women came because they believed in the mission of the college, which
was the empowerment of working-class students. Their background and
training were important ingredients in the school. There were few minority individuals among the faculty, and of the few there were, most
did not have advanced degrees and were therefore not secure in terms
of tenure. This was especially true for the women. A few of the faculty
came as transfers from the original college at the University of Mas-
sachusetts/Boston (UMB) and were either tenured or soon would be.
This was important because they had power that newer faculty lacked
and some of them made it very difficult to develop and implement new
educational ideas and strategies. There were instances of tenured faculty trying to force the college to become a traditional institution. This
would have meant that the new school could not have attracted the
students who fit the original profile: minorities and women who were
not prepared in the traditional way. It also would have excluded relevant experience as a legitimate method of awarding credit.

In the years since its founding, CPCS has grown and changed in
many ways. Approximately 30 percent of its faculty now comes from
minority backgrounds. These teachers are mostly black but there are a
few Hispanics and one Asian. The student body has also changed. It is
older, due in part to the addition of a gerontology program. More students come from Third World cultures of the Caribbean, Latin America,
Africa, and Asia. This means that, like the faculty, approximately 30
percent are from minorities; the majority of these are African Americans. Women make up more than half of the student body, and although
most come from Boston's neighborhoods, an increasing number come
from the suburbs and more distant communities in the state. Some
of these women, divorced or abandoned with children, are the new
"poor." They find themselves having to work but without job skills.
Some come from middle-class families where college education is the

norm, which contrasts with the inner-city students who are often the first in their families to go to college. This has affected life at CPCS in terms of competition among students and completion rates.

The Experience at CPCS and Elsewhere

Education is seen as the "way up" by many groups in the United States. A woman may know as much as her white male colleague but she can accomplish little in terms of advancement unless she can counter gender discrimination with educational credentials. This is especially true for black women. It sometimes takes a court challenge to establish equity, in spite of the fact that there is legislation barring discrimination in the workplace.

When women and minorities gain access to higher education they encounter many aspects of discrimination, some of which they did not anticipate and with which they are not prepared to cope. It has been amply documented that many students from urban communities, especially students of color, are poorly prepared to do academic work. Their language and critical thinking skills have not been developed, usually because the schools they come from have left them ill-prepared. Such neglect is typical of inner-city schools and accounts for some interesting, painful struggles. The older returning students have worked at jobs that do not require abstract theoretical thought. The little writing or reading that is required is limited to official reports filled with jargon and bureaucratese. Some of these people have been called functional illiterates, although this is usually an inaccurate assessment. Although the problem has been defined, no solution has been found and inadequately prepared students remain at a disadvantage and are denied the satisfaction of early success at college.

The Author as Student

My own experience at CPCS as a student is not unlike that of other students. I was middle aged and had not been in school for twenty-seven years. I had worked all that time in the mental health field but was denied advancement because I had no degree. As an RN, I was more fortunate than most because I was able to earn a professional salary. I was good at what I did and was recognized for it but I could go no further, in spite of numerous offers, because regulations required that I have a degree in order to move to the next level. That is why I became the first applicant and student at CPCS. I think I was a good student. I retained some good study habits from my nursing school days. I had always been an avid reader of fiction, current social issues, and literature from the field of mental health. And, perhaps most important, I liked school and learning. Consequently, I was popular with the teachers and moved quickly through the program. My major difficulties were that I couldn't write and that I had personal problems that made it hard for me to give my complete attention to school.

Writing presented a huge problem when I arrived at college and had to write my first essay since grade school. I had taken a course in expository writing while I was waiting for CPCS to open. I did so poorly that the instructor (who couldn't teach) asked me if I had graduated from high school. I was devastated by this question because I had always prided myself on my intelligence. Who was this young upstart of a poor teacher to question me in this way? He was a professional writer but he hadn't a clue as to how to deal with someone like me. I still can't understand it. Another thing about him was that he was black; he should have understood that there are differences in language styles among different social groups; how could he write dialogue for his novels if he didn't know these nuances of speech? He couldn't tell me how to correct my errors and to make matter worse he was disrespectful and acted as if I should not have been in the class. I was able to write a cogent sentence in standard English, punctuate it correctly, and I was an excellent speller. But the writing was awful and he couldn't tell me why. It totally undermined my confidence. I now know that the problem was one of organizing my thoughts and of mastering something called academic discourse, which I had never heard of at the time.

Painful as that experience was, I am glad I had it because it helps me to understand what my students go through when they have writing problems.

Eventually, CPCS opened and, scared as I was, I did enroll. I loved it. The subjects we studied were those dearest to my heart. I was given credit for work that I had done that related to the curriculum and as a result, I was able to finish my work in five semesters. Writing continued to be a problem for me. Teachers, and I include myself, can't seem to help students who know grammar and punctuation but still can't write.

I suspect it is partly a problem of finding one's voice. One teacher told me that for older students it's a matter of knowing too much about a topic and then having to make choices about how and what to say because it can't all be said in one paper, or even in one book. That makes sense and it seems to help when I repeat it to students.

In 1976 I went to graduate school and earned a Ph.D. in social psychology. My writing problems came with me. I made some discoveries about my writing, some cognitive and some emotional. Nurses were not taught to write when I was in training. The only thing I ever wrote were case notes which, like police reports, call for a strange style, to say the least. The prose is truncated with conditional statements: things never "are," they "appear to be." Rings taken from patients when they are admitted are "gold colored." Patients don't "die," they "cease to breathe" (we know a patient is dead, but must say he ceased to breathe because legally only a physician can pronounce a person dead). Because there was never enough time to complete all the work, notes consisted of incomplete sentences, hospital jargon, and abbreviations. Nursing and similar subprofessional fields teach their students and workers not to have opinions. One can describe what one sees but must not draw conclusions. Similarly, in the day-to-day activities one has ideas for improving how the work is done but cannot act on them independently unless one is a physician or a very senior nurse. This institutionalized subservience has the effect of making a person feel that her ideas are unworthy.

In graduate school I was expected to have ideas, express them, write them down, and—horrors—defend them. How does one do that? If you defend them, some hot-shot white male is there to tear your arguments to bits. What manner of discourse is this? Many women, especially older minority students, had this problem. We thought that tearing apart arguments was rude at best and cruel at worst. It was the worst element in the academic environments that I encountered, and it still is. I had been treated very well and was respected at CPCS, and I thought I would receive the same treatment in graduate school, especially because I had been awarded a prestigious Danforth Fellowship. Instead I was treated as a pariah in a place where, clearly, some people thought I didn't belong. I didn't fit the typical student profile. I was not white, young, innocent, nor eager to follow the interests of the professors unless they coincided with mine. I was concerned with the social issues of the day especially those of oppression, but my work was often called polemic. This was crazy! Wasn't I in a *social* psychology program, and weren't the major issues studied those of attitudes, racism, attribution, organizational behavior, small groups, war, obedience to authority, and so on? So why were they mad at me because I wanted to focus on some of those issues? Well, I learned that one has to validate assertions by citing someone who has preceded you in the field. I failed a question on the qualifying exam because I gave an analysis of racial attitudes as my own opinion. The instructor, a wonderful woman who understood what I was going through, told me that my answer was polemic; when I objected, she asked where I got the ideas. I said they were my ideas. She then asked if I had encountered them anywhere else. Yes, I had seen them in the works of three prominent social psychologists, one of whom was Asian. I was told to rewrite the answer in more appropriate language, make the necessary citations, and resubmit. I did not change one line of my text, but simply added the citations and I passed. Later I discussed this with the instructor and she said it was part of paying your dues in the system. This seemed to me, as it must to many students, very childish and trivial, especially for one who had been accustomed to making life and death decisions both at home and at work. I resented having to play these games, but I did because I had to.

As I proceeded through the program my work was frequently questioned, both my original choices and my objectivity. If I chose to write on the topic of how the police handled runaways it was suspect because I had intimate knowledge of the subject.

One senior professor even attacked me on a personal level. My husband was a working-class man and was not a college graduate. This was grounds for disapproval. The professor asked me on several occasions how I would handle the differences that my graduate education would make in our marriage. I finally got angry and asked him if his wife was like him in every respect. This did not help me in my dealings with him but it did get him to stop harassing me. I should say that my experiences in this program were not unique. Women, especially if they are minority and working class, have interests that differ from men's. Since men control the academy, it is an uphill struggle to get our needs and interests recognized. We talk differently, our social behavior is different, we are more nurturing and welcoming to new colleagues, we care what happens to each other, and we help one another with projects and other things when needed. All of this behavior is suspect in the eyes of the controlling males. The prizes they win seem to lose their value unless they are won through cutthroat competition. Women like the prizes but they also value the relationships.

I finally got my degree; it was not easy. "Privacy, Interaction, and Residential Satisfaction in a Low-Income Housing Development" is the title of my dissertation and it should be no surprise that the topic was not well received in my program. I asked the head of the psychology department to chair my defense, which offended the professor who had given me such a hard time; he expected to be given first choice in these things and to keep the committees within the program. I must say that I didn't know this tradition until he told me, but even if I had, I wouldn't have asked him because I was afraid he would refuse me or, worse, read my manuscript at the last minute and demand changes that could only be made by delaying the date of the hearing. He had done this to others. At the hearing, he was rude and upsetting, but my friends on the faculty helped me through by asking relevant questions and cutting him off when he got too obnoxious. At the conclusion, I felt vindicated, partly because the department chair congratulated me and told me that mine was one of the more interesting dissertations he'd read in a long time. I learned a lot that is of value to me in my work and as a person, but I don't know if I could go through a graduate program again.

It seems significant to me that one of my colleagues at CPCS used my dissertation in some important work she was doing on housing the poor. She didn't think it strange that someone would be interested enough in the topic to write a dissertation on it.

My years as a black working-class older woman student have been fraught with anguish, discouragement, mystery, and misunderstandings. This was because I lacked the writing skills required by academicians and had different social experiences and expectations and different educational and professional interests. I was also unfamiliar with the ways of the academic world. As more of us with similar backgrounds enter academic life, things will change.

The Author as Teacher

A teacher brings to the classroom all the experiences, good and bad, that she has accumulated through years of socialization at home, school, graduate school, and daily living. This socialization includes the stereotypes and prejudices that not only define her as a working-class person and woman of color, but which also influence her own view of the students that she encounters. Teachers make judgments about their students' potential that are often quite obvious to the students. Indeed, the students judge themselves by the same measures, which leads to negative self-evaluations that get in the way of learning. Such students are terribly embarrassed by their shortcomings, which adds to their tenseness and anxiety. Even students who have some formal academic experience beyond high school, such as nurses and preschool teachers, have these problems because their training is skill based and requires little creative thinking.

Another problem is that students cannot read critically. There is a common assumption that if an idea is in print it must be "right," which is an attitude that makes it almost impossible to question and evaluate. This is compounded by these women students feeling that they have no right to challenge ideas even though they may have better ideas of their own. A third factor is the misunderstanding of the abstract notion of theory. Students are frequently asked to use theories to support their ideas and analyses. They are mystified even though they may have taken a course that introduces them to theory. They seem to have little capacity to generalize abstract notions from one context to another, which means that they may have done reasonably well in a class on theory but cannot define and analyze problems in human behavior in theoretical terms. Although there is not necessarily intrinsic value in this skill, it is, unfortunately, the lingua franca of professional and academic discourse and one must learn it if she expects to go on to graduate school or to gain credibility for her ideas among professional colleagues.

Finally, there is the problem of personalization. We do get our ideas from personal experience, but when we express them in professional life we cloak them with "objectivity." We don't say that we "learned about human development from raising our children" even though that may be true. Instead, we say we observed a phenomenon and support our assertion by citing someone in the field. Students find this way of discourse weird and don't understand why they can't use the language they are used to. They find the new style pretentious and are embarrassed to use it.

As a teacher, I have found these problems difficult to resolve, but I have learned a lot about discourse since my student days (much of it from correcting student work) and I have developed a few strategies that seem to help. Let me describe the way I teach "Social Science Research for Consumers," a course designed for human service workers who will be using research results and, perhaps, become researchers themselves. The course requires the students to do a good bit of scholarly reading in addition to doing critiques of five research reports from professional journals and designing and implementing of a small research study of their own.

The tasks in this class involve dealing with all the problems I have discussed, and they include reading difficult technical material, thinking critically about abstract ideas, using academic language, and writing reports in which the students must support assertions with evidence from the appropriate literature.

I begin the class by acknowledging that the subject is difficult in its technical aspects but that the concepts are not difficult in themselves. We approach it as a task of demystifying the research enterprise. I use a detailed and specific syllabus and describe every aspect of the work. The first assignment is to do a small survey of a question that interests them. In class we share results and I help them frame the results in an appropriate format. We get into the habit of critiquing each other in this assignment. It is important to establish a way of offering feedback that is not devastating to the writer but is truly helpful. A friendly atmosphere is set by limiting the class to fifteen, which allows us to get to know each other quickly. In order to minimize the power differential between me and the students, we sit in a circle so that I am not at the head of the room. I get the class to treat each other as professional colleagues and to look at the person whose work is being discussed rather than at me the teacher. It usually takes a couple of weeks to get comfortable but soon the students settle in and start to work seriously. One thing that helps is knowing that other people have trouble understanding difficult material; by working together to solve problems, the students help each other learn. At mid-semester the class assignment is to pick a research topic; working in pairs or trios the students must develop a proposal for the project. These proposals are critiqued in class before a final design is chosen. I am always amazed at the sophistication that has developed by this stage. I think one thing that helps is that there is a written assignment every week. The class is told that this is so I can check their

206

understanding of the material and give feedback in an on-going fashion. This encourages them to get the work in on time; anyone who doesn't is quickly identified and I can speak to him or her, giving reassurance. Students who don't do their assignments are usually scared. Working in groups helps to avoid this problem.

By the end of the semester the students are very enthusiastic about the work and some of the projects in every class approach the professional level. Those that don't are usually from students who resisted working cooperatively. I have learned to make this a requirement.

Although I have had good luck in this class because of the nature of the subject, I have not been as successful in other subjects, for instance human development. The same problems of critical thinking and academic discourse occur but I have not been able to overcome them. It is partly because there is much more material to cover and the tasks are limited to writing papers, exams, and classroom discussions. The classes are also larger and so the opportunities for lab activities are very limited. I have come to know a great deal about learning styles and teaching in this environment and although there are still problems to solve, by now I have much to share. I think that some of what we have experienced at CPCS has relevance for younger students, even at the high school level. I believe that those of us who have had success teaching the nontraditional college student have done so because we were willing to take risks and have respected the knowledge our students brought to the classroom. Above all we enjoy the challenges they present.

Teaching the Working Woman

I HAVE ALWAYS believed that students learn best from teachers whom they know well and personally. I think that it is especially important for adult working-class students to know that their teachers face the same problems they face, live the same lives they do, experience the same fears—and joys—as theirs. As a teacher of working-class adults, I do not see myself as a dispenser of wisdom, but rather as a leader of an expedition over terrain that is simply more familiar to me than it is to them. I think that it is important for all of my students to recognize that I have as much to gain from our relationship as they do.

During the past seven years, I have had the good fortune to teach at the City College of New York Center for Worker Education. The Center for Worker Education (CWE), which was founded in the mid-1970s, is a degree-granting program specifically designed to meet the needs of working adults who have had neither the time nor the money to go to college in the traditional way.

Classes at the CWE are offered in the evenings and occasionally on Saturdays, catering to the schedules of those adults who have full-time jobs but still want to pursue their education and the degrees they need for job advancement. As a child of a working-class family, I feel indebted to the effort that the CWE is making to fulfill the dream that was born in 1847 when the Free Academy of New York was founded. The charter of the Free Academy of New York, which later became the City College of New York, specifically states that its goal is to provide working-class people with the quality of education that was traditionally available only to a privileged few. I am honored to be a part of the staff at the CWE as we continue to pursue that goal.

When I began my career at City College in 1960, most of my students were from working-class families and the first generation in their families to attend college. It was then, in my judgment, one of the very best colleges in the country, the alma mater of such luminaries as Jonas Salk.

Although I left to teach elsewhere, in 1982 I had the chance to go back to where my heart has always been and to be a part of the experimental CWE. At the time, I thought that I already knew all there was to know about teaching working-class people; I did not. My recent experience teaching at the CWE has been more challenging, more exciting, and even more rewarding than the teaching I did at City College in its halcyon days.

Among the happiest discoveries that I made as a teacher of working adults is that my students are eager to learn. In most cases they have waited for a college education for a long time; these are not people who must be coaxed into doing assignments. On the contrary, they are eager to work, sometimes, indeed, they are too eager, too willing to accept without question whatever they are asked to do. Curiously, their burning desire to learn is their greatest strength and also their greatest weakness. It makes them, on the one hand, the most highly motivated students one can teach; on the other hand, it makes them accept as gospel whatever the professor, whom they invariably overvalue, says. The temptation—studiously to be avoided—is to think of oneself as the oracle at Delphi. My hardest job has been to convince my students how much I have to learn from them, for these are the people whose lives have often been the stuff of novels: a woman whose father was a guerrilla in the mountains with Fidel Castro; another whose great-grandmother was a slave who "kept a little diary." I give these examples to demonstrate the crucial importance of a teacher's knowing adult students well. In teaching them we are not teaching impressionable adolescents, but adults whose complex personal histories deeply affect their experience in the classroom.

The class I am currently teaching at the CWE is typical of those I have taught in the past. Ninety-seven percent of my students are women. Of these women, 99 percent are black or Hispanic. Typically, the women I teach at the CWE range in age from their mid-thirties to their late sixties. Almost without exception they come from families in which boys are thought to be more valuable than girls and in which intelligence in a woman is thought to be a social defect which should be disguised at all costs.

My students at the CWE are also people who have suffered at the hands of the educational establishment. If they believe they have little or nothing to offer, it is because they have been taught to believe so.

Much of the task of teaching working-class adults consists of unteaching what has been taught to them by incompetent, insensitive teachers. For example, one of my students was told by an elementary school teacher that her name could not really be her name because "Callaghan could not be the name of a black person; it must have been the name of an owner." Another, a child refugee from Cuba, was told that her parents must be "fascists" since they did not stay in Cuba after the revolution. My most brilliant student, one of the two or three passionate intellectuals I have known in my life, was told by his high school guidance counselor that he should take a "commercial" rather than an "academic" program so that he might aspire to work on a word processor. I urged him to transfer to Yale or Columbia and promised to help him get entrance, but he could not go through with the application. He was afraid. These are some of the people who are my students at the CWE. What do they know and what do they seek to know? What are their expectations of college and of me? Increasingly in the coming decades our students will be different from the young people just graduating from high school whom we have taught in the past. More and more we will be teaching returning students—women who have been kept from education by the demands of family and work; men and women who have had to carry two jobs to make ends meet; retirées who at last have the time to devote to study; minimum wage earners, nursing home attendants, clerks and other blue-collar workers who want to better their chances in the job market.

One of the most important functions of the humanities course I teach is to uncover hidden ideologies that have caused my students to think as they do about themselves. The paradox I encounter in assuming this approach is that while they are often more sophisticated and aware of their history than their younger undergraduate counterparts, they are, at the same time, unaware of the ways in which the social forces that operate upon us have affected their own lives. Moreover, so pervasive and subtle is the American mythology that enforces the notion that we have complete control over our destinies, that most of my students resist the idea that social ideologies condition them at all. For example, in teaching "The Death of Ivan Illych," I was exploring the question of how the social structures into which we are born shape our most intimate relations with others. "Not at all," said my student Eugene. "My lady and I don't have a pot to piss in or a window to throw it out, but we don't care what they say. They can't touch us. We don't need them." It is interesting that this Shelleyan free spirit is a career army man stationed at Fort Hamilton in Brooklyn. In response to his observation, we began to test the limits that "they" put on us, and to ask ourselves who "they" are. It was a mutually enlightening, vigorous, and interesting discussion in which the whole group became vociferously involved.

This experience is typical of the course that my students and I have created over the past seven years. On the first night of classes we begin by introducing ourselves to one another, describing our jobs, our families, our reasons for being there. I have learned from the journals my students keep how valuable this short introduction is. It helps them to see that we are all in the same situation, that everybody in the room is equally terrified and equally sure that everybody else is better prepared for this business of college than s/he is. It assures them that although I am the professor, I am also a working woman, a wife, and a madly overanxious mother. It is doubly reassuring for them to learn that, since I too did my B.A. in the evening session at Brooklyn College, while holding a mind-bogglingly boring job as a switchboard operator, I know exactly how hard the sheer mechanics of the task on which they are embarking will be. These initial exchanges begin the bridge building, the establishment of mutual trust, upon which our class, to be effective, must rest.

Humanities I, as it is prescribed, is divided into four ways of approaching literature: psychological, historical, sociological, and mytho-religious. We begin by examining T. S. Eliot's "Love Song of J. Alfred Prufrock" for two reasons: first, because I believe the poem is a particularly sensitive exploration of the inside/outside paradoxical psychological condition in which we exist simply by virtue of being human; second, if I can line-by-line and image-by-image lead them to draw forth their genuine responses to this difficult modernist poem, they will discover that they can read any poem, however superficially impenetrable it may seem. Teaching the poem by reading it closely with them, by drawing their responses from their own experience, their own sense of what "a patient etherized upon a table" looks like, or what "one night cheap hotels" suggests, demonstrates to them that reading poetry, which they have been made to believe is an almost occult art practicable only for the high priests of culture, is really just a matter of allowing a poem to speak to one and responding openly and honestly to its voice.

People often ask me what students in a program like the CWE should be assigned to read. My answer to this question is everything, from classical Greek drama, to slave narratives, to modern poetry. It is a great mistake to restrict any students to reading about people "just like themselves," if by themselves we mean people in the same social stratum, who do the same kinds of work that they do. Therefore, I do not believe that working-class women should be restricted to reading about working-class women. I consider it my charge to show my students that all great literature is about ourselves, about our timeless, perplexing human condition. It is centrally important that adult students learn that the great works were not written for some intellectual elite but for all of us, with all our imperfections. The sense of mastery it gives them when they can make a work of literature their own, can live with it, can use it as a flashlight to explore themselves and their world, is the end and object of the literature course I teach.

That is not to say that all students will like or think important every work their teacher asks them to read. I had a student who groaned aloud that reading one more African-American writer would do her in; I had another who thought that reading Ibsen's *Doll House* was completely irrelevant in the post-NOW age. My thumbnail criterion is that when students feel sufficiently comfortable and are sufficiently analytical to give reasoned arguments for why a particular work should be dropped, the teacher is doing a good job in that class. As long as my students know that I like and respect them, they will believe that what I am teaching is at least worth thinking about.

There are no exams in my classes because examinations test the amount of information a student has acquired, and I believe that acquiring great works of literature is as useless as saving bottle caps or match books. In lieu of exams, I have my students keep journals. They are asked to write a minimum of one page for each class meeting. They invariably end up writing five. They may write their critical, analytical responses to whatever work we are discussing; they may relate a character or event in the work to their own experience; or they may speculate further on some issue or question that has been raised in class discussion. My aim in having them keep journals is three-fold. Primarily, I want to instill in them the habit of thinking aloud in writing, that is, I want to create in them an automatic connection among reading, analytical thinking, and writing. Second, the journal becomes a place in which they can confide ideas and responses which they may feel uneasy about expressing publicly. Finally, their journals become for me, as well as for them, records of their growth in awareness and understanding.

An interesting example of the usefulness of journals is that of my student Vivian, a woman of about fifty. In recent years I have devoted the historical approach section of the course to reading African-American women's writing. In the second of our readings, Frances Ellen Watkins Harper's *Iola Leroy* (1892), Vivian came upon a passage that struck home for her with particular force:

Iola, I see no use in your persisting that you are colored when your eyes are as blue and your complexion as white as mine.

Doctor, were I your wife, are there not people who would caress me as a white woman who would shrink from me in scorn if they knew I had one drop of negro blood in my veins? (89)

Vivian had been a civil rights worker in the 1960s. She considered herself politically liberal. Her daughter, white, is married to a black man. Now that her daughter was pregnant, Vivian was horrified by the thought that her grandchild would "have African features." To further complicate the matter, she was guilt stricken by the finding that she had a deep-seated horror of negritude that she had never been aware of having. She was able to confide her fear and guilt in her journal as she would not have been able to express them in class.

Later in the term we read Nella Larsen's *Quicksand* (1928), a novel that explores the identity crisis of a mulatta woman named Helga Crane. The work raised for us a whole complex of questions about whether a mulatta's self-hatred was innate or socially inflicted. Is it nature or familial rejection that breeds Helga's self-doubt and discontent? we asked. The novel, and our explorations of it, led Vivian to a change of consciousness. Whatever deep-seated feelings she might have, so long as she did not act upon them, she was not guilty. Moreover, hers was a situation about which she could do something; she could be so loving and accepting a grandmother that she would shield her grandchild from social rejection and inner conflict. Writing in her journal not only provided Vivian with a way to make meaningful use of literature, it also allowed her to think through, and grow through, a thorny moral problem. Objectifying her complex feelings in writing made her better able to understand and deal with them.

I collect the journals three times during the course of the term. They allow me to give personal instruction in writing, for which I do not have time in a literature course. Reading the journals also allows me to respond personally and individually to the views and ideas of each student. Furthermore, reading my students' journals is a learning experience for me. Reading over the past several years has enabled me to make some general observations about this particular student population.

I have observed that my young thirties-aged students are apt to write analytically and generally about the works we read and to relate issues they encounter in them to their own political views or social values. On the other hand, older, fifty- to sixty-year-old students are more likely to compare situations and feelings of characters in a novel or poem to those of people they have known. I find no gender differences between people who take an analytical approach and those who feel strongly about characters. For example, one of my older students, a lay preacher, hated *Oedipus the King*, believing Oedipus' worship of pagan gods earned him his punishment. Much against my own expectations, I have discovered that my adult working-class students are generally much better writers than the young people I teach at SUNY Stony Brook, even when the adult students have received their elementary school education in an educationally disadvantaged state like Alabama or Mississippi. Of course, I must collect more data before coming to any conclusions as to why this should be so, but my suspicion is either that they received their primary education before the advent of television, when children read for fun, or that they have jobs that require some minimal writing every day.

At what level should one pitch instruction to working-class students? I have been asked this question but I do not entirely understand it. I feel that a teacher should choose the works that are most meaningful to her and pitch her discussion of the work to what Samuel Johnson called the "common reader." The excitement and enthusiasm she feels about the work will generate excitement in her students and her meaning will become clear to her students whatever their level of experience. Whether I am teaching a graduate seminar or a class of working adults, the process is much the same. I must draw from the community in the classroom whatever examples and illustrations from our common experience will serve us best to make the work available to the minds of us all. I think it is a grave but common error to think that we must give easy works to students or talk to them as though they were mentally deficient because their past educational experience is less extensive than our own.

Often my students at the CWE have lived through the experiences or lived in the setting that a particular literary work describes. It has been tremendously exciting for me to teach Nella Larsen to people who actually lived in Harlem in its heyday, and to teach Zora Neale Hurston to people born and bred in the rural South. In order to be beneficial to our understanding of the literature we are studying, the connection between the student and the work they are studying need not be immediate or simply apparent. None of my students nor I have lived the upper-class life of J. Alfred Prufrock, but all of us know what the process is of "prepar[ing] a face to meet the faces that you meet," and when and why we feel called upon to do that. Likewise, none of us is an incestuous parricide, but we can all sense the same dark terrifying horror within ourselves that rises up to overwhelm good, well-meaning King Oedipus. It is precisely this kind of connection between reader and text that makes the study of literature so exciting.

I like to think of my teaching experience at the CWE as a reciprocal learning process. My adult students have shown me that they are skilled and talented writers. Their enthusiasm and intelligence have inspired me to develop a diverse curriculum specifically designed to expand their literary experience and, I hope, their lives. In return, these students come away from my class with the knowledge that they can read and understand all kinds of literature and that their personal experience is both relevant and valuable to the understanding of the literature they are studying.

Ways In and Ways Out

Recasting the "Politics of Truth": Thoughts on Class, Gender, and the Role of Intellectuals

A CONSIDERABLE amount of Marxist social theory has concerned itself with the problematic position of the intellectual in hegemonic culture, taking up questions of class location and relationship to reproduction of social forces. Yet little explicit attention has been paid to the role of gender in determining the very grounds (and bounds) of the debate.[1] Who is not only allowed—but encouraged—to become an intellectual in our patriarchal, as well as capitalist, culture? What complex of forces works to produce the "typical" mental laborer, whose position can be so critically invested with the potential to undermine, as well as reinforce, dominant ideology? Viewed from another direction, what conditions allow those who are normally excluded from this position to slip through the system's cracks in order to enter (as interlopers) the intellectual arena? I am interested in enlarging the scope of the above debate by searching for ways to begin theorizing about this latter group of individuals—specifically, women intellectuals from the working class. They constitute an unlikely, but nevertheless identifiable, minority in the academic/intellectual community; and their situation, it seems to me, inspires its own set of intriguing questions deserving of further exploration. How might gender, together with class background, shape their identity and determine the "class" they represent? What is their function in the academy (or in other similar spheres of intellectual activity)? What can it be? How might their particular experience revise traditional Marxist—and feminist—conceptions of the intellectual and *her* ability to accomplish social change?

Much of my thinking in this essay is grounded in the work of Antonio Gramsci, Michel Foucault, Nicos Poulantzas, and Erik Olin Wright, whose efforts in this area pose possibilities, as well as problems, for a theory of intellectuals based on both class and gender. Their contributions to the field need not be dismissed in toto, and indeed, their very shaping of that field requires continued attention.[2] I intend to review and build upon their various notions of "organic," "specific," and "contradictory" intellectuals while at the same time making use of feminist approaches to epistemology, such as Sandra Harding's, to expose noticeable gaps in their analysis. My attempt to formulate a new critical direction hinges on a perspective of the family which challenges both Marxist and feminist theoretical models, suggesting that in a working-class context, the family helps to foster a class subculture which aggressively resists, as well as reproduces, dominant ideologies. And this subcultural experience, I want to argue, combines with the working-class female's *gendered* set of subject positions to create a particular ideological matrix that in turn perhaps constitutes the most promising (as well as potentially inhibitory) "training ground" for a new kind of intellectual: one who, by virtue of an upbringing that places her in a peculiar dialectical position to the dominant system, has the ability to develop a radical way of seeking knowledge—of creating a new "politics of truth."

I

Although Foucault and Poulantzas are both concerned in their own ways with the intellectual's relationship to the state, Gramsci's highly influential essay in *Selections from the Prison Notebooks* serves in many respects as the foundation for much contemporary social and political theory. In "On Intellectuals," Gramsci establishes a new "definition" of intellectual activity: the intellectual enterprise is distinguished by its *function*, its place within "the general complex of social relations," (8) rather than by its "intrinsic nature." All activity, he stresses, requires some form of mental work, no matter how "physical" it may be: "all men are intellectuals," however, "not all men have in society the function of intellectuals" (9). According to Gramsci, this function is historically determined and breaks down into two basic types: the traditional intellectual, representative of the retiring hegemonic class such as the aristocracy; and the organic intellectual, who rises out of the newly emerging dominant class (the bourgeoisie) and explicitly furthers its ends in the cultural, as well as economic, sphere. It is the express role of the organic intellectual to *organize* and *legitimize* the dominant class, serving as its "deputy," Gramsci notes, by "exercising the subaltern functions of social hegemony and political government" (12).

I am most interested in Gramsci's specific application of this theory to working-class struggle: Can the proletariat develop its own category of organic intellectuals? If not, can it hope to overthrow the ruling class without means of intervening in and subverting the civil realm of society? On the one hand, Gramsci insists on the necessity of any class "developing towards dominance" to create its own organic intelligentsia so that it can subsequently create a new state: as Giuseppe Vacca elaborates in his study of Gramsci, intellectuals mediate "relations between rulers and the ruled" in civil society, serving a crucial role in building a progressive (socialist) state (45). Gramsci argues that the proletariat must therefore produce what he finally designates as the "new" intellectual: one who will "no longer consist in eloquence . . . but in active participation in practical life, as constructor, organizer, 'permanent persuader'" (10). Specifically, "he" will be "closely bound to industrial labor" and have a "technical," rather than an "artistic," education (9). And ideally, the new working-class organic intellectual will proceed to foster a "new social organization of knowledge" rooted in "the world of production" (Vacca 64) so that intellectual activity will no longer be the province of "professional philosophers," but a "popular, 'mass' phenomenon" (Boggs 224).

At the same time, however, Gramsci argues that the working class can create its organic intelligentsia only after seizing state power, in a transitional socialist state, since its very development depends upon the existence of a different mode of production (one which, in Gramsci's scheme, allows the proletariat to assert cultural dominance in the first place). Within a traditional capitalist state, *individual* members of the proletariat cannot hope to infiltrate the ranks of the bourgeois intelligentsia and remain committed to their class; greater structural change is a prerequisite for the emergence of a new organic intellectual outlook. Within Gramsci's Italy, of course, there were very specific and very real limitations. Nevertheless, Gramsci fails to anticipate in his theory a historical moment in which individual members of the working class might in fact penetrate state apparatuses and become successfully disruptive intellectuals. Further, the gender blindness of his analysis severely limits his theory of intellectual labor. Women's experiences (on any level) simply fail to be taken into consideration. I am therefore interested in extending Gramsci not only by seeking ways that individuals can subvert intellectual positions in the short run, but also by seeking ways in which gender shapes the very knowledge developed by the working class.

Like Gramsci, Foucault struggles with the notion of a working-class intellectual position, recognizing that the intellectual's function is traditionally closely tied to the reinscription of dominant ideology; and like Gramsci, he is concerned with the need to develop a new type of knowledge. But Foucault is much more interested in the individual's struggle to resist and attain power, locating the body as the site of conflict. His interview with Alessandro Fontana and Pasquale Pasquino thus raises the following significant question: If for Foucault the "specific site of confrontation with power" occurs as a local struggle ("on" the body) rather than a global (class) struggle, where, exactly, does the intellectual fit into political conflict and action? His conception of universal and specific intellectuals ostensibly resolves this question. Foucault envisions a historical shift in types of intellectuals: from the writer/man of letters, who had functioned as a universal spokesperson for "truth and justice," to the post–World War II expert, who operates within "specific sectors" and is often aware of "concrete struggles" by virtue of "his" own frequently adversarial relation to the state ("Truth and Power" 126–29). This specific intellectual, typified by the atomic scientist who holds "knowledge of life and death," plays an important role in establishing and codifying the dominant culture's "regime of truth"—its method of constituting knowledge or distinguishing truth from falsity, which in turn is directly linked to its maintenance of power ("Truth and Power" 130–32). He finally argues that the specific intellectual can thus insert "himself" into political struggle by delegitimizing the current apparatus of truth:

The essential political problem for the intellectual is not to criticize the ideological contents supposedly linked to science . . . but that of ascertaining the possibility of constituting a new politics of truth. . . . It's not a matter of emancipating truth from every system of power . . . but of detaching the power of truth from the forms of hegemony . . . within which it operates at the present time. (133)

The above statement has become one well known, and often celebrated, directive for postmodern intellectuals. It is less clear how women and/or the working class fit into Foucault's scheme. He outlines two types of specificity underlying the intellectual's relation to the re-gime of truth: class position and conditions of life and work (132). Gender specificity is notably lacking. And although he allows for the possibility of a proletarian organic intellectual in the class category, his discussion overall tends to assume that the specific intellectual is born of the petite-bourgeois class and only sympathetically linked to the pro-letariat. Foucault's interview with Gilles Deleuze in *Language, Counter-Memory, Practice* further underscores the slippage in these categories. Once more he proposes that the specific intellectual's political function is to extricate "himself" from the current system of truth/power, to re-fuse to be its instrument by devising a new system of knowledge so that the masses may speak for themselves (and "in this sense," he claims, "theory does not express, translate, or serve to apply practice: it is practice" [208]). Yet here he introduces a distinction between exploi-tation and power: exploitation is always force exercised against the masses, while power is also related to desire and the unconscious, and is thus bound up with the individual. Operating with this distinction, Foucault subsequently argues that intellectuals "genuinely serve the cause of the proletariat" (216) by struggling individually against power: for if they struggle against exploitation, they must "totally identify with the proletariat" and struggle directly alongside them; but a struggle against power—"fighting in those places where they find themselves oppressed"—allows them to ally with the proletariat while fully strug-gling "on their own terrain" (216).

All of this implies, of course, that intellectuals are never from the working class themselves, caught as they are in the seemingly uncom-fortable—perhaps impossible—predicament of attempting to identify with it. And significantly, Foucault includes women with neither the proletariat nor the intellectuals, but with others who are marginalized by dominant culture (homosexuals, prisoners) and who struggle specifi-cally against power. I would like to approach Foucault's theory from another direction, however, and, as will be illustrated later, suggest that it in fact places women intellectuals from the working class in a more advantageous position to fight against both exploitation *and* power. Their unique understanding of global, as well as local, conflict might allow them to become a different sort of specific intellectual with a particular stake in dismantling the current "regime of truth."

Much of Nicos Poulantzas's theory of state power and vision of relations between dominant and dominated groups resonates with Gramscian and Foucaultian ideas. Perhaps as a result, he equally underestimates (though in different ways) the endurance of class ties among working-class intellectuals, as well as fails to perceive the gender implications of his perspective. Like the above theorists, Poulantzas conceives of state power as a "condensation of a relationship of forces" (123), yet he particularly stresses that the state contains *within itself* all elements of class struggle. It can thus never be considered a seamless monolith separate from the masses: Poulantzas valuably notes that the state is riddled with internal contradictions and by its very existence replicates class struggle. The dominant class exists within the state specifically through self-sustaining power apparatuses, while the dominated classes assert their presence through the creation of "centers of opposition" (they lack their own power apparatus) and through the state "material framework," which is profoundly "bound up with the relations of production" (141).

How, then, does the intellectual enter Poulantzas's theory? He observes that no potentially subversive group can think of going *outside* the state to organize, since that is (in Poulantzas's terms) "impossible." Echoing Gramsci, he emphasizes that the dominated group(s) must finally transform the internal state hegemonic apparatuses that control the dominant ideology, as well as seize state power, to gain control (138). At the same time, however, he expresses little faith in the emergence either of an organic proletarian intellectual or of any bourgeois intellectuals willing to seek an overthrow of the state, to accomplish this transformation. The intellectual is seemingly designated a full-fledged member of the "state personnel" and of the petite-bourgeois class despite "his" class origin; and though he may forge political alliances with the working class for his own ends, he will never challenge, according to Poulantzas, the very "reproduction of the social division of labor within the state apparatus" (156). State personnel "do not radically call into question their own place and role in relation to the popular masses" (157).

The intellectual thus has little, if any, currency in this scheme, though Poulantzas fails to demonstrate how the masses will subsequently manipulate the state's ideological apparatuses without their own intelligentsia. Like Gramsci, he dismisses too quickly the possibility of a working-class allegiance that can resist co-option, setting up a similar Catch-22 situation for revolutionary struggle. And it is interesting that his own brand of masculinist assumptions again leaves room for a different, feminist, analysis. Although Poulantzas should be credited with recognizing the difficulty of including women's struggle against patriarchy exclusively under the rubric of "class struggle" (148), he generally fails to make gender distinctions among either the masses or state personnel. He can thereby observe that "the masses are directly present in such apparatuses as the school, the national conscript army and (through their representatives) the institutions of the electoral system" (152), when on the contrary it is clear that women as a group are actually far less represented in those institutions than men. As with Gramsci and Foucault, his lack of gender analysis—as well as his shortsighted view of class agency—limits the efficacy of his theory and causes him to overlook alternate possibilities for disruptive activity. What *are* the implications for working-class women, who tend to be excluded from even the most common state apparatuses? Obviously, they are less likely to attain positions of influence in the state. But at the same time, their exclusion might paradoxically place them in a better position for resistance. Less susceptible to assimilation, they are perhaps more likely to see class and gender relations clearly, arriving at a different means of perceiving and articulating truth.

Erik Olin Wright's essay "Intellectuals and the Class Structure of Capitalist Society" gives rise to similar sorts of questions, but he contributes yet another perspective to this debate, as he is less interested in speculating on the "function" of intellectuals in political struggle than in mapping out their precise class identity or "location" in hegemonic society. In many respects, Wright's analysis proves the most interesting and challenging; he directs his attention to exceptions and contradictions, poking holes in Gramsci's and Poulantzas's mass theories. Essentially, he seeks to plot the "class character of intellectual labor" (192): the activity (as Wright defines it) of elaborating and disseminating ideas. He reviews and refutes four standard Marxist interpretations of the class position of intellectuals—all of which link the intellectual to a specific class or category—before arriving at his own more comprehensive theoretical model. Wright argues that intellectuals finally occupy *contradictory* locations within class relations, distinguishing between positions at different structural levels: at the economic level, they appear between the working class and the petite bourgeoisie since they have more autonomy over their labor process than the proletariat, but less than the petite bourgeois producer (who is, as Wright notes, in effect "his or her own boss"); at the ideological level, however, intellectuals occupy a contradictory position between the working class and the bourgeoisie, since they again have more control over ideological apparatuses than the proletariat, but lack the complete control over those apparatuses exercised by the owners, the bourgeois class (204–06). These distinctions are valuable, it seems to me, because they allow for greater complexity and recognize varying levels of power among mental laborers in capitalist culture. Wright successfully demonstrates that one's function as a disseminator of ideology may conflict with one's structural position, which might very well establish sympathetic ties to the working class (201). Finally, he argues, we must envision a nonlocation for intellectuals, rather than insist upon a set class designation that rarely, if ever, fits: intellectuals "share class interest" with each class that they straddle, but "have interests identical to neither" (206). Such an argument suggests, along with Foucault, that there might indeed be a role for intellectuals in day-to-day class struggle, since their loyalties may not be as fixed as Poulantzas or Gramsci propose.

Yet curiously, Wright's comprehensive analysis fails to address the issue of class origin: what particular conflicts do intellectuals from working-class backgrounds experience in this contradictory class location? Are they more likely to assimilate to the bourgeois class strata in order to escape class roots, or will they in fact remain more closely linked to the proletariat? And what of women intellectuals? It is not surprising, perhaps, that Wright also succumbs to an essentially gender-blind approach. How is the level of contradiction further compounded by gender difference? How do gender and class work together to distinguish one's location? His example of the increasing proletarianization of college teachers proves especially interesting in the light of both these neglected categories, since women and working-class academics are much more likely to be employed as instructors in non-elite educational institutions where, as Wright correctly points out, they are rapidly losing control over work loads, curriculums, and the like (210). Wright hints that such teachers might be particularly susceptible to radicalization as the discrepancy between their ideological function and their structural position becomes all the more apparent—and, again, I wonder whether working-class women intellectuals, who may already lay claim to a radical outlook when they occupy these positions, might not lend all the more proof that the mental laborer has the potential to serve an oppositional purpose while enmeshed within dominant culture.

II

Sandra Harding's essay "The Instability of the Analytical Categories of Feminist Theory" complements the above theoretical efforts here in profitable ways. But before I address Harding, I want to lay some groundwork by exploring the potentially unstable, conflicting ideologies confronting working-class females through a variety of subcultural experiences and discourses in order to understand their difference—how their particular upbringing encourages, as well as suppresses, a radical interpretation of reality and relationship to the state.

As Samuel Bowles correctly notes in "Unequal Education and the Reproduction of the Social Division of Labor," working-class subculture is born out of capitalist social relations and, as such, is profoundly bound up with the replication of dominant ideology (as well as the system itself): children in working-class families are usually taught obedience and discipline in a way that prepares them to accept subordinate employment positions, and they are additionally socialized to adopt traditional gender roles. Unquestionably, the family gets caught up in the ideological machine, providing capitalism with a steady stream of trained workers who have a vested interest in keeping their jobs, and men with a ready supply of future wives. Yet the working-class family is clearly more than a passive accomplice to the hegemonic system, since it also tends to rewrite that system's version of class, if not gender, relations. Both male and female children, for example, witness the alienating and demeaning effects of their parents' jobs and as a result are often taught from an early age to see (mercilessly) through the myth of "cooperation" or "teamwork" that frequently characterizes management-worker relations under capitalism. Both are encouraged as well to resist and disrupt—from small, individual acts of sabotage to more obvious collective efforts (walk-outs, strikes, etc.). In fact, successful assimilation to bourgeois culture is often perceived by the family as an out-and-out act of betrayal. In the interest of developing useful theory and successful praxis, it is important to recognize that working-class culture

227

may affirm its difference even as it succumbs to the dominant class's discourse, often providing what I would consider a counterhegemonic vision of day-to-day reality.

Paul Willis's and Angela McRobbie's work on contemporary British working-class culture helps to bear this out. In *Learning to Labour*, Willis sets out to uncover "how working class kids get working class jobs." He studies a core group of male working-class students by charting their progression from the world of education to the world of labor, probing attitudes toward work, their families, and their school experiences. Willis is primarily concerned with delineating the set of ideological forces that gear these students to a life of manual work, focusing specifically on the British school system's role as a state apparatus. And he successfully demonstrates that the school and the family work indeed together to encourage compliance with the dominant culture. Yet Willis suggests that the family (usually the father) also acts as a significant influence to delegitimize and often struggle against the social order: "Stories are told in the home about shopfloor culture, the things which happen and the attitudes which prevail there—especially attitudes towards authority . . . there is an undoubted sense in which working class values and feelings . . . work against the school and provide concrete materials for *differentiation*" (73). The students themselves confirm this statement. One named Spanksy notes that his father "wouldn't want me to be a wanker, sitting there working . . . I'd like to be like him, you know, he can't stand no bull" (74–75); another, Joey, boasts that his children "wouldn't be submissive fucking twits. They'll be outspoken, upstanding sort of people" (12).[3] Willis is particularly interested in affirming the existence of working-class agency, and this study provides exciting (if often disturbingly sexist) evidence for such a project.

McRobbie's similar study of working-class girls in Birmingham during the same period helps to redress Willis's focus on male experience, although McRobbie for her part appears more interested in what she terms the "culture of femininity" than in working-class culture per se. Her study actually foregrounds the wholesale adoption of conventional feminine roles by her working-class subjects, such as "underachievement in school" or the desire to marry and have children early. And when McRobbie identifies a rare, *class*-based form of defiance, it is expressed in problematic "feminine" terms as well: at school, where the girls confront middle-class teachers and students, they accentuate their own class difference by accentuating their sexuality—disrupting class by applying makeup and wearing provocative clothing (104). Thus, even the "oppositional activities" they engage in ultimately work to re-inscribe other kinds of equally oppressive or questionable roles for women.

McRobbie discusses the implications of this traditional positioning with a great deal of insight, and it is important that she links that positioning to specific material constraints, as well as to ideologies reinforced both in school and at home. At the same time, it seems to me that her study does include signs of other, rewarding aspects of working-class culture for women. One girl, for instance (sneeringly) discusses her father's attempts to interest her in union politics, encouraging her to read more and spend less time with her friends "chasing boys." And I suspect that McRobbie could have uncovered a lot more distinctly class-based attitudes that push against the system if she had looked for them. Also, she herself notes that for those interviewed, the family became an arena in which the ideology of romance and marriage was exposed, as well as propagated. Marital violence and the blatant economic necessity of "finding a man" undermined any blissful visions of male-female relations that the girls might have had. I therefore think that the "complex interweaving of class and sex" (102) that she sets out to investigate with her Birmingham population is even more complicated and potentially subversive than her analysis indicates.

Having said that, let me turn to specific instances of American working-class women's confrontations with the academic system—both traditional and nontraditional—in order to attempt to piece together a suggestive pattern of experiences and attitudes associated with a joint class-gender identity. Jake Ryan and Charles Sackrey's 1984 collection *Strangers in Paradise: Academics From the Working Class*, provides a most interesting model of gender difference. To begin with, Ryan and Sackrey (themselves from working-class backgrounds) offer an overwhelmingly negative presentation of working-class culture in their introduction, concentrating upon the antagonistic relationship between working-class existence and higher education. For better or worse, they argue, a working-class background ill prepares a budding intellectual for a successful stint in academia and haunts forever those who finally do emerge as university professionals. It is not surprising that their emphasis is echoed as well in the autobiographical profiles they have chosen for their study: most are written by male working-class intellectuals (more on this curious gender differential in a moment) who either harbor not-so-veiled hostilities toward their pasts or downplay any memories of distinct class attitudes. There are significant exceptions, but overall, the male respondents tend to dwell upon—and begrudge—their misfit status and offer a cynical view of their current intellectual positions.

The hostility toward women that also marks these responses is echoed in Ryan and Sackrey's editorial policy as a whole: they announce in their introduction that they could find only two responses from women academics "good enough" to be included in their study, since they sought contributions from working-class women which were preoccupied with class, rather than with gender, concerns.[4] Fortunately, the editors' narrow vision perhaps led them to overlook as well the comments on female subjectivity that do surface in Jane Ellen Wilson's and Alice Trent's essays, allowing them to incorporate two valuable discussions of both class and gender influences on women academics. Although two women's commentaries can hardly be considered representative of the whole, they pose a striking alternative to the majority of male contributions found in Ryan and Sackrey's volume, offering a perspective of identity and cultural experience that seems to embrace, rather than resist, contradiction.

Wilson in particular demonstrates that she has achieved a workable, inspiring balance between her class roots and her intellectual identity, recognizing at the same time that neither can be completely reconciled with the other. Fleeing a life in small-town Pennsylvania for "intellectual stimulation and community," she progressed through an English degree program to eventually become a graduate student in folklore; in her work, she specifically attempted to remain faithful to the "views of the 'folk,' the peasants, the poor, the disenfranchised" (214). She makes it clear that it was her class background that enlarged her scope of study and originally stirred this interest: "I had always felt there was something missing from academia's view of the world. In literature, for example, I knew that they studied Englishmen writing literature; I knew that people exercised verbal creativity in many more ways than that. My grandfather told stories, my father told stories, every truck driver . . . had a story to tell" (212). Her disillusioning experiences at the university led her to discover that

only by coming to terms with my own past, my own background, and seeing that in context of the world at large, have I begun to find my true voice and to understand that, since it is my own voice, that no pre-cut niche exists for it; that part of the work to be done is making a place with others, where my and our voices can stand clear of the background noise and voice our concerns as part of a larger song. (216)

As she writes her response, she is conscious of finally arriving at a satisfying "sense of community" which "comes from both inside and outside the academy" (216).

But that borderline status—occupying at once the insider and outsider position—is grounded as well in gender difference. Although her parents encouraged her to read and develop her talents, she was raised with limited options. She also experienced sexual discrimination as a student. While she fails to offer a systematic analysis of her oppression as a woman, these memories continually punctuate her commentary, making it clear that gender, as well as class background, forms a significant part of her identity. One of her closing statements illustrates this well: "My intellect, as well as my background, is a part of me that I can't deny. I would rather give a lecture on mythology for an honorarium than work as a waitress for the same amount of money. . . . I'd rather spend the day writing than driving a tractor, five days a week. I would rather do any of the above than be a wife to someone whose support bought my subservience" (217).

Unlike Jane Ellen Wilson, Alice Trent received unusual encouragement from her mother to pursue whatever goals she desired ("Never was anything held as impossible because I was a girl"). Yet she admits to a more troubling sense of conflict overall between her class roots, gender, and intellectual position, situating herself in a highly contradictory space in dominant culture: "When some of my colleagues rhapsodize about the glories of the working class, I feel just as uncomfortable as I do when my female colleagues talk about the Women's movement. The most important thing about my being working-class is that I identified with no group—I don't subscribe to any 'organized religion'" (229). At the same time, Trent seems to value precisely this "non"-location and difference, realizing that (among other things) she can open her upper-middle-class students to "a wider range of thinking" (232–33). She concludes her essay by speculating further upon this sense of contradiction, but although she actually focuses here on the "price" paid for "different-ness," her comments also suggest that she recognizes a kind of multiplicity within herself that is lacking in her male counterparts.

Perhaps this is the crucial element in being a female working-class academic. The male working-class academics I have met are usually extremely driven. They have to "prove something" by succeeding in their careers. Often this makes them rather single-minded. As a woman, I don't feel a career—whatever it is—is enough. I seek emotional fulfillment as well. (233)

Though they provide mere glimpses, both women's contributions begin marking out the possibilities of a gendered, as well as a class-based, vision informed by an acceptance of conflict and a spirit of resistance.

To complement and extend the possibilities suggested by women such as these two who occupy traditional academic posts, I have finally sought out the experiences of explicitly nonacademic women at various schools for women workers, such as the Bryn Mawr Summer School and the Women's Trade Union League Training School for Women Organizers. They serve as another, somewhat different, source of testimony to the positive influence of working-class culture upon women and its encouragement of political knowledge. The schools themselves began as joint ventures between universities and labor unions in the early part of the century and created a new agenda for education—which continues today in contemporary labor programs—essentially training women workers to be more effective labor activists. But although students were hardly being groomed for university posts, the school's programs also often incorporated traditional academic subjects ranging from astronomy to English literature and rhetoric (Kornbluh and Frederickson 43–44). They thus sparked a love of learning in many women normally barred from intellectual activity, as well as capitalized upon their acute understanding of class relations and instinctive ability to perceive "truth" differently.

In *Sisterhood and Solidarity* one student at Bryn Mawr in the late 1920s, Sadie Goodman, offers an especially cogent and moving analysis of workers' education: "The best thing that happens to a [middle-class] student who has worked in a factory is that she has her illusions shattered on how to help the working class. She learns that it is not important to teach workers how to live properly, how to be good Americans or to be good producers . . . but that it is important to awaken workers to the fact of the big role they play in industry and in helping to develop civilization" (Kornbluh and Frederickson 99). She concludes:

What happens to my industrial sister when she gets a taste of the intellectual world? First a dizzy pain in the head. . . . The second thing that happens is that the world begins to stretch out. They begin to see and hear things that have always been there, but to which they have been deaf, dumb, and blind. . . . Some understanding of the history of civilization gave me a feeling of importance as a factory worker. The study of English made speakers and writers out of us overnight. . . . We see books that have always been on the bookshelves but have meant nothing to us. The study of science opens our eyes to the skies and trees. A theoretical understanding of the trade union movement strengthens our faith in it, even when our fellow workers and leaders seem to fail us. (101)

Recognizing that education should be aimed at the deconstruction of dominant ideology and directly linked to social action, Sadie Goodman emerges, it seems to me, as the most appropriate model for the Gramscian new intellectual—a member of the working class intervening in the civil realm while promoting a truly radical and practical "social organization of knowledge." It is important, however, that she and other students at these labor schools also sought to develop the analytic skills necessary to confront and understand the patriarchal component of the state, hoping to mediate tensions between their private and public lives as women: many autobiographical essays in *Sisterhood and Solidarity* speak of a father/brother/husband/boss's domineering control or suggest that husbands were resistant to wives taking on leadership roles in their unions.[5] The schools in fact offered early versions of consciousness-raising sessions and assertiveness training to help the women address their often conflicting gender and class concerns. And it is in this sense that I believe women like Sadie Goodman, along with Jane Ellen Wilson and Alice Trent, might finally represent the kind of theorist that Sandra Harding envisions.

In "The Instability of the Analytic Categories of Feminist Theory," Harding advocates the acceptance of a feminist "non"-epistemology grounded in contradiction, multiplicity, contextual ways of thinking and seeing. She reviews two particular trends that have developed within feminist theory as it has grappled with the difficulty of establishing a distinct feminist epistemology: the "successor science" position asks How can we "scientifically" correct or adjust male theoretical discourses so that they adequately take into account women's experience and reflect a female vision? Feminist postmodernism counters that position by asking whether such a corrective can ever be possible—and whether it is politically desirable. (In other words, can any theory reflect the way the world "really is"?) Harding herself proposes that we need "to see these two tendencies in feminist theory . . . as *converging* approaches to a postmodernist world—a world that will not exist until both (conflicting) tendencies achieve their goals" (657, my emphasis). She, too, asks "Where are we to find the analytical categories for the absent, the invisible, the silenced that do not simply replicate in mirror-image fashion the distorting and mystifying categories and projects of the dominant discourses?" (648) But much like Erik Olin Wright, she opts for a "non"-choice: rather than construct an inadequate overarching conceptual form that presumes to speak for all women, she argues that "we can learn how to embrace the instability of the analytical categories, to find in the instability itself the desired theoretical reflection of certain aspects of the political reality in which we live and think; to use these instabilities as a resource for our thinking and practices" (648). And like Foucault, Harding thus implies that theorists can "detach the power of truth" from hegemonic epistemology by continually disrupting it and refusing to offer another in its place. Ultimately, she takes the position that feminist theory should not seek to articulate generic woman's identity through a central discourse, but should attempt to express and explore different ways to knowing the world from a female position that possesses enough flexibility to capture "what we think at the moment we want to say" (649).

Bringing together the more exciting elements of previous Marxist positions and situating them in a feminist framework, Harding's model suggests a number of possibilities for the current political role of the woman intellectual. To begin with, it validates the notion that gender in and of itself fosters a valuable way of perceiving reality: "This approach to theorizing captures what some take to be a distinctively women's emphasis . . . in which a valuable 'alienated consciousness,' 'bifurcated consciousness,' 'oppositional consciousness' might function at the level of activity theory making—as well as at the level of skepticism and rebellion" (650).

Yet such a consciousness obviously extends as well to other marginalized subject positions. And when those are compounded, the singularly oppositional forms of knowledge normally produced—based upon the experience of being female *or* nonwhite *or* non-Western *or* proletarian—converge and subsequently condition strategies, as well as opportunities, for resistance. As I have tried to suggest, working-class women's joint class and gender identities possibly encourage (or demand) a broader vision and instill within them a sense of the *right* to resist. They might, then—along with others dually or triply marginalized—serve as the most promising theorists for this new convergence of unstable epistemologies, benefiting from a different kind of global outlook and a relationship more markedly antagonistic to the dominant culture. In fact, as bell hooks has stressed, *black* working-class women develop a particularly dramatic "oppositional world view" as a result of their devalued gender, class, and race, and should be at the forefront of such an enterprise.[6]

I am ultimately searching for a way to bridge theoretical and practical approaches to the creation of knowledge in order to envision a viable oppositional function for the intellectual in dominant culture. The Harding-Foucault strategy of delegitimizing the reigning regime of truth offers a place to begin. A theory that moves this strategy beyond the bounds of the academy, however, seems imperative, offering radical epistemologists within the workplace itself a leading role in reconstituting truth. Perhaps the workers' education model poses the most interesting and viable means for such a project, bringing together university women intellectuals in semi-autonomous positions with those on the shop floor, in offices, and in unions to establish connections between both spheres, and allowing a new feminist/working-class politics of knowledge to be passed on through a variety of activities—teaching (at universities, community colleges, and community centers), organizing, speaking out. Like many others, I return finally to Gramsci: I seek a theory that extends, or redefines, the concept of intellectual work and recognizes the need for an organic proletarian intellectual to intervene at all ideological levels directed by the state. Yet with my efforts here, I hope to begin a new tradition as well: a return to feminist theory for confirmation that such an intellectual can be—and in light of her particularly marginalized relation to the dominant culture, indeed should be—female.

Notes

1. For more extensive discussions of the gender blindness that pervades Marxist theory as a whole, see *Women and Revolution*, ed. Lydia Sargent (Boston: South End, 1981), particularly Heidi Hartmann's now classic essay "The Unhappy Marriage of Marxism and Feminism: Towards a More Progressive Union"; Michele Barrett's *Women's Oppression Today: Problems in Marxist Feminist Analysis* (London: Villiers, 1980); and Nancy Hartsock's *Money, Sex, and Power: Toward a Feminist Historical Materialism* (New York: Longman, 1983). All three challenge Marxism's hegemony as a theory that explains relations of domination and subordination and attempt to redress its neglect (or trivialization) of gender concerns specifically by mapping out the relationship between capitalist and patriarchal systems. Also see Julia Swindells and Lisa Jardine's *What's Left? Women in Culture and the Labour Movement* (London: Routledge, 1990) for a more recent critique of British Marxism, and see Linda Nicholson's essay, "Feminism and Marx: Integrating Kinship with the Economic," *Feminism as Critique*, ed. Sayla Benhabib and Drucilla Cornell (Oxford: Polity, 1987).

2. As the above citation attests, feminist theorists interested in class issues have certainly attempted to take Marxist studies in different directions, yet few, if any, have undertaken this specific area. Spurred by my own working-class background, my efforts here will, I hope, stimulate further discussion within feminist scholarship about theories of intellectuals, particularly as they relate to working-class women both inside and outside the academy. See, however, Janet Zandy's introduction to the anthology *Calling Home: Working-Class Women's Writings*, ed. Janet Zandy (New Brunswick: Rutgers UP, 1990); and the anthology, *Making Face, Making Soul*, ed. Gloria Anzaldúa (San Francisco: Spinsters Aunt Lute, 1990).

3. Willis's interviews with the students' parents prove in some cases even more fascinating and revealing. Here, one father and mother complain about "parents' night" at their son's school:

FATHER: The headmaster irritated me, I can't put me finger on it now . . . 'cos I could see . . . could see, I was 'im, I was 'im, I was standing there, and I was 'im. I thought, 'Aye, aye, he's talking to hisself,' you know, wa'nt talking to me [. . .] he put my back up [. . .] . . . See now, I can't get up in a room and talk against teachers, like, I couldn't talk against you, because I'd be flabbergasted, I'd be 'umming' and 'ahhing,' and I'd be worried stiff you know [. . .] I dunno how to say it, how to put it, 'cos I'd look around me and I'd think, 'These people don't want to know anyway' [. . .] If I could have been in a room with 'im [the head] on his own . . . I could have said. . . .

PW: Could have said what?

FATHER: You're full of bull.

MOTHER: They say, 'Children's night', go down, they ain't interested really in what you'm saying, am they? They don't want to know.

PW: What's the whole thing in aid of then?

MOTHER: I don't know.

FATHER: I think it's trying to show you what good they'm doing for your kid [. . .] They don't tell what they'm doin' wrong for him, they tell you exactly what they're doing right for 'em, what good they're doing. (73–74)

4. To wit:

As we have said, everyone knows . . . why more women, from all classes, are not in the academy in proportionate numbers, and, even more so, why such barriers would be particularly great for working-class women. Yet, in our own gathering of autobiographical essays, we ended up with two exceptionally good ones from women. Had the two women, whose essays we have used, focused on matters of *gender*, rather than on *class* issues, we might have considered not using them, for in such a case they could not have been anything remotely representative of the opinion of academic women on that dimension of their experience. However, as our readers eventually will see, our two women contributors mostly concentrated on experiences and feelings that we believe are common to the academic from the working class *as an outsider* rather than *as a woman*. (9)

To add insult to injury, Jane Ellen Wilson's name is misprinted in the Table of Contents as *James* Ellen Wilson!

5. In a 1982 interview, Barbara Kohn of the United Auto Workers notes: "I had always been involved with the union as a silent majority. My husband was president of his local union. . . . So I lived union, but I lived it through him. Because of *his* involvement. His idea was for me not to get involved" (309). Speaking of her reasons for attending the Michigan Summer School for Women Workers, she states, "The role of a woman in the generation I was brought up in was to be a housewife first, subservient to her husband. To be seen but not to speak. Or if you did speak, to speak softly. Decision-making was the male's job. You just didn't make decisions. . . . You were locked into your own little world. You were dominated by others. I didn't want to be part of those 'yes' people. I wanted to be part of the people in the decision-making, but I didn't know how to do it effectively" (310).

6. hooks's entire *Feminist Theory: From Margin to Center* serves as an invaluable examination of black women's marginality, as do her other works, such as *Talking Back* (Boston: South End, 1990). For additional texts emphasizing the need to incorporate multicultural and working-class perspectives into the academy—particularly into feminist studies—see Barbara Smith's numerous essays, including "Racism and Women's Studies," in *All the Women Are White, All the Blacks Are Men, But Some of Us Are Brave: Black Women's Studies*, ed. Gloria T. Hull, Patricia Bell Scott, and Barbara Smith (New York:

Feminist P, 1982); Maxine Baca Zinn, Lynn Weber Cannon, Elizabeth Higgin-botham, and Bonnie Thorton Dill's "The Cost of Exclusionary Practices in Women's Studies," *Signs* 11, no. 4 (1986): 290–303, and *Making Face, Making Soul*, ed. Gloria Anzaldúa.

Works Cited

Boggs, Carl. *The Two Revolutions: Antonio Gramsci and the Dilemmas of Western Marxism*. Boston: South End, 1984.

Bowles, Samuel. "Unequal Education and the Reproduction of the Social Division of Labor." *Review of Radical Political Economics* 3 (Fall 1971): 1–30.

Foucault, Michel. "Intellectuals and Power." *Language, Counter-Memory, Practice*. Ed. and trans. Donald F. Bouchard. Ithaca: Cornell UP, 1977.

——. "Truth and Power." *Power/Knowledge: Selected Interviews and Other Writings, 1972–1977*. Ed. and trans. Colin Gordon. New York: Pantheon, 1980.

Gramsci, Antonio. "On Intellectuals." *Selections from the Prison Notebooks*. Ed. Quintin Hoare and Geoffrey Nowell Smith. New York: International, 1971.

Harding, Sandra. "The Instability of the Analytic Categories of Feminist Theory." *Signs* 11. 4 (1986): 645–64.

hooks, bell. *Feminist Theory: From Margin to Center*. Boston: South End, 1984.

Kornbluh, Joyce L., and Mary Frederickson, eds. *Sisterhood and Solidarity: Workers' Education for Women, 1914–1984*. Philadelphia: Temple UP, 1984.

McRobbie, Angela. "Working Class Girls and the Culture of Femininity." In Women's Studies Group, Centre for Contemporary Cultural Studies. *Women Take Issue*. London: Hutchinson, 1978.

Poulantzas, Nicos. *State, Power, Socialism*. Trans. Patrick Camiller. London: NLB, 1978.

Ryan, Jake, and Charles Sackrey. *Strangers in Paradise: Academics from the Working Class*. Boston: South End, 1984.

Vacca, Giuseppe. "Intellectuals and the Marxist Theory of the State." *Approaches to Gramsci*. Ed. Anne Showstack Sassoon. London: Writers and Readers Publishing Cooperative Society, 1982. 37–39.

Willis, Paul. *Learning to Labour: How Working Class Kids Get Working Class Jobs*. Westmead, England. Saxon, 1977.

Wright, Erik Olin. "Intellectuals and the Class Structure of Capitalist Society." *Between Labor and Capital*. Ed. Pat Walker. Montreal. Black Rose, 1978. 191–211.

Vestments and Vested Interests: Academia, the Working Class, and Affirmative Action

M UCH contemporary literary and cultural criticism aims to privilege what has long been ignored. As a result, in such criticism one finds invoked again and again a trinity (and sometimes, a quartet) of the marginalized, those excluded from social and political power because of race, gender, or class (and in some writings, sexual orientation as well). These are groups, the argument runs, that must be empowered in the interests of positive social change. And more definitively than society generally, the academy (the institutional locus of such criticism) has recognized and embraced the postmodern decentering of "man" and eurocentrism by acting affirmatively to bring women, blacks, Hispanics, and Asians into the mainstream of its institutions. "Affirmative action may be out of favor at the Supreme Court," says Andrew Hacker, "but it is becoming a stronger force on the nation's campuses" (63).

Given the theoretical prominence of class in literary and cultural criticism, one would think that literary intellectuals in particular would embrace the notion that class distinctions create people whose disadvantages are as real and as significant and as long-standing as the disadvantages suffered by those who have been subject to discrimination because of race or gender. One would think we would work to extend the benefits of affirmative action to another group traditionally underrepresented in academe, another group that lacks the wherewithal to negotiate successfully with institutions of the elite.

Instead, what I hear from colleagues is that the influence of class is "so very hard to tease out," a true assertion, perhaps, but one that also might be called cowardly and one that certainly legitimates our abandonment of the working class. Thus, if affirmative action is a strong force on the nation's campuses, as Hacker claims, its power focuses on only two of the three groups in that trinity of the marginalized. The academy theorizes class, but unless it is subsumed by gender or race, and particularly by race, it does not figure in the practical calculus by

239

which we assess our efforts at creating equal opportunity. In this essay, I want to unpack this fact by describing the conflicts of interest I see looming behind it, which will deepen our understanding of explanations commonly offered to account for it, such as guilt or a failure of moral will on the part of academics (or, if you prefer, intellectuals, or the new class, or the knowledge class).

Before addressing these conflicts of interest, however, I would like to examine in the next few pages some of the mystifications they result in, some of the arguments colleagues use, and some of the attitudes they hold that lead them to resist recognizing class as an issue comparable to race and gender and to resist recognizing further that class can cut across other markers of advantage or disadvantage. In countering such arguments and attitudes, I hope to support the notion that class distinctions may create real advantages or disadvantages with respect to achievement in school or society, advantages and disadvantages that may thus compound or reduce those associated with, say, race or gender. My focus here is on class alone, partly because race, class, and gender are, as the social scientists say, independent variables; partly because I wish to understand why some intellectuals resist seeing them as such; and partly because for me personally the difficulties and advantages associated with my class background have been more significant for my professional development than have been those associated with my gender. A research report published in 1991 by the American College Testing [ACT] Program suggests that my experience is not unusual. In the last twenty-five years women's access to higher education has increased substantially—"the gains are broad, significant, enduring, and continuing"—and in light of this, ACT concludes that in terms of access "women are about to reach . . . equity with men" (Mortenson 116, 117).

To begin, then, with some mystifications about class: some colleagues and the academy generally seem to assume that if a writer or critic or scientist is black or Hispanic (or, even more astonishingly, a woman), he or she is also working class. Yet of course, many women and persons of color are middle or upper class, especially those who matriculate at the nation's colleges and universities; and Harvard University, for one, ensures "that most of its black students come from middle-class families and predominantly white schools" (Hacker 64). This strategy allows Harvard to keep up what black economist Thomas Sowell calls "a good-looking 'body count' of black students" (cited by Hacker 64). As an admissions officer at Harvard explains, "It is right for Harvard and better for the students, because there is better adjustment and less desperate alienation" (Hacker 64).

Other colleagues seem to think that the working class is part of the problem of oppression, or at least that the working class is aligned with or co-opted by the ruling, hegemonic elites. The working class has voted and is voting Republican, and yet, rather than consider the relationship of this fact to possible social and economic realignment in this country, rather than consider whether old labels and old oppositions—left/right or radical/conservative—remain viable, we literary intellectuals trivialize the working class's anger and resentment by attributing this phenomenon to, for example, the charisma of politicians or the false consciousness of workers. By doing so, however, we free ourselves from considering the history of the working class's marginalization and its relation to the marginalization of other groups. It is a long and difficult history, if recent work by New Historicists is correct. For example, in her work on narrative form and the industrial revolution, Catherine Gallagher points out that by the early nineteenth century, the incompatible "interests of colonial slaves and British workers" were openly asserted in English debates about both colonialism and industrialization (8). Even more prominent in these debates was a charge of hypocrisy leveled at "a middle class that had exerted itself to end black slavery in the colonies but remained apathetic to the plight of British workers" (8). After passage of the Reform Act of 1832 and throughout the 1840s, radical working-class writers and activists made these points themselves, often using a rhetoric less civil than that of their middle-class allies, or of their late twentieth-century chronicler. Feeling themselves betrayed by middle-class liberals, the working-class radicals, Gallagher explains, "were often very disrespectful of what they considered a middle-class cause: the emancipation of black slaves" (31). Focusing on an even earlier time, New Historicists working in my period of specialization, the English Renaissance, have suggested rather convincingly that the lower or working classes were the guinea pigs on which the elite practiced techniques that later would be used quite effectively in colonies across the globe. As Stephen Greenblatt concludes in an essay on Shakespeare's Henriad: "One man's tinker is another man's Indian" (49).

Still other colleagues, those, say, whose parents own a business (even a small one), are reluctant to acknowledge the crucial difference between possessing and not possessing capital. Colleagues whose parents are salaried managers, not capitalists, are reluctant to acknowledge the perhaps even more important difference between possessing and not possessing power, which is the ability to give orders and receive deference. Randall Collins, following Ralf Dahrendorf, calls this "the most crucial difference" among occupations, which are "the major basis of class cultures" (62).

Barbara Ehrenreich, too, sees as fundamental the difference in power between managers or professionals and the working class. True, she observes, work for the salaried manager or professional is "seen, and often experienced, as intrinsically rewarding, creative, and important" (132), while for the working class—"defined broadly and crudely as people who work for hourly wages" (109)—work is, in the words of John Kenneth Galbraith, "fatiguing or monotonous or, at a minimum, a source of no particular pleasure" (cited by Ehrenreich 132). Yet, she argues,

the difference . . . goes deeper than comfort. Relative to the working class, the holders of middle-class occupations are in positions of command or, at the very least, authority. Their job is to conceptualize, in broad terms, what others must do. The job of the worker, blue or pink collar, is to get it done. The fact that this is a relationship of domination—and grudging submission—is usually invisible to the middle class but painfully apparent to the working class. (132–33)

Noting an "antiworking-class bias in the [sociological] literature, presented as it is by middle-class researchers" (70 n.7), Collins does not malign working-class culture that is "loyalistic, cynical, and oriented toward the immediate present" (71). Workers, Collins explains, distrust

the abstract rhetoric of their more cosmopolitan superiors. . . . The viewpoint of workers is largely confined to what is physically present to themselves and their immediate circle of acquaintance. Thus, we find that workers tend to confine their social relations to their own family and groups of childhood friends. The middle-class cosmopolitanism expressed in joining political, social, and charitable organizations is largely absent in the working classes, as is the pattern of sociability in which strangers are invited to the home for dinner or parties found commonly in the upper- and upper-middle classes. (71)

Like those of everyone else, Collins reminds us, "working-class values . . . emphasize the virtues of their own life situations: in this case, physical toughness, loyalty to friends, courage and wariness toward strangers and superiors" (71). And the life situation that spawns the "cynical and defensive" attitudes of the working class, or their "localistic and unrefined" behavior, is one influenced heavily by work situations in which they almost always take orders and have little or no say in the channels of organizational communication that govern their work lives (72).

A professor, indeed any professional, in contrast, certainly must fill a position of authority and must assume an active role in abstract networks of communication. The professor, for example, must behave authoritatively toward students and colleagues and must expect deference from those who are not experts in his or her field, especially from students and the general public, and even from colleagues. Authority, then, reveals that the professor's occupation is not working class. And it follows, too, that people brought up to be "cynical and defensive" or "localistic and unrefined" will find it difficult to become comfortable in the role of professor, with its requirements of autonomy, authority, and sociability.

Some other colleagues, musing, perhaps, on their own salaries, which are, of course, rather low for professionals, seem to think that such cultural disadvantages linked with class are no longer relevant because organized labor unions have negotiated increases in the wages of the working class. But this conclusion ignores the fact these wage increases are more perceived than real: in the 1980s organized labor saved its jobs by giving back bit by bit the advantages it secured during the inflationary 1970s. More fundamentally, as sociologists point out, wage earnings are an independent variable, a link "between occupational position and many aspects of lifestyle that sets classes apart; as such it can have some independent effects" (Collins 66). The possibility of "independent effects" does not obliterate differences in, say, power or assets; and so, despite my own low salary, I find I agree with Lillian S. Robinson, who holds that "the realities of a class-stratified system . . . are disguised by such phrases as 'Middle American,' 'lower middle class,' and 'blue-collar middle class'" (35).

In short, in the thinking of some colleagues I find a bizarre contradiction, the kind of contradiction Ehrenreich isolates in the professional middle class as a whole: "'Enlightened' people, who might flinch at a racial slur, have no trouble . . . caricaturing the white or 'ethnic' working class: Its tastes are 'tacky'; its habits unhealthful; and its views hopelessly bigoted and parochial" (7). On the one hand, like many "knowledge workers" in postindustrial society, such colleagues firmly endorse left-liberal politics and support almost unfailingly affirmative action for minority groups and the historically marginalized. On the other hand, these same colleagues are reluctant to acknowledge in a practical way the historically marginalized position of the working class. This odd refusal on the part of intellectuals to recognize class as an issue comparable to race and gender results, I think, from largely unexamined but powerful conflicts of interest.

One conflict of interest is, perhaps, rooted in a "perceptual" problem: policymakers in academia and elsewhere ignore the marginalized position of the working class because unlike women and racial minorities, people of the working class are not clearly and obviously working class. A glance does not tell a bureaucrat or a hiring committee that a professor is working class. A glance does not tell a working-class student that a role model is directing business in the classroom. In fact, by definition, because of education, socialization, and occupation, the working-class professor is no longer working class—he or she may "pass" rather easily (and, perhaps, willingly, which may point to the possibility of class shame in contrast to racial or gender pride); whereas, of course, the black professor remains (proudly) black, and the female professor remains (proudly) female.

So, to anticipate part of my conclusion, acknowledging the claims of the working class as marginalized and disadvantaged would throw wrenches into the machinery of academia's programs of affirmative action. Bringing class to bear on the practical calculus by which we create equal opportunity would cause practical and theoretical problems that are easier to avoid. Verification on all levels, from recruitment of college freshmen to annual campus-wide assessments of faculty, would be made confusing and difficult. Admissions and hiring committees would have to balance even more competing claims, especially since the numbers of the white working class in particular are enormous. Who is the more disadvantaged? Or the more historically disadvantaged? The son of, say, a black lawyer who practices in Gadsden, Alabama; or the son of a white mechanic who works somewhere in southern Pennsylvania; or the daughter of a Japanese grocer who owns a small market in Fresno, California; or the daughter of a single white woman who works as a data entry clerk in Boulder, Colorado?

Sociologist Peter Berger offers another perspective on academia's failure to recognize the marginality of the working class. Isolating a conflict of interest that could affect academics' willingness to promote the interests of the working class, Berger describes the "curious symbiosis," the convergence of political and ideological interests, between intellectuals on the one hand and the underclass—but not the working class—on the other (70). Perhaps less surprising is another sociologist's contention that the interests of the underclass conflict with those of the working class. Anthony Giddens points to "a basic division of interest" between the urban underclass and the working class, and even if, like Giddens, one wishes to question "the proposition that the working class . . . is the main repository of irrational sentiments of prejudice against ethnic minorities," one cannot avoid his conclusion that the division of interest between the two groups will increase (289).

Doubtless, many literary intellectuals do not question the proposition Giddens cites, and Ehrenreich insists that during the 1970s "the working class became, for many middle-class liberals, a psychic dumping ground for such unstylish sentiments as racism, male chauvinism, and crude materialism: a rearguard population that loved white bread and hated black people" (120). Such beliefs in themselves are enough, I think, to explain literary intellectuals' attachment to the underclass and their dislike of the working class. It is easy to relegate the Archie Bunkers and Al Bundys of this country to the dustbin of history.

But Berger pushes the link between intellectuals and the underclass a bit further and demystifies it by rooting it in economic self-interest rather than moral selflessness. To begin, intellectuals are part of the rising new class of knowledge workers in postindustrial society, and "like all rising classes, the knowledge class rhetorically identifies its own class interests with the general welfare of society and especially with the downtrodden (just as the early bourgeoisie did in its conflict with the ancien régime)" (70). Further, like the underclass who often must find assistance from social services funded by public monies, intellectuals find their livelihoods primarily in the public sector, including those employed by private institutions, whose budgets are supported to a considerable degree by public monies, in the form of, for example, student financial aid, faculty research grants, and various kinds of tax exemptions. Both intellectuals and the underclass, therefore, hold a vested interest in the expansion of the welfare state. Both groups, that is, have "an interest in the distributive machinery of government, as against the production system," and this in turn accounts for "a tense relationship with the industrial working class, especially as represented by organized labor, which has very different interests" (69, 70). As more than one colleague has pointed out to me, "*they* vote for Republicans."

Berger's thesis that intellectuals are politically, economically, and ideologically antagonistic to the industrial working class is disturbing. It brings to mind Robinson's complaint that the studies of high culture she disseminates to her working-class students have for the most part nothing to do with their lives. This irrelevance has not been lessened by the democratization of the canon, which

retains . . . a certain investment in the assumptions of high culture. It does not address itself to the leisure activities that *take the place* of art in the lives of most people, including most students. It does not provide students with critical instruments that they can apply to their other cultural experiences. And it does not speak intelligibly to anyone who lacks its own initial commitment to the subject. (77)

Literary critics have a vested interest in maintaining the canon, or some canon, insofar as their own teaching and research interests are concerned. Even more fundamentally, they—and intellectuals generally—have a vested interest in privileging work of the mind over work of the body, a value judgment and moral commitment revealed not only in the business of our own lives but in our bottom-line sense of what education does for the dispossessed, lifting them up from and out of their oppression and into comfortable middle-class lives.

Despite its arguable irrelevancy to the larger society, squabbling about the canon has become quite loud and public recently—witness William Bennett, Allan Bloom, E. D. Hirsch, and Camille Paglia among others—and much of the squabbling concerns the functions of higher education in this society, which are numerous and not the focus of my discussion here. Relevant to it, however, are two functions, one conserving and one progressive, which can work against the empowerment of the working class and, of course, other historically marginalized groups. The conserving function of higher education, its transmission of the "best" of "our" heritage, is, I think, obviously at odds with the interests of many of the marginalized. More important, one progressive function of higher education—its invention and dissemination of technology—is a blessing and a curse for the working class. Training in business and engineering, for example, has offered working-class children an excellent avenue of upward mobility. But do not forget the working-class children who will become working-class adults; they will be managed by people who have been trained in the universities (some of whom, not incidentally, will be upwardly mobile working-class youth). In fact, Ehrenreich observes, the professions developed in this country "on the front lines of the early-twentieth-century battle between labor and capital" (135); one of their functions "was in fact 'to keep the workers in line'" (133). Higher education is, perhaps, the best route out of working-class life; higher education also helps keep the majority of the working class firmly embedded there.

Yet of course, these people who are not served by higher education must support its work by contributing through taxation to the pool of money that funds the nation's universities and colleges, whether public or private. It is surprising that thinkers from both the left and right make this point: public expenditures on higher education transfer wealth from one socioeconomic class to another, in this case from the working classes, who make less use of these services, to the middle and upper classes, who use them much more heavily.

Neoconservative and libertarian academics who support the market economy—such as Milton Friedman, F. A. Hayek, and Walter Williams—tend to object to public support for anything, arguing about education subsidies that no one has the right to insist that others be taxed to bolster one's own cultural preferences. But in doing so, they also argue that public subsidy of higher education, again whether public or private, transfers wealth from the poorer to the richer. As economist Sam Peltzman explains, "if one easily identifiable socioeconomic class is benefited by subsidized higher education, it lies at the upper end of the income distribution. Well over half the students come from families with above-median income" (12).

Academics on the left make this point, too, even those committed, like Jonathan Dollimore and Alan Sinfield, to "the transformation of a social order which exploits people on grounds of race, gender and class" (Dollimore and Sinfield viii). Sinfield urges us to see the subsidization of education as part of the system of welfare capitalism, in which by delivering to all classes "the kind of provision which the middle classes have historically made for themselves" (164, 165), the state intervenes to temper inequalities created by the market economy. Rather paternalistically, the state assumes the desirability of offering education or high culture to all; yet, Sinfield observes, in Britain such paternalism fails, as the middle class rather than the working class tends to benefit from public expenditures on social services of all types, and perhaps especially, education.

In different ways, Berger, Giddens, Robinson, Ehrenreich, Sinfield, and I wonder who is paying for whose edification—and at what cost and according to what justification. Without begrudging the gains made by and afforded to the racial minorities and women, I point out that another group, alas a numerically very large group, has been left to fend for itself. Also historically oppressed, also lacking skills and postures to perform with ease in middle- and upper-class environments, the working class is effectively ignored by official and unofficial attempts to create equal opportunity, especially through programs of affirmative action (which, Hacker notes, have been extended in certain cases to the disabled and to Italian Americans [63]). And the working class has been ignored by such attempts, even as it supports both voluntarily and by taxation, institutions that not only publicly espouse affirmative action for the historically marginalized but also promote—or may be seen as promoting—the values and interests of a culture quite alien to those working-class taxpayers or the working-class children who hope to benefit from higher education.

Where, then, does this argument lead? Some readers see in it a plea to extend affirmative action to the working class, and one reader urged me to organize a working-class caucus at the MLA, a move that if successful would begin to legitimate the working class as a social category and as a group to be reckoned with. That is not a serious option for me—I haven't the personality for it—but I will admit to musing on it, if only briefly and for selfish reasons: perhaps as a founding mother of the working-class caucus and with the help of class-conscious affirmative action, I might land a job at a nice campus of the University of California. Maybe Santa Cruz.

Other readers have recognized the subversive implications of the argument. One reader suggested I send this piece to *New Criterion* and another was appalled that I would so sneakily use left-liberal arguments to undermine affirmative action. I have been amused though not surprised by the way the argument can be read as both for and against affirmative action. Yet it seems to me that the argument is subversive of affirmative action and critical of left-liberal intellectuals as well.

Those who see subversion in this argument recognize that any practical attempt by universities to extend to the working class the benefits of affirmative action would meet certain and vigorous resistance from groups already invested and institutionalized in such programs, a public relations nightmare, if nothing else. More important, those who see subversion here feel the weight of numbers; including class as a variable in affirmative-action decisions would change the pool of the underrepresented and marginalized, by including more Caucasians and excluding some well-to-do minorities. Class as a variable implemented and not just theorized would underscore the potential folly of this kind of social engineering, potential already apparent in the ongoing conflicts over representation of Asian Americans.

Of course, that left-liberal intellectuals fail to address in a practical way the marginalized position of the working class gives rise to charges that they lack the moral will to effect the kinds of meaningful social change glimpsed fleetingly in the sixties or that programs like affirmative action allow intellectuals to occupy a cozy moral highground, assuaging the guilt they feel over their own privilege. My argument here both supports and complicates such charges, making both more damning by rooting them in economic self-interest and an elitism that, while always denied, never goes away. What we see in the abandonment of the working class is the academic's, the intellectual's, the new class's astonishing agoraphobia, its fear of the market and its fear of the people.

Works Cited

Berger, Peter L. *The Capitalist Revolution.* New York: Basic, 1986.

Collins, Randall. *Conflict Sociology.* New York: Academic, 1975.

Dollimore, Jonathan, and Alan Sinfield. "Foreword: Cultural Materialism." *Political Shakespeare.* Ed. Jonathan Dollimore and Alan Sinfield. Ithaca, NY: Cornell UP, 1985.

Ehrenreich, Barbara. *Fear of Falling.* New York: Pantheon, 1989.

Gallagher, Catherine. *The Industrial Reformation of English Fiction.* Chicago: U of Chicago P, 1985.

Giddens, Anthony. *The Class Structures of the Advanced Societies.* New York: Harper, 1973.

Greenblatt, Stephen. *Shakespearean Negotiations.* Berkeley: U of California P, 1988.

Hacker, Andrew. "Affirmative Action: The New Look." *The New York Review of Books* 12 October 1989: 63–68.

Mortenson, Thomas G. *Equity of Higher Educational Opportunity for Women, Black, Hispanic, and Low-Income Students.* Iowa City: American College Testing Program, 1991.

Peltzman, Sam. "The Effect of Government Subsidies-in-Kind on Private Expenditures: The Case of Higher Education." *Journal of Political Economy* 81 (January/February 1973):1–27.

Robinson, Lillian S. *Sex, Class, and Culture.* Bloomington: Indiana UP, 1978.

Sinfield, Alan. "Royal Shakespeare: Theatre and the Making of Ideology." Dollimore and Sinfield. 158–81.

Language: Closings and Openings

SCHOOL? Yea, I know what you mean. My friend Mary—the one who works with me down at the place?—is having a rough time. Can't figure out what the teacher wants from her. Isn't it so? The teacher keeps telling her she should use her woman's intuition or something when she writes and Mary can't figure that one out. And when she tries to get things just generally right—spelling and commas and all that stuff?—the teacher tells her her writing's dull and that she's a more exciting person than that. I feel really sorry for her. She's sure the teacher thinks she's dumb. She's beginning to wonder if she shouldn't just forget it. Don't you know? Her job's pretty good and her mother keeps wondering what good all that stuff you learn in college is anyway. I don't know. Is it worth it? Books are just books and she's never got time to go out with us anymore.

Almost everyone has trouble learning the kind of language their teachers want them to use in school—particularly when they're writing. In this article, I am mainly interested in how this common problem affects working-class women, who may have it hardest of all because they bring into the school with them a language that seems out of step in two ways: it is both women's language and working-class language. What might help them develop the strengths of their female language often works against what helps them turn their working-class language into a more school-oriented language. To make matters worse, their teachers often think they're not suited for college because of the way they talk.

Patterns of language use—in terms of both competence and performance—reflect the gender and class status of the language user and are crucially important in determining the language user's success in the academy. Working-class women thus face, when they encounter the language demands of the academy, a double-pronged threat which is always already present at that point where their language engages that which they read and hear in the classroom: as they attempt to negotiate around the Scylla of their relationship-based female language and ways of knowing, they may well collide with the Charybdis of their material-based, working-class language. Those strategies that nourish the growth of their female-language potential are not necessarily—and may even be in direct opposition to—those that might serve to bring about elaboration of their working-class language. To complicate their acculturation to the academy, their teachers often evaluate them as unfit because of that language.

> A woman like that is misunderstood
> I have been her kind.
> —Anne Sexton

Women, whose language evolves out of their bodily labors and loves, contest the language of the academy. All of us struggle, strive, and search for our place when we enter a new con-text: when we seek to make ourselves heard and listened to, respected and nurtured, in a place where our ways counter, act inappropriately, disconcert, call into question the ways of the place we entered. But the working-class woman is doubly wound(ed) in her language. The body of her word is ill(-/,)constructed in the eyes of those who rule within the academy. Judgment, negative assessment of the mind and spirit and ways of being and knowing crush. Sigh-lent.

Class and gender as each relates to language acquisition and use and to success in school have been at the center of significant educational debates of the past century. Those focused on gender have tended to concentrate on describing woman's language, or comparing boys' and girls' acquisition of language, or analyzing female style in literature. On the one hand, not many have focused on the presence of female students' language in the classroom and how that interacts with the expectations of faculty and of the academy in general. And there is very little evidence that what we have learned and are learning about women's language has been translated into pedagogical strategies. On the other hand, the problems of school performance and class, particularly as class relates to speakers of nonstandard languages, have been fairly exhaustively analyzed, mostly in terms of the elementary school classroom, somewhat less in terms of the high school classroom. In terms of the college classroom, such studies have created a group of students labeled "basic writers" or "nontraditional" or culturally deprived students.

These discussions on the role of nonstandard language in school have been engendered both by teacher observations and grades and by statistical studies that demonstrate fairly conclusively that children from the lower classes of society rarely do as well in school as children of the middle classes. In an effort to discover the causes of this school failure, sociolinguists have focused on the differences between lower-class and middle-class language. Basil Bernstein's research into these differences has served as the basis for vigorous debate. He concluded, after analysis of the language of working-class and middle-class children in England, that the former functioned within a "restricted" code and the later within an "elaborated" code.[1] Both codes are products of a child's socialization in the home environment. A "restricted" code orients its users "toward particularistic meanings," whereas an "elaborated" code orients its users "toward receiving and offering universalistic meanings." According to Bernstein, the "restricted" code "creates social solidarity at the cost of the verbal elaboration of individual experience" (28–29). The elaborated code

contains longer sentences with a vocabulary that is more varied and more explicit, especially with respect to logical connections, which are often left implicit in "restricted" speech. The syntax of elaborated speech is more complex and the delivery is usually more paused, more edited, and generally less fluent. Restricted speech tends to contain formulaic expressions such as *Don't you know* and *Isn't it so,* which are, in effect, appeals to the hearer to fill in from background knowledge those parts of the message the speaker has not made explicit. (Kay 77)

Labov characterizes the difference between middle-class and working-class language in similar terms:

A number of studies show that middle-class speakers use longer sentences, more subordinate clauses, and more learned vocabulary; they take a less personal verbal viewpoint than working-class speakers. Our own studies of narratives of personal experience show that middle-class speakers interrupt their narratives much more often to give evaluative statements, often cast in an impersonal style. Middle-class speakers seem to excel in taking the viewpoint of the generalized other. (*Study* 37)

Educators have been quick to form judgments based on these descriptions, but Labov warns us that we do not know what, within the traits of middle-class speech, might be educationally enabling. "Before we train working-class speakers to copy middle-class speech patterns wholesale, it is worth asking just which aspects of this style are functional for learning and which are matters of prestige and fashion" (*Study* 37). Labov also questions the negative traits ascribed to working-class language, concluding that "there is nothing in the vernacular which will interfere with the development of logical thought, for the logic of standard English cannot be distinguished from the logic of any other dialect of English by any test that we can find" ("Logic" 229). In fact, in reference to narrative skill, "the vernacular used by working-class speakers seems to have a distinct advantage over more educated styles" (Labov, "Transformation" 396). More on storytelling anon.

Subjective reaction tests demonstrate that it is not just the academy that judges on the basis of language, although those outside the academy probably react in terms of social prestige rather than intelligence (Labov, "Logic" 203). Given the connection most of us make between intelligence and class, however, the reactions of academics and nonacademics are not that different in the end.

Certain dialects that differ from Standard English in their phonology, grammar, or lexicon are devalued, and persons who speak them are considered to be ignorant, unschooled, unintelligent, or provincial. We send our children to "grammar" school so that they may escape such stigmas. Our notion of language, as it functions in the determination of social status, is one of correctness of linguistic form. (Kay 35)

Thus, whether in school or out, working-class speakers suffer from the poor estimation of others. Once teachers have made this judgment, consciously or unconsciously, the expectations so engendered become self-fulfilling. Sharp and Green claim that tracking of this sort serves our economy by assuring that the lower class will continue to supply the peoplepower for the unskilled labor our economic structure demands. "Children of socio-cultural backgrounds which are perceived to be less prestigious are channeled into lower paying, lower status positions in the economic hierarchy. . . . schooling does not iron out social stratification, but promotes and maintains it" (Edwards 11). Do we academics, I wonder—in a comparable way—assign C's and D's to those papers whose language does not sound academic? I suspect we do.

The conclusions of sociolinguists such as Labov about the possible merits of nontraditional language, however, are largely ignored, for most academics are concerned not with the language students bring to the academy (whether middle or working class) but with the language

254

they think all students need to acquire in order to enter fully into the life of the academy. Most of them would probably agree that academic language makes higher thought possible. This conclusion is not as harmful in the classroom as its corollary: inability to use academic language is an indication of stupidity. The problem here is that middle-class speech is closer to academic language than lower-class speech (Heath 270–72). Thus, usually without knowing anything about their students' social backgrounds, faculty will come to conclusions about their students' intelligence based upon the speed with which they learn the "right" language.

Everyone adjusts their language toward the formal in certain situations (Joos 35–36), but such adjustments are not independent of social class or gender—particularly when a speaker feels disapproval in a school environment. The lower middle class (with which, in Labov's labeling system, the working class shares traits) exhibits the most radical shift toward the formal, that is, the most language insecurity. But

when we examine the full spectrum of stylistic behavior for men and women, it appears that the crucial differences lie in the steeper slope of style shifting for women: in all but the lowest status group[2] they may actually use more of a nonstandard form in their casual speech than men, but in formal styles they shift more rapidly and show an excess of hypercorrect behavior at that end of the scale. (Labov, *Study* 32–33)

Furthermore, working-class men's language has a value within its own culture and perhaps without as well because many equate its speech traits with masculinity—certainly a quality our society rates highly, for men, that is.[3] The need felt by women to move toward prestigious forms of speech moves them away from their natural dialect and also, as I will discuss later, away from satisfying their needs to learn in ways compatible to women's ways of knowing. Women thus expend energy that males and members of the middle class can direct elsewhere.

Despite an apparent willingness to shift styles toward a formal register, students—both male and female—may experience an undermining tension. Labov, in his studies of speakers of nonstandard English, observed that those students who were the most popular among their peers were the least successful in school and those who were the least popular in the streets were more likely to be successful in school (*Study* 43). Most adolescent peer groups do not overtly approve of doing well in school. Working-class women, it would seem only rational to conclude, come to school because they want to be there. Thus, the resistance characteristic of adolescents would not be a factor. However, there is another kind of subtle, probably largely unconscious, resistance which may be at work.

Being successful in college has its drawbacks. "The disruption that it forms is dangerous, a separation from all that makes life possible at the margin: the material and emotional support of friends and family, the internal sense of doing what is right, that is, acceptable" (Holzman 29). Our native way of using language is, for all of us, a survival tool. We do not abandon it lightly. We sense that such an abandonment may mean the loss of the social and interpersonal support of our home community. Jacqueline Mitchell, an academic sociologist, attests to this in descriptions of her personal reactions to returning to her native environment:

My professional attire identified me in this community as a "middle-class," "siddity," "uppity," "insensitive" school teacher who had made her way out of the ghetto, who had returned to "help and save," and who would leave before dark to return to the suburbs. My speech set me up as a prime candidate for suspicion and distrust. Speaking standard English added to the badges that my role had already pinned on me. (31)

With the potential of such rejection, most of us need to have some assurance of a new social group before we will leave the old one. Thus, even students beyond their adolescent years may well work unconsciously against their own educational success.

> "What remains of me at the university,
> within the university?"
> (Cixous and Clement 145)

The issue of class language collides directly with one of the currently most debated issues in the field of composition and rhetoric research and practice. This is, stated at its most simple, a debate between those who advocate teaching methods that encourage individual voice and the academic relevance of storytelling and validate whatever culture students bring with them and those who emphasize teaching methods that encourage the adoption of language appropriate to the academy—impersonal, conceptual, organized, and abstract—regarding the acquisition of such language as the most significant intellectual task of students, particularly students who are the least prepared for college.

256

THEM: Students cannot participate in the life of the mind developed by the university if they cannot use the language of the academy. Knowledge is a socially constructed result of such collaborative language use (Bruffee 646–47).

ME: Hmmmmm.

THEM: "It's no good just saying, 'Learn to write what's comfy for you, kiddies,' if that puts them behind the eight-ball in their college careers. Discourse carries power . . ." (Elbow, Reflections 135).

ME: Hmmmmmmmm.

THEM: One who wishes to be heard in the academy must adopt the language of the academy because Otherwise No One Will Listen.

CHORUS: (Addressing itself to no one in particular) Is rhetoric the expedient employment of whatever works or an attempt to approximate truth of some kind, even if that truth is context bound and personal?

THEM: "That right to speak is seldom conferred upon us—upon any of us, teachers or students—by virtue of the fact that we have invented or discovered an original idea" (Bartholomae 10).

CHORUS: (Looking directly at me) Unduly harsh, I hear you say? Let's consider for a moment. The academy has—if even with soul-grinding, bull-bellowing, breast-beating, and dragging of the *d(r)oits*—altered its can(n)on to admit the works of Women, Minorities, and Third-World writers and philosophers into course syllabi. That is, the academy has shown an oxy-moronic coerced willingness to alter its subject matter—but it has shown no willingness to alter the language in which that context is contained. The "requirement that students master academic literacy in order to continue their education is still institutionalized in the great majority of writing programs in this country" (Bizzell 141).

ME: Sure, we'll assign *The Color Purple* in literature classes and slave narratives in history courses, but we do not permit our students to talk and write about these in the language in which they are written. The truth is that it *is* our language that constitutes our world; we will admit into it (our world/our language) anyone who proves they can use it: we will listen to them. But we will not listen to those who do not address us in our language.

257

THEM: Ergo, it is hypocritical of us to "graciously" allow students their own language. When we do this, we are simply assuring that they can never compete in our world; we are con-signing *them* to remain wherever it is they are.

ME: But if knowledge is socially constructed through language, if we never change that language we cannot change the knowledge. All we are doing when we draw students into our discourse communities is limiting them to the thoughts *we* have already had and ensuring that they will be neither creative nor original. We are creating little parrots (in smaller type), extending the hegemony of our own ideas. We need to teach students to name *their* world so they can then control it (Freire).

THEM: Nice sounding, but too simplistic. Pablum. Overlooks the real issue. (With a knowing smirk at colleagues) Students have to write papers too. It's a matter of standards.

ME: Why? Most of the "papers" they write in school are nonpapers. School forms that are just displays—proof to a teacher they can do what they do, which is generally useless and seen by no one except the teacher and the student. Performances for an audience of one.

THEM: (Aside) She talks too much.

ME: Why on earth would anyone encourage students to sound like most academics anyway? "I think that America has made itself a bit ridiculous in the international academic world by developing distinctive disciplinary jargon. It's the last thing we want to inculcate in the freshmen" (Olson 7).

THEM: Is she still talking?

ME: Besides, no one of us ever belongs to just one discourse community. We belong to a number of overlapping discourse communities and the idiosyncratic nature of each individual's overlapping discourse communities assures her of some uniqueness of voice. And since each of us has that, we need to assure that each of our students does also. If we direct our students solely toward the acquisition of our language, we neglect whatever it is they want to say.

THEM: A romantic and romanticizing notion: "what *they* want to say," as though they existed apart from culture and context. Adherence to form has cultural value. Those whose language is inadequate are "more comfortable with a composition curriculum that reduces writing to a set of distinct subskills and that rewards and punishes performance according to a fixed set of ground rules—a curriculum which in the public mind is associated with the teaching of 'basics'" (Tuman 45).

ME: Disempowering. It's difficult to do genuine authoring (Macrorie 8) or rigorous exploration of ideas for ourselves (Elbow, "Closing" 50) while worrying about audience reaction to our language. By focusing classroom activities on the acquisition of the conventions of academic writing, we may well return to the prescriptive teaching that most modern composition theory disparages—but instead of being prescriptive about grammar, we will now be prescriptive about discourse features (Fontaine 90). And the truth is we lack any comprehensive knowledge of the features of particular kinds of discourse (for example, what *are* the discourse features of writing in sociology?).

THEM: Oh, come now, we all know what's best stylistically *and* grammatically.

ME: Such teaching is often quite self-serving: "Purifying the language of the tribe—whether as a project subsumed within modernism or as a hope kept alive by embattled New Criticisms surrounded by mass culture—always moved further from the really big existing tribes . . ." (Said 6); certainly the working class is one of "the really big existing tribes."

THEM: The fact that we and others have and can be charmed by superior control of syntax, diction, and appropriate stance—by the outer trappings of academic style—does not necessarily negate the arguments of the social constructionists.

CHORUS: There is a far deeper sense in which their theories ring true, for we do need to share language with others if we are to converse meaningfully with them—if we are to collaboratively create knowledge with them. The more aspects of language we share, the better we can talk and construct together.

ME: We must walk a very fine line, for if we allow our students to join our conversation only with *our* language, might that not mean that we cut off other conversations they might have had which would better serve their needs? How might they know if the conversations never happen?

The rest is silence.

THEM: (Aside) More romanticizing.

CHORUS: (This is normal discourse for a chorus) The self is socially constructed; it's a vestige of romanticism.

ME: All the more reason why the self's experiences speak for all of us.

CHORUS: Hmmmmmmmmmmmmm.

ME: Allowing students to be expressive allows them to stand back and gain perspective on the various social and political voices peopling their own heads. In seeking their own voices, students at the same time confront these other voices and can begin to understand their power (Railey 7). The imposition of discourse conventions which students have not yet mastered is inhibiting and *silencing*.

> It is reported their singing resembled
> the flight of moths in moonlight.
> Who can say? It is silent now.
> —Denise Levertov

THEM: What you want them to do is to dump emotion on a page all the time. They can do that outside of school. Besides they already know how to express their feelings. In school we need to encourage them to *think*, to present rational arguments.

CHORUS: Well, that brings up issues beyond those of class.

BOTH OF THESE debates (Does the language of one's social class determine success in school? Must our goal be the sacrifice of individual voice to the exigencies of academic discourse or vice versa?) intersect with concern for the differences between male and female language.[4] Today's traditional teaching of rhetoric is an outgrowth of classical rhetoric, which itself was developed in a society that educated only men and which flowered into its present form in a society in which school and church language (A-men/A-women) diverged from the vernacular. That is, the history of the development of rhetoric as a school subject is the history of progressive movement away from natural language toward an artificial language. The language one (read "men") learned at school was exclusive to males and different from the one both they and their sisters learned at their mothers' breasts. Thus, as Ong points out, when women first began to write (themselves) outside school walls, it was not the traditional patterns of rhetoric that shaped their pieces.

Much of women's writing consisted of diaries, journals, letters, and other sorts of personal writing, such as autobiography (111–12). But this was not the writing schools valued then nor is it valued by schools today as highly as the impersonalized, argued by plan, generalized discourse that is shaped to match predetermined genres of form and mode. These distinctions again echo those I set forth earlier as distinctions between speakers of an elaborated code and speakers of a restricted code in one sense: like those who speak a restricted code, women tend to keep more of their meaning implicit rather than explicit. In schools,

certain forms of discourse and language are privileged: the expository essay is valued over the exploratory, the argumentative essay set above the auto-biographical; the clear evocation of a thesis preferred to a more organized exploration of a topic, the impersonal, rational voice ranked more highly than the intimate, subjective one. (Caywood and Overing xii)

"Male" style is generally synonymous with the accepted style of academic discourse. Farrell describes the male mode of rhetoric as "copious or abundant, formal and distanced, and public" (915); it begins with its conclusions and then elaborates on them; it "seems to assume that antagonism is all right because intellectual life presumably proceeds agonistically" (916); it requires "that one have the ability to distance oneself from the situation at hand, to recognize a boundary, to differentiate between oneself and the subject of the discourse"; furthermore, it is "playful" (917).

CHORUS: It is important to note that Farrell is not necessarily identifying the male mode with men and the female mode with women—although he does comment on women's use of the female mode.

THEM: But, although he concedes value to the female mode, he still advocates that college composition courses teach a male mode because "the male mode of rhetoric is probably better suited than the female mode for written discourse." One reason for his advocacy is that the positing of antitheses "helps development of ego-consciousness" (918).

ME: I thought I was part of this debate. (Actually I thought it was over—strange that the CHORUS started it again.) What Farrell is espousing is exactly the gender-based attitude that Chodorow decries in "Being and Doing," in which she demonstrates the extent to which theories of maturation reflect only male models.

261

THEM: Aha, Farrell has evidence, for he has uncovered the truth that "all of the women that I know who are able to use the female mode have told me that they write in the male mode whenever they write for publication, and those who teach composition teach students to write in the male mode" (920).

ME: (Under my breath) I guess it's time to ditch this article. (Aloud) He obviously considers these women's attitudes as proof that the male mode is superior. But, alas, he is probably correct about how we women write; most of us are thoroughly acculturated, but I do hope that he is not quite so right about the way we teach composition.

CHORUS: Yes? Well, listen to this woman talking about the general characteristics of female students:

whether they are honors or remedial students, more often than not [they] limit, even thwart their intellectual development by employing exclusively intuitive analysis. They rely *solely* on personal experience in their thinking, in their focusing on topics, and, most notably, in their writing, scribbling a world of particulars within which the incident is isolated, individual, non-generalizable, and stunted because it does not relate to universal concepts which could give it meaning. . . . (Pigott 922)

ME: (Whispering) I always thought it was the particular that gave meaning to the general.

THEM: "Most untrained women do not break through the remembrances of experience to search for intellectual relevance and often rot in their nests of particularity" (Pigott 922).

ME: Wonderful word, that "scribbling"! And how about "stunted" and "rot"?

CHORUS: This same writer urges us to be aware of "the limitations of the woman student," to "sympathize" with her, and "thus begin to lift [our] sister-student out of that confining nest into the world of twirping, chattering, and clattering, to begin to partake and debate in the grand parliament of fowls" (926).

ME: Whose side are you on? Sounds like a parliament of fools to me.

CHORUS: Women's ways of writing and learning do not mesh well within academia. "Patriarchal expressive modes reflect an epistemology that perceives the world in terms of categories, dichotomies, roles, stasis, and causation, while female expressive modes reflect an epistemology that perceives the world in terms of ambiguities, pluralities, processes, continuities, and complex relationships" (Thorne et al. 126).

ME: The authors of *Women's Ways of Knowing*, based on their interviews with numerous women, conclude "that women often feel alienated in academic settings and experience 'formal' education as either peripheral or irrelevant to their central interest and development" (Belenky et al. 4). In the course of their study, these authors "became aware of the fact that, for many women, the 'real' and valued lessons learned did not necessarily grow out of their academic work but in relationships with friends and teachers, life crises, and community involvements" (4). They conclude that women's ways of knowing contrast with what schools value: "Looking back on our experience and talking with other women inside and outside the classroom reinforced our feeling that education and clinical services, as traditionally defined and practiced, do not adequately serve the needs of women" (4).

CHORUS: It is small wonder that women often speak in terms of having lost their voices.

Modern feminist theorists [I think particularly of Kristeva, Irigaray, and Cixous] have gone far beyond Ong in describing language that they call "feminine." Rather than concentrating on what such language is *not*, they focus on what it *is*. These authors, particularly the latter two, practice a feminine style that explodes academic style. I do not know what working-class style exploded by feminine language would look like. And if schools continue to set themselves the goal of eradicating working-class language, I may never find out. Nonetheless, the principles set forth by these feminist theorists remind us that language is more than rational and linear and that we should not be quick to criticize the writing and language of working-class women because it does not adhere to established academic forms. Women far more educated than they, are also breaking molds—it's mold-breaking that matters, not just which molds and how.

Having just examined aspects of women's language in general, I need to recognize that working-class language traits are not limited to women. Nor are they totally defined by the grammatical and syntactical traits that I have—with the guidance of Bernstein and Labov—already examined. Working-class students, both male and female, bring into the classroom not only a world most of us are unfamiliar with, but also a way of looking at the world that is unfamiliar to us. They have not learned as we have to separate the world of school and nonschool. Working-class literature demonstrates this lack of separation, for it is primarily functional and communal (Coles 673). Working-class students (male and female) have learning habits that align them with nontraditional college students. They tend to be "highly gregarious and social," "more comfortable in an oral rather than a written mode," and "holistic" and "deductive" as thinkers (Troyka 256, 258, 259). Such students are destined to have difficulties in lecture-based classrooms where they are judged mainly through their writing by faculty who "tend to be inductive thinkers" (Troyka 259). We cannot expect our working-class students to abandon these learning habits or their notion of the functional and communal aspects of writing and reading in their lives because they have walked through the doorways of our classrooms. Just as such students tend not to see art "as a means of lifting people outside of the world in which they live" (Lauter 18), so they are likely to respond to classroom material in terms of "particular problems in a particular time" (Lauter 19). In this sense, the impulse toward "story" is likely to be the same for working-class women both as women and as members of the working class.

Academics who espouse a literacy that is depersonalized, distanced, logical, and objective see the classroom as "a separate world of its own, in which teachers and students relate to one another undistracted by the classism, racism, and sexism that rage outside the classroom" (Brodkey, "On the Subjects" 139).

THEM: Yes, "the American Academy" needs to "preserve its identity as an intellectual sanctuary from the so-called real world, where the economics and politics of racism, sexism, and classism are thought to interfere with or distract from the processes of disinterested, intellectual inquiry" (Said 22).

ME: Sure, these people would obviously frown on female and working-class tendencies to introduce personal experience. Thus as the academy pushes working-class students toward depersonalized language, it is forcing women to submerge their natural abilities to learn through personal connections.

DIANE TRILLING: "Our serious intellectual culture may think it strange of me to assume that our personal lives have bearing on our intellectual lives, or even that our experience as individuals is significantly related to our experience of society. That isn't the way that people are now thought about, is it?" (Koch 1, 26).

ME: If a writer of Diana Trilling's status is sensitive to such criticism, working-class women in college classrooms who feel the criticism are likely not just to feel it, but also to be silenced by it, to be driven to adapt a foreign language in which it is very difficult to express what the/she/y want(s) to say.

Stories undermine generalizations because they never quite fit; academics do not want their generalizations undermined by the students in their classes. "Stories introduce inconsistencies of one kind or another into our desire to represent experience as wholly accounted for by our respective ideologies. . . . The Academy has a limited tolerance for lived experience, which it easily dismisses as 'stories' . . ." (Brodkey, *Academic Writing* 107).

A story. Two years or so ago Elizabeth walked into my office and said she and Michelle were going to get up a collection of articles on working women and the academy and would I contribute something. I told her I really didn't know too much about working women in the academy but perhaps I could do something about language and how proprietary we all are about it and how this can be exclusionist. She thought that was good. I promptly pushed the idea back in my head until one day Michelle called me and said how was the article going and I had to admit it wasn't and she said she wanted it in about two weeks and I said I'd try but couldn't promise anything. I felt like I was leaving my little corner of secure knowledge and practices and didn't want to make a fool of myself and so I went to the library and requested an ERIC search. The three concepts I gave them were one class and language two women and language and three language in schools. Well I really only got 10 articles and the machine wasn't working very well and so I started reading some other things and they led me to others and I must have read 10 books at least and 50 articles and I still know there's lots I should read but I did promise Michelle an article before the year 2000 and so I put all my notes together and listened to all those voices and began to put a piece of my voice in but theirs were still stronger and as I revised theirs receded and mine came out but still there's lots of quotes and now I'm just about finished and I know all those people are speaking through me and I hope I'm speaking through them too. And as soon as I get some feedback from some good readers and do a little bit (i hope) of revising and some copyediting and proofreading I'll be able to mail off the article and that will bring my story to the end.

But of course that wasn't the end; it never is. Because the article was too long; i (oops!) always do that—get started and can't stop. And so I got feedback from them and from Sheryl and Dennis and Peter and I had to cut it and make unpleasant decisions and realize where things hadn't come off that I thought were so clever and then of course I had read some other things and wanted to include them and now here's this story getting longer and adding length. But I'm almost finished with this revision and so that will be the end a second time.

Not all stories are created equal though. Brodkey reports on a study she set up in which teachers wrote to working-class students whom they didn't know and never met. All contact was through writing. The teachers' narratives in their letters are about trying to resolve conflicts in the demands on them—they felt guilty. The working women told narratives of external threats, not internal conflicts. One of the working women inserted a reference at one point to violence in her neighborhood. The teacher barely referred to that violence (that story) in his reply.

And while this is admittedly one of the more dramatic examples, it suggests the extent to which unacknowledged tension over the control of subject positions contributes to rather than alleviates class antagonism, for we see that the teacher's desire to be preserved as the unified subject of an educational discursive practice that transcends class overrides the student's desire to narrate herself as a subject unified in relation to the violence that visited her working-class neighborhood. ("On the Subject" 133)

Ensuing letters between these two became increasingly unsuccessful as communications.

But, at the same time such students feel alienated, they also want—if they are women—to be "good girls": "sociolinguistic research on gender and language suggests that women are more aware than men of the link between social status and speech" (Penfield 176). This can produce speakers and writers who ignore themselves and think too much about the reader, the patient Griseldas, as Bolker names them. Such students are too anxious to please, to the detriment of their own thinking processes:

A style that aims to please all and offend none, one which "smiles" all the time, shows very little of a thought process, but strives instead to produce a neat package tied with a ribbon. Ambivalence is out, changes of mind are out, the important nagging questions are out, because they are not neat, and they might offend—and because they involve paying some attention to one's own state of mind when one is writing. Such papers are highly published, so much so that it is hard to catch a human voice in them. And, like Griselda, they are dull; competence is all. (907)

Bolker believes (and I agree) that we must somehow disrupt this imbalance of concern for pleasing the reader, for what it produces is women who have "learned how to write papers," but who "have not yet learned to write" (906).

THEM: Rigor is what's needed—ability to present ideas clearly and in an orderly structure. "The quality of an argument is more favourably perceived when presented in a standard accented voice. . . .

ME: ". . . but when it comes to attitudinal (and perhaps behavioral) consequences of an argument, listeners may be more convinced and persuaded by a speaker with whom they can identify—an ingroup member" (Giles and Powesland 99).

CHORUS: "Formal logic essentially strips away all specific connections to human affairs and things of the world; it allows us to represent relations and interactions within a wholly abstract system" (Rose, "Language" 285).

ME: (Who am I arguing with anyway?) "Our elevation of this procedure blinds us to the overwhelming degree to which powerful and effective reasoning can be practical, non-formal, and concrete" (Rose, "Language" 285). Doesn't the intuition. . . .

THEM: But we're talking about teaching students to succeed in school according to the rules of the school's game.

ME: They'll never need to write the way you do once they get out of school. They need to forge links between their lives in and out of school.

THEM: But teaching them our language is teaching them how to think our way and *that* is valuable.

ME: Not always. Reminds me of what Mary told me about her experience in that classroom with that awful snobbish teacher, . . .

THEM: Generalize please.

Simultaneously (almost):

THEM: Thinking is logical, rational, impersonal, paradigmatic. . . .

ME: Thinking is associative, intuitive, personal, narrative. . . .

(You'll notice the chorus didn't join in.)

Given this simultaneity of truths, what can we do in our classroom? Pushing students toward academically privileged language and male rhetoric may well work against the strengths and abilities of women. "Women students need to stop learning primarily how to translate their own experience into a foreign language and instead to spend some time learning their mother tongue." That mother tongue includes (but is not limited to) "an emphasis on the particular, the contextual, the narrative, the imagistic" (Annas 371). Pulling students away from the particulars of their lives, their stories of themselves, may create crippling disjunctions in their lives outside of school. And acceding to the possibility that we cannot change any of this until the world outside changes may cripple us.

I have no answers either for myself or for others—only some thoughts I've collected from both sources, which seem to be relevant right now. "The best way to accomplish those things that are impossible today is to do today whatever is possible" (Freire 64).

First, we need to realize that "our own scholarly practices have contributed to the marginalization of such politically and often economically disfranchised groups as minorities and women, not to mention the vast and undifferentiated group commonly referred to as the working class" (Brodkey, *Academic Writing* viii; see also Rose, *Lives on the Boundary*). Unfortunately, "The Academy is by all accounts a conservative culture" (Said 22).

Second, we need to realize that "teaching students to use formal written language for analysis, synthesis, reflection, and the like is not teaching Literacy but only a certain kind of literacy, linked to the practical enterprises, traditions—and biases—of academic inquiry" (Brandt 138). Only when we truly believe this will we be able to see value in the literacies students bring into our classrooms. Composition teachers are crucially important because we " 'always already' function as the custodians of the discourse of mastery so treasured at the university. We are, in other words, the author-ities our students must salute in order to get their identity papers. As gatekeepers, however, we are also singularly suited to finding or creating the gaps and cracks in the (sign) system in which difference(s) might blossom" (Cixous 51).

Third we need to recognize this issue as a permanent one within the academy; we cannot solve it for the future.

Each generation of academicians facing the characteristic American shifts in demographics and accessibility sees the problem anew, laments it in the terms of the era, and optimistically notes its impermanence. No one seems to say that this scenario has gone on for so long that it might not be temporary. That, in fact, there will probably *always* be a significant percentage of students who do not meet some standard. (Rose, "Language" 355–56)

As teachers, we can never be secure in our knowledge of our students' cultures. But even without the diversity of culture, our students' culture will always differ from academia's. Min-zhan Lu, writing of her struggles to find her own language and wondering about her daughter's education, finds herself

especially concerned with the way some composition classes focus on turning the classroom into a monological scene for the students' reading and writing. . . . When composition classes encourage these students to ignore those voices that seem irrelevant to the purified world of the classroom, most students are often able to do so without much struggle. However, beyond the classroom and beyond the limited range of these students' immediate lives lies a much more complex and dynamic social and historical scene. To help these students become actors in such a scene, perhaps we need to call their attention to voices that may seem irrelevant to the discourse we teach rather than encourage them to shut them out. (447)

These "need to's" I have listed above are directed at what I think we as teachers "need to" understand about our classrooms. If we do not understand these, we cannot implement educational activities in the classroom aimed at change—we will only be going through motions, and our own attitudes will override whatever gimmicks we use. If, however, we genuinely realize the problem and if we genuinely want to move to do something about it, then we can profit from the suggestions of others.[5]

We do not need to settle for teaching students the discourse of the academy and thus invalidating their personal discourse; we should not even be acquiescing in the academy's dichotomizing of discourse into

269

academic and nonacademic. Whose idea is that anyway? Both we and our students can foster and produce a multiplicity of discourses which all of us can learn to control.

The task facing our students, as Min-zhan Lu has argued, is not to leave one community in order to enter another, but to *reposition* ourselves in relation to several continuous and conflicting discourses. Similarly, our goals as teachers need not be to initiate our students into the values and practices of some new community, but to offer them the chance to reflect critically on these discourses—of home, school, work, the media, and the like—to which they already belong. (Harris 19)

And, finally, I believe that modern composition theory with its emphasis on a "process model, insofar as it facilitates and legitimizes the fullest expression of the individual voice, is compatible with the feminist revisioning of hierarchy, if not essential to it" (Caywood and Overing xiv). In the process model

much more emphasis is given to the act of writing, to both revealing and examining the private process of discovery. One important result of this change of emphasis should be the validation of the private voice in that of the process of discovery becomes as important, if not more so, than the summarized product of discovery. Revisionist writing theorists also affirm the importance of the inner voice, its forms of discourse, and its language: pre-writing, free writing, rough drafts and their revisions, learning logs, reading diaries, journals, and exploratory essays are as valued as the more traditional linear modes of expression. (Caywood and Overing xiii)

I will not cover this issue further, but recommend to anyone who has gotten this far in my article that she looks at the essays collected in the Caywood and Overing book, the only book I know that brings together composition theory and feminist theory. A recent article does however pick up on some of these connections and concludes that "in a sense, composition specialists replace the figure of the authoritative father with an image of a nurturing mother" (Flynn 423).

I find I cannot *not* say one more thing about the place of writing in education. Writing needs to be a part of all classes because it generates; students spend far too much time in school being receptors. They cannot struggle through to their own place in or out of the academy if they do not produce discourse of some kind. Talking is good, of course, but it is not enough. Writing is doing.

But there is more, for we need to be conscious of the social networks in our classrooms also. We need to think about how we as faculty can help students caught between their comfortable world and a new, somewhat frightening one. One way is to work at making our classrooms a supporting environment, an environment in which students work collaboratively and thus begin to trust and depend on one another. It is quite difficult—if not impossible—for such an environment to develop in a lecture format. Students remain isolated from one another in worlds of their own. Small wonder they return to the warmth of their own worlds and cling, even if unconsciously, to the language of that world. In such instances, they may "put on" our language, but I suspect that what they say through such put-on language will seem quite separate from them; they will have little investment in it. As a result they may write acceptably, but they will never write well; that is, they may learn to write papers, but they will not learn to write, not learn to "author" their writing.

Notes

1. I cannot help wondering if sociolinguists are always talking about the same group when they use the label "working class." It is a slippery term and as a nonsociologist I will not risk a definition. I will though quote the following from Lauter:

I would designate as "working-class people" those who sell their labor for wages, who create in that labor and have taken from them "surplus value," to use Marx's phrase; who have relatively little control over the nature and products of their work; who are not "professionals" or "managers." I refer to people who, to advance their conditions of life, must move in solidarity with their class or must leave it (to become, for example, managers). I would include those who work in the home, whose labor though not salaried is sold as surely as that of those who work in the mills or the streets. I would also include those whose labor was or is extorted from them by slavery and peonage, as well as farm laborers. (16)

Labov separates the working class from both the middle class and the lower class, placing it between the two. The working class thus has some traits of the lower middle class and some traits of the upper range of the lower class (Labov, "Stages" 86). At times, though it is not easy to determine whether he is speaking of the working class as distinct from the two classes at its borders.

2. Labov includes in the lowest status group women who do not work outside the home and who thus have little contact with speakers of other classes. Once such women leave their homes to go to school or to work, they become a part of that group of women who demonstrate severe style shifting.

3. "The working-class style of casual speech has values strongly associated with masculinity" (Labov "Stages" 94). This has not gone undebated. Giles and Marsh disagree; Cameron (49) and Trudgell agree.

271

4. The degree to which differences can be attributed to actual differences in brain structure is hotly debated. Tanner apparently accepts the possibility as do some of the researchers whose work Goleman summarizes. I cannot enter that specialized debate.

5. I recommend highly Kyle Fiore and Nan Elsasser's description of a curriculum they developed and the outcomes of it. What happened in their classroom demonstrates what *can* happen when teachers want it to. Quite different but worthy of attention is Flynn's analysis of what it means to compose as a woman.

Works Cited

Annas, Pamela L. "Style as Politics: A Feminist Approach to the Teaching of Writing." *College English* 47 (1985): 360–71.

Bartholomae, David. "Inventing the University." *Journal of Basic Writing* 5 (1986): 4–23.

Belenky, Mary Field, Blythe Clinchy, Nancy Goldberger, and Jill Tarule. *Women's Ways of Knowing: The Development of Self, Voice, and Mind.* New York: Basic, 1986.

Bernstein, Basil. *Class, Codes and Control: Towards a Theory of Educational Transmissions.* Vol. 3. 2nd ed. Boston: Routledge, 1977.

Bizzell, Patricia. "Arguing about Literacy." *College English* 50 (1988): 141–53.

Bolker, Joan. "Teaching Griselda to Write." *College English* 40 (1979): 906–08.

Brandt, Deborah. "Review: Versions of Literacy." *College English* 47 (1985): 128–38.

Brodkey, Linda. *Academic Writing as Social Practice.* Philadelphia: Temple UP, 1987.

——. "On the Subjects of Class and Gender in 'The Literacy Letters.'" *College English* 51 (1989): 125–41.

Bruffee, Kenneth A. "Collaborative Learning and the 'Conversation of Mankind.'" *College English* 46 (1984): 635–52.

Cameron, Deborah. *Feminism and Linguistic Theory.* London: Macmillan, 1985.

Caywood, Cynthia L., and Gillian R. Overing, eds. *Teaching Writing: Pedagogy, Gender, and Equity.* Albany: State U of New York P, 1987.

Chodorow, Nancy. "Being and Doing: A Cross-Cultural Examination of the Socialization of Males and Females." *Women in Sexist Society: Studies in Power and Powerlessness.* Ed. Vivian Gornick and Barbara K. Moran. New York: New American, 1971. 173–97.

Cixous, Hélène. "Castration or Decapitation?" *Signs* 7 (1981): 41–55.

——, and Catherine Clement. *The Newly Born Woman*. Trans. Betsy Wing. Minnesota: U of Minnesota P, 1986.

Coles, Nicholas. "Democratizing Literature: Issues in Teaching Working-Class Literature." *College English* 48 (1986): 664–80.

Edwards, Frances L. "Sociocultural Dialects and School Achievement." ERIC ED183662.

Elbow, Peter. "Closing My Eyes As I Speak: An Argument for Ignoring Audience." *College English* 49 (1987): 50–69.

——. "Reflections on Academic Discourse: How It Relates to Freshman and Colleagues." *College English* 53 (1991): 135–55.

Farrell, Thomas J. "The Female and Male Modes of Rhetoric." *College English* 40 (1979): 909–21.

Fiore, Kyle, and Nan Elsasser. " 'Strangers No More': A Liberatory Literacy Curriculum." *College English* 44 (1982): 115–28.

Flynn, Elizabeth A. "Composing as a Woman." *College Composition and Communication* 39 (1988): 423–35.

Fontaine, Sheryl. "The Unfinished Story of the Interpretive Community." *Rhetoric Review* 7 (1988): 86–96.

Freire, Paulo. *Pedagogy in Process*. New York: Seabury, 1978.

Giles, Howard, and Patricia Marsh. "Perceived Masculinity, Androgyny and Accented Speech." *Language Sciences* 1 (1978–79): 301–15.

Giles, Howard, and Peter F. Powesland. *Speech Style and Social Evaluation*. New York: Academic, 1975.

Goleman, Daniel. "Special Abilities of the Sexes: Do They Begin in the Brain?" *Psychology Today* 12 (1978): 55–56.

Harris, Joseph. "The Idea of Community in the Study of Writing." *College Composition and Communication* 40 (1989): 11–22.

Heath, Shirley Brice. *Ways with Words: Language, Life, and Work in Communities and Classrooms*. New York: Cambridge UP, 1983.

Holzman, Michael. "The Social Context of Literary Education." *College English* 48 (1986): 27–33.

Irigaray, Luce. *Speculum of the Other Woman*. Ithaca: Cornell UP, 1985.

Joos, Martin. *The Five Clocks*. New York: Harcourt, 1961.

Kay, Paul. "Language Evolution and Speech Style." *Sociocultural Dimensions of Language Change*. Ed. Ben G. Blount and Mary Sanches. New York: Academic, 1977. 21–33.

Koch, Stephen. "Journey's Beginning: A Talk with Diana Trilling." *The New York Times Book Review* 19 February 1989: 1, 26–27.

Kristeva, Julia. *Desire in Language*. Ed. Leon S. Roudiez. Trans. Thomas Gora, Alice Jardine, and Leon S. Roudiez. New York: Columbia UP, 1980.

Labov, William. "The Logic of Nonstandard English." *Language in the Inner City*. Philadelphia: U of Pennsylvania P, 1972. 201–40.

——. "Stages in the Acquisition of Standard English." *Social Dialects and Language Learning*. Ed. Roger Shuy. Champaign, IL.: NCTE, 1964.

——. *The Study of Nonstandard English*. Urbana, IL.: NCTE, 1969.

——. "The Transformation of Experience in Narrative Syntax." *Language in the Inner City*. 354–96.

Lauter, Paul. "Working-Class Women's Literature: An Introduction to Study." *Radical Teacher* 15 (1979): 16–26.

Levertov, Denise. "What Were They Like?" *The Sorrow Dance*. New York: New Directions, 1967.

Lu, Min-Zhan. "From Silence to Words: Writing as Struggle." *College English* 49 (1987): 437–48.

Macrorie, Ken. *Searching Writing*. Rochelle Park, NJ: Hayden, 1980.

Mitchell, Jacqueline. "Reflections of a Black Social Scientist: Some Struggles, Some Doubts, Some Hopes." *Harvard Educational Review* 52 (1982): 27–44.

Olson, Gary A. "Social Construction and Composition Theory: A Conversation with Richard Rorty." *Journal of Advanced Composition* 9 (1989): 1–9.

Ong, Walter J. *Orality and Literacy*. New York: Methuen, 1982.

Penfield, Joyce, ed. *Women and Language in Transition*. Albany: State U of New York P, 1987.

Pigott, Margaret B. "Sexist Roadblocks in Inventing, Focusing, and Writing." *College English* 40 (1979): 922–27.

Railey, Kevin. "The Democratic Potential of Elbow's Pedagogy." Unpublished manuscript.

Rose, Mike. "The Language of Exclusion: Writing Instruction at the University." *College English* 47 (1985): 341–59.

——. *Lives on the Boundary: The Struggles and Achievements of America's Underprepared*. New York: Free, 1989.

Said, Edward. "Opponents, Audiences, Constituencies, and Community." *Critical Inquiry* 9 (1982): 1–26.

Sexton, Anne. "Her Kind." *To Bedlam and Part Way Back*. New York: Houghton, 1960.

Sharp, Rachel, and Anthony Green. *Education and Social Control*. Boston: Routledge, 1975.

Tanner, James E. "The Ethics of Literacy Training." *College English* 44 (1982): 18–24.

Thorne, Barrie, Cheris Kramarae, and Nancy Henley. *Language, Gender and Society*. Rowley, MA: Newbury, 1983.

Troyka, Lynn Quitman. "Perspectives on Legacies and Literacy in the 1980s." *College Composition and Communication* 33 (1982): 252–62.

Trudgell, Peter. "Sex, Covert Prestige, and Linguistic Changes in the Urban British English of Norwich." *Language in Society* 1 (1972): 179–95.

Tuman, Myron C. "Class, Codes, and Composition: Basil Bernstein and the Critique of Pedagogy." *College Composition and Communication* 39 (1988): 42–51.

Dissent in the Field; or, A New Type of Intellectual?

Wherever there is a general attempt on the part of the women of any society to readjust their position in it, a close analysis will always show that the changed or changing conditions of that society have made woman's acquiescence no longer necessary or desirable.

—Olive Schreiner, *Woman and Labor* (1911)

THIS ESSAY analyzes the roles academics engage in in their struggle to identify themselves—to provoke identity—in the institutional network (as in fabric, netting) they learn to call home. I use the bounds (or ceilings and room dividers) of the humanities and social sciences to define my argument and assume that the "hard" sciences operate within somewhat different bounds.

The Field

Graduate school is the place of our professional birth. Graduate education comprises the institutionalization of the novice scholar.[1] This process involves: an initiation into a new order and ideology, and therefore a new identification; a displacement of old ways of speaking, interpreting, behaving; learning a new way of thinking and articulating thought with concision, logical structure, and self-consciousness. In short, it means transforming oneself into a member of the intellectual class. The novice proceeds not without pain. Students face a double bind in graduate school, where they are simultaneously infantilized (washed of any knowledge, authority, skills they bring with them) and depersonalized (placed clonelike in a writing or intro classroom or section as an authority figure). The intention of this double whammy, derived from ancient (Eastern and Western, religious and military) pedagogy, is for the master to knock each initiate down and then in an identificatory process, pick him or her up; during this bonding with the authority figure, the student transcends a prior identity. The new, unitary bond thus delivers them from the threat of the double bind. When realized, this mentoring relationship produces a fully inculcated scholar who has been not only inducted into the profession, but also institutionalized to his or her current rank. Each successive change of rank will entail another shake-up in the scholar's identity and way of thinking as he or she readjusts to the new level of institutionalization, at least until the middle stages of associate professorship.

This modeling of our profession came home to me through a preliminary study of working-class women graduate students in literature departments and of their special problems inherent in their gender, social class, and student status. The two histories I begin with shared so many traits and details with so many other stories I heard from students, former students, and ex-students from all kinds of backgrounds and schools that I reorganized my polarized field of class/gender versus institution. Now I want to begin at both ends and work toward the central or inner space: the student's experience and academe's machine are interlocking, and we need to find the fit between the inward process of how a student metamorphoses to faculty, and the inner halls of the buildings where we work and where we talk ourselves into ways of being and thinking.

Some Players

On this field, the younger of two players, Shari, had gone from a floundering sense of self-orientation in her first year of graduate studies to a shaky sense of professionalism. Marjorie, the older player and a divorced mother, had vacillated for several years over whether to continue the program at all. These two stories allegorize the experience of graduate students in research institutions. Working-class graduate students within the humanities, regardless of gender, tend to acknowledge anxiety over performance and expectation as they intrude on the bastion of canonized culture and elitist tradition. Class issues in the academy are informed by women's social experience within masculinist culture; at the intersection of these factors lies the crippling self-doubt of these two students. But is their anxiety idiosyncratic or is it due to the same fears more privileged (whether by gender or class) students face?

Both graduate students have the same ethnic and social backgrounds, both come from the same geographic location, both chose to go to the same state university. Shari experienced a loss in her sense of self-sufficiency when she moved into her parents' house in order to afford graduate school; family tensions and arguments affected her commitment to the program, making her question personal and career goals and defer program deadlines. The decision to be on her own again in her fourth year meant taking on several extra part-time jobs; Shari's new found self-worth crumbled by mid-year after continued lateness, absence, and bad reports at each part-time and stipend job. In her fifth year, when stipend support ended, she moved back to her parents' house; although she has not officially dropped out of the program, nearly all ties with the department have been cut.

The second graduate student, Marjorie, returned to school in order to discover both herself and a career. However, when her mentor left the profession altogether, she experienced conflict and doubt over the profession's adequacy to meet her own aspirations. Immediate financial needs and heavy student debts led to a series of full-time campus jobs in administration as Marjorie explored career options, all eventually disappointing. Although she took several years leave from the program, she recently became disgruntled with nongrowth office jobs and, lowering her expectations of her own performance, quickly took her comprehensive, submitted her dissertation proposal, and found a non-tenure-track teaching job several states away. Marjorie readily admits that had her mentoring professor not become dissatisfied himself, she would not have questioned pursuing an academic career or her own ability to perform.

Neither Shari nor Marjorie discovered mentors of their class or gender; their lack of role models meant their concepts of self within an elitist profession never found firm ground. Although their department has women faculty of working-class backgrounds, both students dismissed these professors as possible models. The choice of mentors who bespeak privilege and authority signifies a distrust of faculty who have not held what Pierre Bourdieu calls "cultural capital" from birth.[2] It may also signal that the working-class faculty were not recognizable as role models—that is, they are no longer working class yet they lacked cultural capital; they now have what Bourdieu calls "intellectual capital," but this does not seem to be what either woman student is seeking.

Two male graduate students who are superficially Shari's and Marjorie's counterparts—both working class, one young, one older and divorced (though childless)—differ interestingly in how they experienced similar doubts and similar difficulty in finding concerned and attentive mentors. Shari's peer and good friend, Joe, has taken and failed his comprehensives, but has continued his ties with both peers and newer graduate students in the department, is studying to retake the exams, and supports himself as an adjunct at a nearby school. Although his years in the department were marked by aggressive displays and outbursts of bravado, throughout he maintained his relationship with his mentor: a full professor near retirement with a national reputation. Marjorie's friend, John, also explored extreme self-doubt, with bouts of intense, self-imposed periods of alienation. Like her, he took several years leave before his comprehensives and also resolved to find teaching posts elsewhere. Although he is less committed to finishing the degree and admits that he probably will never begin the dissertation, John's leave-taking was the result of a newfound confidence, gained from having passed his exams, a confidence Marjorie did not experience because she is convinced her performance was shamefully poor.

Shari's shakiness, Joe's tenacity, Marjorie's eventual commitment to teaching but not to scholarship, and John's confident leave-taking reflect the levels of response typically found in humanities departments of working-class universities. The question becomes Are these responses of doubt, anger, inferiority, and diffidence—all forms of resistance to the overarching authority of academia—common to all graduate students? Or do students from privileged backgrounds, whether social or educational, confront the forces that blanket working-class students? Or are they immune to academe's patriarchy because they know how to operate gainfully within it? In other words, does academe temporarily release students from the privilege and confidence they enter with (that is, disable them as adults), only to endow them with another form of privilege upon successful completion of their trial by fire? There are far more success stories at elite institutions than not (in inverse ratio to state schools), but in fact, I could tell four similarly scenarioed stories of graduate students at ivy-covered institutions. We need, then, more than a theory of class oppression or of social patriarchy in the medieval cloister: we need to understand our professional work as labor in and among the multiple discourses with which we engage, including that of industry, politics, family, and culture. In short, when we are enmeshed in our professional identities as belonging to a class and world apart, we forget our need to engage with the world at large.

The Fiction

The mystique of academe is that it is a world unto itself constituting a community of the wise and the soon-to-be-wise. This utopian vision, however, is both medieval and unfortunate; the reality can only be fallen by comparison. Elitist or not, campuses are divided by each of the diversities—race, ethnicity, gender, class, age, sexual orientation, handicap—insidiously or overtly replicating the social field and its hierarchies. Campuses also impose their own hegemony on this socially structured marginalization, a pecking order wrought in an earlier history. Indeed, this should come as no surprise since the ivy-educated, who have been trained in the old power relations, dominate university systems whether private or state operated. This dominance results from the organization of state universities from their inception along traditional stringencies for tenure, tracking, and preferment in a mirror-imaging of the elite schools themselves; therefore, hiring practices favor candidates with particular credentials. How else to lure faculty of "quality" to an institute of higher education than by assuring them that power can and will come their way?

What mucks up these hierarchies and relations that rule our academic lives are our own ideologies: each of us has political affinities that we hope impede or sustain the armature holding up our hegemonic walls. Each of us hopes/knows that the fictions/truths we tell in class will reform/hold up those walls unto the next generation. What we can't see, for all ideology is blinding, is that liberal or conservative, feminist or patriarchal, Marxist or capitalist, deconstructive or humanist—we cannot change the shape of those walls. They are impervious to perestroika for the very reason that faculty pretends either they are not there, or they were there from the dawn and will outlast us. The academy, whether an institute where language is preserved from change or a place where artists reward their most conservative members, has always been a bell jar.

I would like to propose that the Schreiner epigraph at the beginning of this essay, if modified to read "wherever there is a general

280

attempt on the part of the students of any university to readjust their position in it, a close analysis will always show that the changed or changing conditions of that social system have made students' acquiescence no longer necessary or desirable," will describe academe in the twenty-first century. Student agitation (working class or privileged) cannot redistribute or even topple power imbalances between administration, faculty, graduate students, and undergraduates; it cannot because of the strictures of the hegemony that wall students off and hedge them in. They experience in small the same frustration and tenuousness that working-class academics feel before they are secured to the mast with tenure and promotion: it is they who are in danger of sinking, not the ship. Both groups have difficulty voicing their marginalized status and this is part of their instability; it is difficult to detail and then circumnavigate how one is pegged by class, gender, ethnicity, race . . . when academe works so hard to make the bias against difference invisible but keenly felt. These two groups can be compared in another, this time mirroring, way: despite their struggle with class identity, working-class faculty have transformed themselves into the intellectual class through the doctoral process and therefore no longer belong to the class into which they were born: graduate students, despite the class into which they were born or the educational opportunities they have enjoyed, are (for the most part) transformed into working-class laborers during their graduate career in preparation for their transformation into the next generation of the intellectual class.

The Factory

The patriarchal imperatives of our profession, which determine this transformative process of decentering the student's world only to provide a different, more compelling center (promise me gold, promise me anything), include indoctrination of our students (both undergraduate and graduate), a dissociation from their needs and their lives, exploitation of not only our students but also ourselves, and a bowing to authority despite ourselves. This patriarchy, no matter how we set out to fight it, provides the terms in which we learn to think and speak academically, the terms under which we are allowed to achieve a degree. Regardless of one's prior inculcation into language, itself dependent on the particularities in which one is raised, one must learn to conform, deform, transform thoughts and words until they serve a different purpose.

The continuation of this hierarchy is made possible in the following way: in academic institutions, we operate within a complex model of feudal, oedipal, and capitalistic power formations as played out in faculty, teacher-student, and administrative groups; this model creates needless pain in our lives, yet demands our complicity for its continued functioning. These points need further elaboration:

(1) Departmental faculties function in a medieval mode of feudal authority which follows the master-apprentice arrangement, modified by the recent inclusion of growing numbers of faculty with nontraditional backgrounds in the profession.

(2) The basic analogy for this newly modified power relation is that of the nuclear family, and while the mentor-to-student relationship has long been experienced as a father-to-son ratio, the addition of women mentors and graduate students confuses the issue of patriarchal power relations. For the mother is not merely the equal but opposite version of the father; she also must fight hard for her own place, and on several fronts. In this analogy, there are parents and children: graduate students are slightly older than undergraduates, but they are still children who achieve adolescence only after having passed the initiation rites of the orals. And their lengthy adolescence, whatever their actual biological age, extends to the passing of that final rite, tenure.

(3) In capitalist institutions there is necessarily another analogy operating, that is, the industrialization of the academy. This translates into the administration and higher powers that orchestrate university affairs as the ruling class; the various levels of faculty as the middle classes; and graduate students, adjuncts, and part-timers as the working classes (with alienated directors of English department writing programs as the factory foremen). The production of knowledge, consumable in different degrees by different sectors of the academic community, becomes the prime directive of this institution. The vast increase in knowledge production is historically determined as the market value of our scholarship fluctuates, and the speed with which we write directly determines the value of our intellectualizing.

(4) Graduate students as a class thus occupy two related yet disjunctive positions: that of a working class and that of children—and neither is valued. These positions are in dialectical opposition, since

working class implies laborers who remain laborers, while children grow up to become adults. Thus grads are on the one hand anonymous beings, automatons who replace each other in four-year cycles and who are then class-identified as they labor away at the factories of freshman introductory courses. And on the other hand, they are real individuals who grow up to become real professors. Meantime, they occupy that nebulous child or adolescent status which in our society denotes a position of powerlessness and a reputation for irresponsibility, both of which invite, at worst, faculty attitudes of deprecation, patronization, and scorn, and at best, a recognition in itself a kind of inattention wherein the student is assumed to be unknowledgeable and, outside of seminars, a drain on the professor's resources. This differential engenders enormous conflict for graduate students; for those who are adults long before entering graduate programs, it causes self-questioning, repeated humiliation, and a reexperiencing of the child's oedipal attitude toward authority which cannot but be unhealthy for the institution as a whole.

(5) This dual and conflicting analogy, finally, is no longer acceptable. As Evelyn Fox Keller and Helene Moglen note in their article on feminist scholars and academic competition, what is most necessary is to break out of traditionalist assumptions: "our relationships as colleagues are not," they note, "those of mothers and daughters . . . we can at the very least recognize the inappropriateness of those expectations of each other as colleagues in a world beyond the family."[3] We might well, in addition, recognize the inappropriateness of a class segregation that only encourages abuses of authority and disregard for individual worth.

Let me pursue this along slightly different lines, for the question of gender escalates the stakes of this argument. We cannot deny that innate intelligence as a quantitative material resource plays a large part not only in the production of knowledge, but also in faculty's choice of students to mentor. Who identifies with whom, and who feels threatened by whom shapes our academic careers, yet these dynamics too often follow traditional analyses of intelligence. Nancy Chodorow has argued for a different growth model for women, and Carol Gilligan, for a different moral model;[4] there are also different modes of thought and expression, which are available to all classes and groups whether marginalized or central, yet which receive greater or lesser value based on a group's position and identity. Intelligence is not a homogeneous force

283

that finds expression in a univocacy we can all appreciate. The brain, in fact, works in a variety of modes, but it is the male-identified and elitist modes that are valued—symbolic logic, highly contiguous linear thought, dialectical thinking, the capacity for recall when used solely as another form of naming, and a certain amount of mimicry. These modes test well, they win respect and authority for their practitioners, and they are integral to the establishment of the authoritative speech and writing that we must all be able to exercise as the hallmark of our profession. Nowhere is the push to excel in these modes of thinking, speaking, and writing more stressed than in graduate school: our diplomas signify that we are masters, indeed, doctors and practitioners of these cognitive and expressive skills.

But are these elitist modes the ones valued, or even much practiced by other groups, particularly women (as a class), with their socialized and inculcated ethics of care, cooperation, and community?[5] The rites of passage—the orals, where we prove we can speak authoritatively, and the dissertation, where we prove that we, too, can inscribe the patriarch as we assert our own arguments against those of others—with their ritual humiliations in the oedipal struggle between paternal and filial authority, test one's competency in the male arena. These exclusionary tests, which ensure the revalidation of male thought, force us to ask two questions: How can faculty step outside the mastery of academic discourse? but, more immediately, How do women graduate students, regardless of background, survive intact the process of transformation such tests demand? I am suggesting here, based on our four case "players," that women internalize a different pain (or intensity of pain) than men because they continue to attend to or value more levels of discourse than graduate programs approve.

As intellectuals, we need to recognize the pain involved in our self-transformation from marginal to dominant modes, and to admit complicity in the demands for this pain. In addition, we might do well to attend to Julia Kristeva's proposal that the one energizing intellectual pursuit is that of "the writer who experiments with the limits of identity, producing texts where the law does not exist outside language. A playful language therefore gives rise to a law that is overturned, violated and pluralized."[6] Kristeva's conception of intellectual activity is related to Bourdieu's theory that the only way to escape the strictures of the social field is to rewrite the rules of the game, thus transforming the field ("overturned, violated and pluralized").

Those entering graduate school have never been asked to alter themselves so radically at such a conscious level to conform to a particular model. When we agree to alter the way we perceive the world and our interaction with that world, it is called learning. The implication is that we had interacted incorrectly before we acquired this new mode of being, which we learn more or less well.

The Problem

We also learn through cultural changes, and we induct new ways of being in the world through new political rhetorics. Young people now learn that they live in a multicultural world, or that drugs are not as acceptable as they were, or that women are now equal to men and have access to the same jobs and salaries.

There is a quiet crisis in American education of the last few years. Its most disturbing manifestation—a crisis of credibility on the left—is visible in movements such as the new "postfeminism." This last may well be directly related to the recent absorption in women's popular magazines in such topics as "Why Smart Women Are Staying Home," or "Why Careers Are Not Always the Answer." Why have young women, undergraduate and graduate students, recently lost interest in feminist issues, considering such issues no longer relevant to their needs? Even while acknowledging the huge impact of Reaganomics on feminism itself, neoconservatism cannot fully account for student disinterest in feminist theory and politics. The institution itself is to blame, and as teachers, we must accept some blame for continuing its ideological practices. Mary Wollstonecraft pointed out that America's revolution for independence was a hypocritical project based on the institution of slavery. Academic feminism may also be construed as somewhat hypocritical, and we all have occasion to recall "feminist" professors unable to translate feminist theory into daily practice or to mentor feminist students. What we need, as individuals and as intellectuals, as Bourdieu advocates, is a way to revise the rules and thereby change the game and its demands for pain and deformation. We want a beginning, a way to think differently about our profession and our intellectual domain.

Once the thought process is no longer fully patriarchal, then the possibility of revising the game and those invisible walls that align our academic lives might be remodeled.

A New Game

If we consider that we operate within concentric circles of consciousness and vision, circles that do not hold us in place and among which we do have the freedom to range, we can stop institutional reduction of our complex lives to simple hierarchical positioning and the resulting identification with that place. Of the three circles I am initially positing, the central one represents that site from which we interpret ourselves in relation to the social whole as educators of that society, utterers of a cultural consensus. This circle conserves tradition, the history of the dominant culture, protecting it from philistine appropriation or transfiguration by popular culture. It is from here that we conceive our individuality and autonomy, our particular genius in isolation from cultural currents, the uniqueness of self in opposition to another. It is from here that we feel most empowered to speak.

A second circle, which both encloses the first and extends beyond it, is the place of local conversation, incorporating what we say—our manufacture of educational knowledge—with surrounding, disruptive discourses. These alternate ways of speaking are heard from students, friends, other professional discourses, the media, literature, art. The result is a vital realization of our individual and class or group participation in the ruling ideology—whether social (as in patriarchy), political (Reaganomics, capitalism, Western imperialism), or institutional (for instance, the codes by which business, government, or education operates versus the codes by which the family is constructed).

The third circle tells the master narrative of our culture, present, past, and future in all its patterns and rhythms. It also provides the fullest sense of the community as a whole, while locating individuals as the molecules that constitute that whole. This narrative comes to us via art, film, talk shows, retrospects, political speeches, and our gross national product.

Traditional ontologies keep us locked into a single way of understanding the self, but I see this model as dynamic; we are simultaneously

286

in all circles, and the greater our awareness of the circles that define us, the greater our awareness of the roles we ourselves play. If we transfer this concentric structure to patriarchal thought, we find that women are trained to see men as inhabiting that first circle, the locus of liberal humanism, the center to whose margins women have traditionally been relegated. Against this static center-to-margin arrangement we can place the multilevel awareness of self and community,[7] a wider ranging consciousness of the dynamic model. As a conceptual frame, these expanding circles help structure thought in and against the ideologies that rule us. I will construct these circles in feminist terms, but by using the same kinds of shifts, the model can be constructed in the terms of other single or interacting differences.

We can still map the first circle as the center, where texts and readers interact at the level of the knowing self and representable experience. American feminist theory has thoroughly examined the circumference of that first circle, performing archeological and restorative feats while culturally situating women's activities. Women's version of this first circle differs in purpose from the masculinist model, wherein it would be the center of power, the concept of self that informs a patriarchal world concept. It becomes here a circle in which women's voices are sought and recognized. It is not a place of self and other, but of the recognition of foremothers and a women's historical community. Because inhabiting this first circle statically means nonawareness of the surrounding circles, American feminists have been accused by European theorists as being as blindingly liberal humanist as their masculinist peers. Again, moving between circles and making use of their dynamism answer such critique, whereas obviating that core circle as the French have denies the female continuum that provides our identity beyond patriarchal dictum.

French feminist theory has lyrically explored the second circle, with its focus on language's limit and its failure to represent experience. This circle pulls us out of the dangerous nonawareness of patriarchal ideology that the first circle fosters; it is here that we find the tools with which to understand the mechanisms of our complicity and resistance.

The third circle calls on the first two as it tells its complex narrative of our political and social history across class boundaries into the lives of women and men. This is not history as it was, since history itself is nonrepresentable, but as we partake of it, as we have both created and been created by it. For we not only accede to, but also help create the ideologies that control us.

To investigate women's and men's texts in the first circle, to theorize the various levels of their functioning in the second, and to recognize the cyclical patterns of our culture in the third provide a totalizing vision, a way out. Feminists in academia are peculiarly situated in relation to an ongoing women's vision, for we hold the strands, the tapestry threads of this vision's history. We can fill in the gaps, the sublations, the losses of memory, and we can understand why these losses happened and continue to happen. To fall victim to the patriarchal trap of power and suppression of others, the institutional ideology to which we are indeed vulnerable, to which our doctorates indoctrinate us, is to blind ourselves to this third-circle history.

Revising the Fiction

The web of meaning such a history generates invokes a caretaking of the collectivity, a validation over hegemony, a connectedness that should form the skeleton of a feminist academia. Feminine-identified graduate students initially operate within the context of this third circle until it is trained out of them and replaced by institutional thinking. Once we are so invested in the ideology of our profession, we lodge ourselves into that first level of reading the self into society and transmit to our students a professional blindness that denies what we had known. In one of my first seminars as a graduate faculty, I unintentionally insulted a student I thought I knew rather well when he insisted on repeatedly debating feminism *per se* in a course that was not about feminism, and without reference to our assigned readings; in exasperation I finally told him that, as a working-class man, he did not represent the patriarchal power feminism attacks, and so he was responding to something not aimed at him. That is, "men" does not equal *all* men. Concerned with silencing his difficult voice, I confirmed what he had believed about feminists and power. My professional knowledge that this student's questions delayed our discussion and acquisition of syllabus material blinded me to the possibility that we may have needed to go where he wanted to lead us. Not surprisingly, student evaluations marked me on that day's insensitivity.

Ensconced in that first circle, which without the other two produces a necessary but forcibly restricted reading of situations and debates, we can only be agents of the institutions that legislate our lives, running classrooms and granting grades based on indefensible first principles, unable to step back and see that we have become the texts, have been written upon, for a way of thinking that contradicts what we hope to live for. We need to refuse to consent, refuse to hand our individuality over to the institution, refuse to textualize ourselves. It is only in this way that we can avoid the recurrent losses in any feminist vision that must stretch its desire over time, passing its goals on from mother to daughter and from radical to conservative until the entire project is lost from view with only discontented whispers remaining.

Subversive discontent often surfaces in women's restrooms, where gender segregation allows for whisperings, shared secrets, unabashed meditations on the nature of sexuality scrawled on walls. Yet in academe, even restrooms can be sites of oppression. Attending a feminist conference as a graduate student several years ago, I overheard a group of women professors in the restroom complaining about tenure pressures; one said that she was fortunate, she had "several graduate student slaves to help her." Kristeva, in her article "A New Type of Intellectual: The Dissident," argues for a political stance that would speak always from a position of marginality in order to escape the Hegelian master-slave dialectic. Kristeva notes that "the future of Western society will greatly depend on a re-evaluation of the relationship of the masses to the individual or intellectual, and on our ability to break out of the dialectical trap between these oppositions and to recast the whole relationship" (*Reader* 293). Elsewhere Kristeva sees this reevaluation as a redefinition of terms such as "woman," "child," and "adolescent," lifting them out of their first-circle semantic horizon and a master discourse. We need to apply this notion to our own position as women intellectuals and rethink our attitudes toward students as children, and graduate students as working-class laborers and naive adolescents; we also need to rethink our attitudes toward institutional thinking and toward alternatives to master discourses, master rhetorics, master grammars. To cite Kristeva once again,

It is the task of the intellectual, who has inherited those "unproductive" elements of our modern technocratic society which used to be called the "humanities," not just to produce this right to speak and behave in an individual way in our culture, but to assert its *political value*. Failing this, the function of the intellectual strangely enough turns into one of coercion. (*Reader* 294)

Respecting other modes of speaking and inscribing the self become political acts, acts that can protect us from consenting to institutional coercion. Learning is a collaborative process; the hierarchical institution can devolve into the community of peers if we remember that our students are indeed ourselves—not in the master-apprentice relation, but in the peer relation. I am speaking here not of master lectures but of peer tutoring. Kristeva writes, "You will have understood that I am speaking the language of exile. The language of the exile muffles a cry, it doesn't ever shout" (*Reader* 298). Why should we live in exile, perched on the lonely rungs of our academic ladders? In the same terms, graduate students—as a marginalized yet eventually central group—need not live an oedipal existence of bitterness, exile, and muffled anger. The apprentice needs not to become the master, but to become the peer who participates in a cooperative and unending conversation of learning: "Failing this, the function of the intellectual strangely enough turns into one of coercion."

Notes

1. The concept here is that institutions construct the individuals who participate in them. See Mary Douglas, *How Institutions Think* (Syracuse: Syracuse UP, 1986).

2. This essay is premised on Bourdieu's notion of the social "field," of class privilege that enables through the bestowing of "cultural capital," and of the power of institutions to form and transform us as social beings. See particularly *Distinction: A Social Critique of the Judgement of Taste*, trans. Richard Nice (Cambridge: Harvard UP, 1984).

3. This is a painful and wonderfully introspective essay that more fully than my own analyzes case studies to explore different relationships between women in academe. (Evelyn Fox Keller and Helene Moglen, "Competition and Feminism: Conflicts for Academic Women," *Signs* 12 [1987]: 493–511).

4. Interesting pedagogical explorations of Chodorow's and Gilligan's important, though class and culture restricted, studies are *Women's Ways of Knowing: Self, Voice and Mind*, Mary Field Belenky, Blythe Clinchy, Nancy Goldberger, and Jill Tarule (New York: Basic, 1986), and *Teaching Writing:*

Pedagogy, Gender, and Equity, ed. Cynthia L. Caywood and Gilligan R. Overing (New York: State U of New York P, 1987).

5. Women's bonding and caretaking faculties are the result of social expectations imposed on us during our years of subject formation. Those few who escape are either male-identified or radicalized. The majority of women remain locked into female-identified, "womanly" roles unvalued by our profession and unrewarded in the classroom or department.

6. Julia Kristeva, *The Kristeva Reader,* ed. Toril Moi (New York: Columbia University Press, 1986), p. 295.

7. The value of such awareness is that it combines women's sense of community with the masculine sense of self grounded by community for a more comprehensive perception of social functioning.

Telling Tales in School:
A Redneck Daughter in the Academy

M Y FATHER didn't write to me often. Just by looking at his hand-writing, with its heavy touch and too large letters, you could tell that he was impatient with a medium that couldn't keep pace with his thoughts, frustrated that his thoughts didn't come out exactly as he was thinking them. I guess it's because his letters were so rare that I saved one of them, written while I was a college student away from home for the first time and not happy about the experience. "Honey, there will always be things that make us disgusted with everything but remember normally its only just one thing that does this," he wrote. "We have to have enough faith in ourselves to overcome the things which make us unhappy. Belief in our own lives is absolutely a necessity." And then he stopped himself. "Enough of that." He ended the letter with a little story of an ice storm that had canceled a church meeting he and Mama were supposed to attend and his laughing "suspicion" that she had "wanted to stand me up anyway."

Maybe another reason I saved this letter is because I don't ever remember Daddy philosophizing about life. Oh, he told stories like the one about the ice storm, and he applied the Bible pretty literally to his days (and to mine) and he was ready enough to jump into any political argument around, but direct talk of life to his daughter? Not hardly, as he would say. But writing this essay about the effect of my family background, as the child of a redneck farmer, on my academic career has made me speculate about what my father thought about life. Belief in our own lives is absolutely a necessity. I think in some ways that statement defines the word "redneck" for me. I realize that the definition is miles away from the Hollywood version of the southern farmer. Remember *Easy Rider* and the shotgun-toting idiots who gunned down Peter Fonda and Dennis Hopper? When V. S. Naipaul spent some time in his recent book on the South trying to describe the "mythical" redneck, he talked to a new-South Mississippian, who defined "redneck" for Naipaul with a list of defining traits that Hopper and Fonda would have agreed to. It's a list that much of the country, I suspect, believes to be accurate:

A redneck is a lower blue-collar construction worker who definitely doesn't like blacks. He likes to drink beer. He's going to wear cowboy boots; he is not necessarily going to have a cowboy hat. He is going to smoke about two and a half packs of cigarettes a day and drink about ten cans of beer at night, and he's going to be mad as hell if he doesn't have some cornbread and peas and fried okra and some fried pork chops to eat—I've never seen one of those bitches yet who doesn't like fried pork chops. And he'll be late on his trailer payment. (206)

When I began to teach in the Northeast, I discovered to my surprise that many people—even some enlightened academics who would staunchly fight the stereotyping of other minorities or "fringe" cultures in American society—pretty much accepted the stereotype of the southern redneck as racist, sexist, alcoholic, ignorant, and lazy. Some of them even told me southern jokes (redneck jokes may be the last acceptable ethnic slurs in "polite" society). I understood that few had come into contact with any rural southerners; the academic community, especially in the Northeast, is seldom called on to respond to the redneck as a group. Yet the term "redneck" identifies a class group shaped by a strong oral and rural tradition and by a status of outsider in the hyperliterate world of academe. To the academic, the word carries only the negative connotations that Naipaul reported. But as he kept trying to get a fix on the term, Naipaul talked to an older southerner who told him that "when he was a child, the word redneck 'was not a pejorative; was the opposite, in fact, and meant a man who lived by the sweat of his brow'" (208). The redneck was defined by his work on the land, the sun beating on his back and burning his neck day after day as he tended his field. This redneck was not a hard drinker who ate greasy food, parked refrigerators in his front yard and moved from trailer to trailer to escape his debts, but a decent farmer who worked hard and who loved the land he worked even when, as was nearly always the case, it was not his to love. The more antique meaning of the word describes the kind of redneck my father was. I guess he was not a true redneck at that; he had not lived on the farm since he married, served in the army, took a job with TWA, and moved north to Louisville, Kentucky. But he was never far from the farm in his mind. We went back to Northern Florida every summer to visit the relatives, and when I was twelve, my father, two of his brothers, and one sister bought the 350 acres just south of the Okefenokee swamp where their father had tenant farmed with his thirteen children during the twenties and thirties. I can see him as I write this, back against the blue Suwannee sky, the two of us riding in the tobacco sled that hitched to the tractor my Uncle Joe was maneuvering through the corn rows—talking about the land. The story I want to tell here is the story of the redneck I know, the working-class farmer, and what I've learned about the ways the redneck managed to believe in his life (it's hard to think of redneck females, though of course that's just another part of the stereotype), which has, willingly or not, become part of my persona as a teacher and a writer.

The story I'm telling is about the rural and oral tradition that defines the redneck's life. Of course, narrative is deeply embedded in all human communication, not just the rural southerner's. Much of the content of our language—our gossip and our memories, the ways we remind, scold, cajole, seduce—takes the form of stories, with the stories woven so tightly into the fabric of the conversation that we hardly ever examine the threads of narrative. "Stories infuse and inform our lives to such an extent that we generally take them for granted, because they are simply there like the air we breathe," Geoffrey and Judith Summerfield tell us as they talk about the usefulness of narrative to the teaching of composition (101). In my father's backwoods community, the story was often just what the Summerfields indicate it to be, an uncrafted or even unconscious strategy to make sense of experiences and events of the day. Uncle Joe might be telling Daddy that they needed some new fence posts, and he'd lead in by telling a story: "You know what that mama sow did today? Hauled off and knocked down the blamed fence again. Remember that old brindle sow Pa had in Lake Wales? She was exactly like this one. I'd put it to a judge that she was a direct descendant." Or Uncle Cecil would be arguing a point about government at dinner and tell a story about the better past: "Before the Corps of Engineers got hold of all the blamed land in this country and started *digging ditches* every blamed where you could get enough water for your corn of a summer. When we worked this land in thirty-five, was it? When old Joe Costy lived over there next to Ponce? There was water standing in the field after a rain. Why one night Dan and Jesse and all Ponce's brothers and sisters got out between the rows and jumped in the puddles like they were at Ocean Pond. It was that deep."

But in the farm country in North Florida, country that was disappearing even when my father was a young boy and was threatened with extinction by the time I was a teenager, narratives were much more than unconscious reflexes or offhand anecdotes. These stories served another purpose: they were deliberate parables, tales told with implicit but nonetheless clear messages about the way to live life. "Tell about the South," Shreve McCannon says to Quentin Compson in Faulkner's *Absalom, Absalom!* "What's it like there. What do they do there. Why do they live there. Why do they live at all." The stories the redneck told answered Shreve: they explained his life. And they were passed along to the young, who learned the messages that preserved the past by making it a part of the present. Without any straightforward moral code to complete them, the stories told by the people in my father's family subtly taught values and ideals, strategies and subterfuges. Of all the things I have learned from being the child of a redneck farmer, the most useful and important to me has been this emphasis on the story as a tool for teaching.

I think the intimate connection between narrative and religion is one reason that the story is so much a part of the rural southerner's way of explaining "what it's like there" and why they live. One part of the redneck stereotype is close to truth: religion is important in the rural South; in the small fundamentalist churches that hug the sandy roadsides in redneck country religion is personal, and that means that the preacher knows how to tell a story. Suzanne Langer explains this connection between the story and the church in her introduction to *Mind: An Essay on Human Feeling:*

Religious thought. . . . operates primarily with images, by the long-sanctioned "principle of analogy." Images originally made us aware of the wholeness and over-all form of entities, acts and facts in the world and little though we may know it, only an image can hold us to a conception of a total phenomenon, against which we can measure. . . . (xii)

It's this connection between image and idea that Geneva Smitherman picks up as she characterizes black English in *Talkin' and Testifyin'.* She is defining "sacred speech" of the black preacher when she describes the importance of image-making to black English. "The figures of speech created in black linguistic imagery tend to be earthy, gutsy and rooted in plain everyday reality," she says (92). And, as Smitherman shows, that explains their power for listeners in the churches. When Rev. Jesse Jackson told the story at the Democratic National Convention of his grandmother's patching material to make a quilt of "power and beauty and culture" he was using both the image and the story to teach a lesson, one that he made quite explicit in the speech: "America's not a blanket woven from one thread, one color, one cloth. When I was a child growing up in Greenville, S.C., and grandmother could not afford a blanket, she didn't complain and we did not freeze . . . don't despair. Be as wise as my grandmama. Pool the patches and the pieces together, bound by a common thread. When we form a great quilt of unity and common ground we'll have the power to bring about health care and housing and jobs and education and hope to our nation" (651). Jesse Jackson combined his own story with those of his listeners and then encouraged change based on the applications the audience derived from both stories, his and theirs. Jackson, like the good rural southern preacher he is, teaches the universals by telling stories: the congregation believes in universals because they grasp them personally, actively connecting the tales to truths. I remember lots of times sitting at Sunday dinner while Daddy and the family talked over the sermon we all had just heard. Their discussion of the preacher's rhetoric and lesson always centered on application, on making the general personal. If the preacher hadn't given them enough images to hang on to, they created them for themselves. As a redneck farmer or the child of one, all the stories you told and heard, of quilts or tractors or bright leaf tobacco, in church and on the porch, established who you were by making your small world part of a larger scheme, and that allowed you to find power and worth in the life you lived.

The stories my father told my sister and me were stories of his background that set him in a context he lived only partially but remembered fully. He was the only child of the thirteen to have left Florida, and so when he went home the stories he told established once again common ground between him and his siblings, between him and his environment. And his stories pulled me into the background so clearly it seemed almost as though I were remembering with him as he talked. One of the stories I remember best was told by many members of the family, female as well as male, but often begun by my father, whose high-pitched laugh usually signaled the story's beginning. Typically, the story started with the kind of call-and-response opening that Smitherman defines as a characteristic element of black English dialogue, where the teller or leader or teacher asks a question to elicit an answer the group already knows (216). A group would be sitting on the porch and some topic would come up—the government maybe or how overgrown the path leading to the river had gotten—and somebody would start to chuckle. This was the call. Then Uncle Joe or another would respond to the laugh: "Well, I guess we better call in Redmond to consult about those palmettos. He knows more about them than anybody else wouldn't you say?" Aunt Fanny might add "I'd say he has intimate knowledge." And then the story of Redmond, my aunt Gertrude's handsome bootlegger son, would begin. Redmond had been notoriously good at eluding the law by never letting them get close to his operation. One day, however, they nearly caught him, and Redmond arrived at the farm with the revenuers in hot pursuit. He escaped by running them ragged through all the fields and tangled swamps on the farm, and his panicky delight at the chase became a family legend.

"He ran through the house like the Lord himself and when he got to the kitchen stopped to say hello just like he had no place he was hurrying to get to. 'Hello, Aunt LulaMae. Am I invited to dinner this afternoon?' he said. I said how you doing, Redmond? and he laughed 'just like the pudding, ma'am. My-T-Fine.'"

"And then he grabbed a biscuit, didn't he, Aunt Lulamae?" I would add. Everybody was invited to put in a line.

"Yes he sure did. But only after he asked. No time for fig preserves though. And then he lit off through the corn so fast you couldn't even hear its ripple. But they would have gotten him anyway if it hadn't been for those palmettos. He got hunkered way back down in a patch of them, and they got so lost in all that grown-up mess they couldn't follow him—and didn't want to follow him if they could. Their skin's a tad delicate, those boys. You could hear them holler all the way back here every time one of them palmettos hit a little too close to home. But not Redmond. He hid in that swamp till they just gave up and came sloping back up the road, sweaty and all bitten up and mad as Mama's rooster. Still, he repented later, didn't he? When he got home and found his own mama waiting for him on the porch. She told him she intended to hurt him worse than any revenuers the state of Florida might provide."

Lounging on the front steps of the porch, our feet rubbing the worn gray boards, my sister and I listened to the adults, and we learned the message of the story without having been told it, something about family and the land and the power of wit. I've heard nine or ten people

297

tell this story over the years, and each time it's a little different, varying with the teller and with the audience. The language changed to accommodate the varying rhetorical situation; who happened to be the primary teller, who was listening, how close to supper it was. The syntax shifted as details got suppressed or added. If a visitor was there who had never heard the story, the climax was heightened: there might be physical descriptions of Redmond and his pursuers or maybe some background on Redmond's wild behavior as a little boy to lead up to the final chase. Sometimes we heard the aftermath of Redmond's promise to reform, and Aunt Gertrude's methods for checking on the progress of the reformation.

Redmond's story, and all the others my father's family told, made me unconsciously aware of the way language shapes and controls meaning. The stories let me, in other words, comprehend the "metalinguistics" of the language. My father would have hooted at the word "metalinguistic," and I have to admit to being uncomfortable with writing it myself—it's another of the things I learned from him, to watch out for words that people don't generally use when they're sitting on a porch. But metalinguistic it is, a clear sense of language as language that's necessary to a writer and to a teacher of writers.

A "metalinguistics" involves an ability to connect words and images, to see images as analogues for experience. In *Mind*, Langer argues that there is value in images apart from their use in religion or emotion: "only an image can hold us to a conception of a total phenomenon against which we can measure the adequacy of the scientific terms wherewith we describe it" (xii). Langer suggests that theorists are "suffering from the lack of suitable images today," particularly in quickly developing disciplines like biology and psychology and that this lack blocks the development of systematic thought. I think we lack a metalinguistics in the developing discipline of composition, the connections through images that would give us a holistic theory about what reading and writing contribute to the way we know. We've got terms for such a theory, too many of them, but not enough images, and, as Langer indicates, that lack limits our ability to create philosophy. As a brand new assistant professor, I wasn't consciously aware of what I now see as the need to create images for the ideas we explore in our discussions of reading and writing, but unconsciously I was guided by that belief, or maybe it was by the lessons on the front porch in Florida. The first article I sent out for publication tried to use the power of the story to make a connection between my experience and the need to make writing-across-the-curriculum a theory as well as an administrative program in English departments. Its opening was a little story of a conversation with a history professor on the train about the difficulties with writing-intensive courses. Our talk had laid out what I thought were the salient issues English departments had to take seriously if we were ever to make cross-curricular writing programs sustainable. I thought readers would make their own connections between image and theory. But like Bogart in *Casablanca* I was misinformed. "Must we have these 'a funny thing happened-to-me-on-the-way-to-the-cocktail-party' openings?" the reviewer wrote in what seemed to me at the time to be the most condescending tone of voice I had ever heard on a page. I was effectively chastened for using the narrative in the way I had done, and for a long time afterward I didn't use it much, or if I did, I hid it in the middle where it would not distract the academic reader who expected to see the clear thesis-and-support document that her training had prepared her to read and to write herself.

As academic writers we don't tell stories much, and my experience with the reviewer is pretty clear evidence of why. But even in the classroom, where the communication is overt and direct with no middle person reviewing the connection between speaker and hearer, I don't think we tell stories. Maybe it's that we don't trust the power of analogy or symbol to provoke conceptual thinking, or maybe we don't trust the interest or ability of students to make connections between story and generalization. Maybe we fear being personal, even if the story is not ours but someone else's or conjured at the moment, feeling that story-telling is something apart from the real business of the class which, we tell ourselves, is to help students master a body of information or a group of skills. But the traditional academic approach, which categorizes, generalizes, abstracts, is not always, or even usually, the most effective method to teach students who increasingly come into the classroom from communities apart from the mainstream. In many cultures on the margin of white male middle-class America, the personal and the narrative are the ways to come to know. Like some of these other cultures, the redneck teaches the way the fiction writer does, by making the story so good that the "thesis" is laid bare by its very telling.

My students in the northeastern institution where I taught were always surprised, and somewhat disconcerted, by my storytelling. They weren't used to the southern redneck sensibility that regarded the story as method, and I'm afraid they often thought of the stories at the beginning of a semester's work as simply time out or time wasted. Geoffrey and Judith Summerfield argue that teachers have used narrative only as a kind of lead-in writing assignment that gets quickly abandoned in favor of more analytical tasks. "[But] a composition is a story, a construct," they explain, and linking what students know about narrative to what they do in writing creates more powerful interpreters. The Summerfields suggest finding ways to tap into students' unconscious familiarity with plot and character, with symbol and foreshadowing in assignments and in responses to students' writing. But what my background has taught me about the narrative is more profound than my simply making room for it in the assignments I give in English classes, though that's crucial. The stories I tell are the real teaching tools because the stories become analogues for the way a writer writes, the way a learner learns, the way a student becomes a teacher of herself. I've begun to believe that learning by analogue might be the best way to learn, and I'd like more teachers to risk telling stories to teach. The story makes what goes on in the classroom personal. I believe it goes far toward creating the scene where knowledge can get made.

Sometimes I tell stories about other students or other writers; every once in a while I tell a nice made-up story about Hawthorne meeting Trollope and talking about composition. I tell a good story about my son Nick and his writing in school, where he was required to write 250 words and stopped in the middle of a sentence, to make a point to freshman students or to student teachers that creativity can get stifled or lost when writing becomes nothing more than filling in the blanks. I usually don't tell what the stories mean. I invite students to decide meaning and significance, and I encourage them to connect the stories to concepts they're learning and to other stories they're hearing. I invite them to tell me stories too, in writing and discussion, about school, about their own communities, about what they felt when they were reading some text. I believe that's how learning happens in my classes. The story is my most effective way of creating active learners who make the connections, as well as my most effective way of reminding learners of who they are.

As I've suggested, the story is a powerful tool to help rural southerners—rednecks—preserve who they are, to believe in their own lives. And it's important to remind yourself of who you are if, like rednecks set apart from a culture that vilifies them or like students adrift in an academic culture that ignores them or like new members of that academic community only tentatively accepted by a culture that certifies them, you feel threatened or powerless. As I think about the stories that got told over the years by Daddy and his family, I realize that a lot of them were rather defiant stories, with messages about preserving yourself in the face of danger or trial. I remember some poignant and funny Great Depression stories and a few Civil War stories and many stories of the gamble of the harvest. From the women, I remember stories of confronting ghosts under the live oak tree (which I'm tempted to tell now but will resist). Holding your own against the odds, that's what a lot of them were about. The odds, of course, were then as now almost always stacked against the small farmer, and the group doing the stacking was usually the government in some form or another. That's the reason the redneck maintains a tradition of suspicion of the outsider, especially the institution of government in whatever form—TVA, Corps of Engineers, subsidy agents, or revenuers—it might take. Just about everybody who told the Redmond and the revenuers story, for example, was a nondrinker who disapproved mightily of Redmond's line of work. But each of them loved his ability to put one over on the institution.

The defiance of the redneck to the strictures of government comes out of a suspicion that the power the institution wields is not at all just what the farmer has ceded to it. The small southern farmer exists on the fringe of progressive American culture, "the poor, defeated, guilt-ridden member of a prosperous victorious and successful family," as Fred Hobson describes it in his book on southern narrative (3). Power has been stripped from the southerner, especially the rural farmer, and more than other Americans, Hobson argues, the southerner "has felt he had something to explain, to justify, to defend or to affirm" (3). The explanation often takes the form of a defense against the powerful Other of the in-group, represented by a northeastern sensibility that has placed the redneck so far at the edge of American culture. So the redneck affirms a place in the culture by undercutting the institution responsible for his own powerlessness. My own reaction to the institutions in my profession—tenure, evaluation, the forms of academic discourse—has developed in part from my comprehending my father's profound distrust of institutions that saw him as no more than the stereotype that mocked him. One reason Paulo Freire's work on literacy is so appealing to me is that like the farmer Freire looks critically at institutions and exhorts those he teaches—often farmers themselves—to do the same. "Conscientizao," Freire's term for critical understanding of self in society, is something my redneck background taught me to hold in great esteem. As Freire argues, when one looks in this critical way at institutions one becomes the doer rather than the "done to." To question institutions in the way my background has taught me to do is to challenge a larger culture that is often uncaring and sometimes downright hostile.

I realize now that the stories I heard about institutions constituted what Linda Brodkey calls a rhetoric of resistance, a way of fighting from the margins the powerless positions in which the small farmers in redneck country felt themselves placed. Brodkey defines this rhetoric by saying that those who are ambivalent or threatened by their subject positions in a given discourse interrupt "the very notion of the unified self. . . . in their spoken and written texts" by representing "a stereotype as an agent in a discourse the least committed to the preservation of the stereotype" (127). According to Brodkey, these rhetorics of resistance not only shift subject positions but lend support to postmodernist speculation that language and discourse materially construct reality, not simply reflect it. "Knowledge of multiple subject positions makes possible both the practical and the theoretical critiques that interrupt the assumption of unchanging, irreversible, and asymmetrical social and political relations between the privileged and unprivileged subjects represented in a particular discourse," Brodkey says (128). Now my father would have had trouble with that sentence, regarding it with the same cocked eyebrow that he would have heard "metalinguistic." But I think Brodkey is making an essential point that Daddy would agree with: knowing who you are in the society. The stories of bravery, persistence, humility, and humor I heard confronted and denied the stereotypical version of the redneck farmer. For the small farmer, fighting the institution through stories and tales was a way of seizing control, of refusing to be muted or silenced by outside power.

I try to take this institutional awareness into the classroom, to teach my students to be actors in their own learning. It's more than simply making them active, rather than passive, learners. Through close

inquiry and self-examination of their strategies in writing and communicating in groups, students come to know the political dimensions of
the forms they choose to write in, of the words they use as well as the
sources they cite, of the metaphors—consumer, artist, soldier—they apply to their own education. I want students to believe in institutions and
fight them at the same time. I want them to have my father's cocked
eyebrow, the redneck's suspicion and belief. In this way I know they
won't lose their own voices.

Hearing your own voice is another way of saying believe in your
own life. You hear your voice in the stories you tell, in your consciousness of the effect of institutions on your group. But until recently I
thought that hearing your own voice put you in direct conflict with the
part of my rural redneck background I feel the most ambivalent about
because it may be the most ingrained in me, and that is knowing how to
behave. Naipaul found in his sojourn in the South what he considered
an almost neurotic emphasis in the rural southerner on codes of behavior, on being polite. "That had been the great discovery of my travels
so far in the South. In no other part of the world had I found people so
driven by the idea of good behavior and the good religious life. And that
was true for black and white" (164).

The movie version of the redneck, the engine-gunning loudmouth
cracker whose primary characteristic besides racism is rudeness, is far
from the reality I knew. My family were quiet because they knew how to
behave. To outsiders, to representatives of institutions, even or maybe
especially to those you disliked, you nodded and talked calmly, asked
them if they'd like to sit if they came to your house. In *White Trash
Cooking*, before he gives recipes for potato chip sandwiches and rain-
bow icebox pie, Ernest Mickler lays out some of the values of the community he grew up in: "But where I come from in North Florida you
never failed to say 'yes ma'am' and 'no sir,' never sat on a made-up bed,
or put your hat on it, never opened someone else's icebox, never left
food on your plate, never left the table without permission, and never
forgot to say 'thank you' for the teeniest favor. That's the way the ones
before us were raised and that's the way they raised us in the South" (1).
Mickler grew up in the same area as my father did, and I expect his
people were very much like mine. With one difference: the people in my
father's family would never have called themselves white trash precisely
because they knew how to behave. We knew of course that you didn't go

303

into somebody's kitchen without being asked, that you were courteous to salespeople and neighbors, that when a guest was in your house you went out of your way to make her comfortable, encouraging her to stay to dinner, and arguing only good-naturedly (and then only if you knew her well enough) with her opinions no matter how wrongheaded you thought they were. In short, being polite was another way of showing who you were and that you had been brought up right.

I used to think there was some duplicity about that quiet politeness, that getting-by mode, not at all coincidentally like blacks who got by in the white man's oppressive world by "knowing how to behave" to keep from provoking any kind of reprisal. For me, knowing how to behave has often been helpful, if duplicitous. It's helped give me access to an academic world that was far from my experience. (I do remember having to fight the impulse to call my first department chairperson, a fine scholar who was to retire at the end of the year, "ma'am".) Knowing how to behave has meant that I can follow the path to tenure and promotion because I can be quiet, not open other people's iceboxes. And in my teaching too, knowing how to behave has some advantages: I know about codes, registers, and I can teach appropriateness in writing.

I begin to realize, however, that my knowing how to behave is different from the redneck's. Rural southerners know when to get angry and when not to show it because their sense of self is clear, and behaving becomes a way of asserting a position. But the farther you drift from the community where similar values are nurtured, the harder it is to maintain that sense of self, the harder it is to make politeness be a political statement. I worry about behaving too well in an academic environment whose codes are not like my own. Maybe I am quiet when I should speak; maybe I am taken advantage of for being genial. I have a hard time saying no even to requests that interfere with work I know needs first attention. This inability to be thought impolite may be a female problem in general; it's just magnified for a woman who has been raised to believe that it's a flaw to "show yourself," the redneck term for thinking so highly of yourself that you might cause others inconvenience. Far from my own southern community and the values I learned from my father's rural background, I worry that behaving costs too much. My reaction to the rejection of narrative in my academic essay, for example, was me behaving in spite of myself. And even in teaching, where my serious attempt to provoke students' imaginations made me believe that I called into question "good behavior" of predetermined forms and predigested information, I realize that I often unconsciously have encouraged my students to act "right" instead of act up.

Jeffrey was a student in my freshman composition class, and on the first day of class a few semesters ago he responded to an in-class writing in which I had asked students to write about "what's important to you on the first day of class." I had expected the assignment to let me know something about the group mind that semester, to tell me something about writing abilities, to give me a hinge for the beginning discussion in the class to follow. I know now that I expected my students to behave and replay the assignment as I envisioned it, and as I was certain they all could do. Jeffrey didn't behave.

What is important to me on Sept. 6, 1987. What an interesting question, one that I feel lacks an answer. I mean I have plans and goals but at this exact moment they don't seem extremely important. I am having real difficulty in writing this essay. I guess it has to do with the fact that I am very personal and find it hard to write about my own experiences. When I discuss this with my peers they tell me to make something up. I've tried this and have always felt that something was lacking in my paper, personality. I know that I have a lot that I would like to say and share but it never seems to deal with my own experiences. What a dumb way to start off the semester, I can't even do the first exercise right.

I apologize to you for not writing what you asked, but again I must emphasize that I don't know what to write. If I think about something that is important by the time I'm done with the paper it may no longer be important.

Jeffrey's response—his rhetoric of resistance—made me see suddenly that my assignments and my expectations prescribed my students' behavior in quite constricting ways. After I read his paper, I wrote a comment on it that said in part, "Maybe one thing you'll discover this term is that you write from your experience or from your observing without giving too much of yourself away. Your writing here is so fluent; that often happens when you write about something that is important to you." One reason I remember so well what I wrote is that I still have the paper. Jeffrey never came back to class, and so I never got to show him that all his assignments wouldn't invade him or force him to behave in the way this first one had seemed to do. Jeffrey was challenging the expected relationships between himself and his audience and his subject when he wrote to me, placing himself as an actor in the classroom plot. I wish I had been able to show him that I valued that.

If you and I were sitting on the front porch in White Springs, Florida, I wouldn't have told you nearly this much. I would have talked about my father and then the two stories of my career might have come up—the one of my failed writing strategy and the one of my failed teaching strategy, and you would have connected all of it as you wished. You might have put the stories together with what I've told you about my father's values and how I've carried them with me. But the important thing would be that you'd find your own ways to apply it all, or any part of it you wanted to keep, to yourself. Still, I know this is more of an academic essay than a story on the porch. So it should have a real conclusion.

A woman, a compositionist, a southerner, a farmer's daughter—I have known myself to be on the edges of academic respectability, and that fact has worried me. When I began this essay I didn't know what I would end up thinking about the significance of my own background to my career except that it put me there, on the fringe. But I know more clearly now how deeply embedded my father's values are in my character as a writer and a teacher. And writing this essay, remembering the ways my father believed in his life, has made me begin to believe that there are some good things about being southern and female and the daughter of a redneck small farmer, that being on the fringe can help me write and teach in a way so that others on some fringe—students, basic writers, high school teachers—can learn to write rhetorics of resistance of their own. All those stories of the farm and the farmer must have done their work over the years. I never really have strayed very far from the porch. And at the risk of sounding too much like my renegade cousin Redmond, maybe that's like the pudding. My-T-Fine.

Works Cited

Brodkey, Linda. "On the Subjects of Class and Gender in 'The Literacy Letters.'" *College English* 51 (1989): 125–41.

Freire, Paulo. *Pedagogy of the Oppressed*. New York: Herder, 1970.

Hobson, Fred. *Tell about the South: The Southern Rage to Explain*. Baton Rouge: LSUP, 1983.

306

Jackson, Jesse. "Common Sense and Common Ground." *Vital Speeches of the Day*, September 1988: 643–54.

Langer, Suzanne. *Mind: An Essay on Human Feeling*. Baltimore: Johns Hopkins UP, 1988.

Mickler, Ernest. *White Trash Cooking*. Berkeley: Ten Speed Press, 1986.

Naipaul, V. S. *A Turn in the South*. New York: Knopf, 1989.

Smitherman, Geneva. *Talkin' and Testifyin': The Language of Black America*. Boston: Houghton, 1977.

Summerfield, Geoffrey, and Judith Summerfield. *Texts and Contexts: A Contribution to the Theory and Practice of Teaching Composition*. New York: Random, 1986.

Epilogue

By the Rivers of Babylon

I BEGAN working on this anthology at about the same time I arranged to have a maid clean my apartment every other week, and I was particularly conscious of the irony that having a maid was giving me the time to reflect on the meaning of working-class origins. I was also particularly conscious of the maid's Jamaican lilt, an accent that I had come to love during my vacation in Jamaica. Upon returning home from there, I nostalgically looked through my records for reggae music, and found the only reggae I own, Jimmy Cliff's, "The Harder They Come." I had not listened to this album in years, and my mind went back to the time when I played it frequently, at age twenty-four. One of my favorite songs, "By the Rivers of Babylon," I'd listened to over and over again:

> By the rivers of Babylon
> There we sat down
> And there we wept
> When we remembered Zion.
>
> But the wicked carried us away, captivity
> Required from us a song
> How can we sing King — a song
> In a strange land.

At the time I was listening to this song I had stopped attending graduate school at Stony Brook full time because I had run out of money. I was working at odd clerical and factory jobs, trying to complete my master's at night and contemplating going on for the doctorate. Aspiring to be an academic while working in the kinds of lower-level jobs my parents had held made me feel extremely odd. But years later I learned my situation was not so unique. In informal discussions and correspondence about this anthology, many women academics from the working class have indicated that at some point in their journey they returned to working-class jobs—either from economic necessity or from a profound sense of displacement. Displacement is a recurring theme in conversations among working-class academics. I once told Valerie Miner that I didn't feel I belonged to either the working class or the academic world; she stated (correctly, I believe) I never would fit into either. My response as an academic is often to deal with personal conflicts intellectually. I theorize that there could be constructions of class that would be less wrenching, that would incorporate class of origin as well as the class to which one migrates. Yet I am aware that such theorizing itself comes out of the intensely painful experience of feeling pulled between worlds, between my working-class and academic status, between a future of some economic security and memories of continual poverty and—very specific to me—between my secure status as a woman married to a successful vice president in a corporation and my insecure status as a faculty member who for years worked in temporary appointments.

The one pervasive metaphor, suggested by the reggae song I quoted, that comes to me is the metaphor of exile, homelessness. It is the sense of being uprooted, of being wrenched from the world of one's parents and siblings, with only a tenuous possibility of ever putting down new roots. It is a sense that shows itself every day in my inability to convey the realities of academic life to my parents or my working-class friends. To them, I've achieved something; I've made it. I have a Ph.D. and teach in colleges and universities. I, in contrast, realize my vulnerability as a nontenured faculty member, a person who spent her first years after she received a Ph.D. in non-tenure-track positions with little status or security. This kind of employment is, of course, common for many recent Ph.D.s in the humanities. Young doctorates of my generation have been expected to string together a series of one-year or, if they're lucky, as I was, three-year terminal appointments, teach four courses a day and write all night to qualify for a tenure-track job. I did it. So did most of those who didn't get discouraged enough to find alternative careers. But for women from the working class, the chances of getting out of this rut are far fewer. Women from working-class backgrounds are more likely to have degrees from state schools (as I do), and thus at many prestigious institutions they do not make the first cut of candidates. They often have to work through graduate school, work through the summers when they get their first teaching jobs, and thus have less time for the crucial writing, the crucial publishing that will indeed keep them from perishing. Perhaps most problematic, working-class women have a set of values that is often in conflict with the academy's values.

But I'm generalizing too much. My sense of these problems comes from my own life and the lives of women I know well (as well as from my reading in Marxist and feminist theory). My experience is in many ways typical of working-class women. Even some circumstances that are specific to me, I think, nonetheless highlight the unique marginality of working-class women in the academic world.

To begin with my childhood: my father was different from many working-class men in that he was an avid reader of the classics. As a child I loved literature, and many people assumed I would teach it at the high school level. However, I was apprehensive about finding work, and in 1971 the prospects for teachers at any level were dismal. At the time, social work was considered a good field, and I wanted the work I did to be socially relevant. So when I entered one of New York City University's colleges (which then charged no tuition) I planned to major in sociology and go for an MSW. One day as I walked to the library I had what I can describe only as an epiphany (I was a great admirer of James Joyce). What I actually wanted to do, I realized, was to major in English and teach in a college. But at the back of my mind were my father's words "The Ph.D. is a really big deal." At the front of my mind were my dismal job prospects. I hedged, majoring in English and minoring in sociology. Finally, I decided I would go to graduate school in English, but applied to as many terminal masters' as Ph.D. programs. I never even told my friends (much less my family) my real goal—to teach in a college or a university. Perhaps, I said, I would teach in a community college, or get my education certification and teach in high schools.

As an undergraduate at Lehman College, I never thought about class; most of my friends were also from working-class families. But going on to graduate school was different, I sensed. In my application essay to Columbia, my first words were "I was born in New York to working-class parents." When I began my master's work at SUNY, Stony Brook (with the hope of later applying to the Ph.D. program), I felt arrogant for assuming I could pursue graduate work and very uncertain of my abilities. No one I'd grown up with was getting an advanced degree, and the other students in this program seemed to come from solidly bourgeois backgrounds. I was so obviously intimidated that

313

one of my teachers told me I behaved as though Stony Brook were an Ivy League school. I might have been better able to deal with my emotions if I had not been under a severe financial strain. Since I was not in a Ph.D. program, I could not get a teaching assistantship; I had to rely on work study, a system not designed for either graduate students or students with no other source of income. I was required to take twelve credits a semester (four courses) while working fifteen hours a week. My salary was forty-six dollars a week. I could keep up with neither the course work nor my bills. And I found few supports for students in my situation. It was an unexpectedly cold winter and my fuel bills were astoundingly high. In February I realized I wouldn't have enough money for March's rent. Frantically, I went from one university office to another trying to arrange for a loan. One administrator asked me "Couldn't you just ask someone for the money?" Saying no, I felt at a loss to explain that I didn't know people who could lend that much money. And I wanted to say more than that, to indicate that his very question was rooted in privilege and served to exclude people like me. It seemed this administrator had never met someone from a working-class family and had no idea of how to deal with me. When I left his office, I felt as though I wasn't supposed to be in graduate school.

Unable to deal with the financial pressures, I left Stony Brook at the end of the year to finish my master's part time. It wasn't easy to find work, so I scraped together a living from a variety of temporary jobs. I made so little I received food stamps. After a city-wide blackout in this summer of 1977, I lived in constant fear that I would lose the food in my refrigerator during another power outage and would not be able to get additional food stamps from social services. Once the food stamps came late. Two days after they were due they still weren't in the mailbox. I did have food in the house, but not much, and I was terrified at the prospect of not having any. In a panic I tried to make an emergency call to social services. No one could give me any indication if I could be helped the following day, if I had any recourse if my stamps didn't come. My logical questions quickly gave way to screams and tears. Finally, I threw the receiver against the wall.

Desperate for a steady income, I took a quasi-permanent job in the garment district. I got a half hour for lunch, one hundred dollars a week take home (except for weeks when I paid health insurance, when I took home seventy-five). There was no talking allowed; you had to get permission to go to the bathroom, and you were questioned if you were in there for longer than ten minutes. This was my closest experience to working in a sweatshop, but the real sweatshop workers weren't "college girls" in the bookkeeping office. They were foreigners (some, I suspect, illegal aliens) who had little sense of how they should be treated in America and less power to demand decent conditions.

Eventually, my life turned around. I found a reasonable job. I fell in love and got married. Two years after having left Stony Brook, I applied to and was accepted into the Ph.D. program there. A few years later, I received my degree. In a sense, I'd made it, achieved a dream. However, I have never forgotten the poverty and the humiliation I endured. As I walk down the streets of New York, I constantly look at the homeless lining the sidewalks. Part of me thinks I could have been there. At such times I wonder about their, and my own, relationship to a society that considered us disposable. A few months ago I was invited to deliver a paper at a conference in Hungary. Many participants queried me about my obviously Slavic last name and wondered if I had any knowledge of Ukrainian. When I explained that it was difficult for my grandparents to pass down the language because they were illiterate, people at the conference were astounded. I was, one of them responded, an example of American upward mobility. Yes, in a way, I answered. But I never want to be viewed (although I realize I may be) as a symbol of American success. I know the price of that success. And I don't trust it.

Recently I spoke with a British academic from a working-class background. Most of us know that the British have a much keener sense of class consciousness than we Americans do, and this particular woman contrasted her attitude toward upward mobility with that of her working-class American husband. Her husband looked at his change in class status with pride and a sense of personal accomplishment. She, in contrast, believed that if she or her husband had experienced a change in class status, it was because their "mobility" served the interests of the larger society. Society is very fickle. It may be that many of us tell ourselves our talents have brought us success because we cannot face the implications of living in and being complicit in a society that had once been brutally indifferent to us.

Those of us who have been told our skills are unnecessary and superfluous, retain, I think, a strong sense of being treated as commodities, always on the verge of being disposed of. We yearn for a sense of security and rootedness; hence, the word "tenure," to those of us who have spent time in temporary positions, connotes a rootedness, almost a sense of family.

It is not surprising that women especially should long so for home, since they have been trained to try to provide homes for others, and I suspect that many, like myself, try to offer one in academia. When I entered the doctoral program at SUNY Stony Brook, I already had some teaching experience and looked forward to plunging into my classes. I loved working with students and gave a great deal to them, tried to make them feel at home in my class and, indirectly, in the large, necessarily impersonal state university. If there was a choice between giving priority to my work and my teaching, I gave it to my teaching without question. I did not see myself as making sacrifices; I thought such dedicated teaching would boost my academic career. I had carried my female, working-class values into the academy and expected to be rewarded for nurturing others and serving my community. According to the academy's standards, I was doing the wrong things. When I think of this conflict of values I am reminded of an episode in Valerie Miner's *Murder in the English Department* in which the protagonist, Nan Weaver, an assistant professor of English with an excellent teaching reputation, expresses her apprehensions about coming up for tenure. Her working-class brother-in-law confidently asserts no one would dismiss such a hard worker. Similarly, one of my former professors at Stony Brook who is from a working-class family tirelessly serves on committees, directs numerous dissertations, and heads the job placement of new Ph.D.s in the English Department. Reportedly she was frustrated when yet another faculty member declined to be on a dissertation committee. "What do these people think they're getting paid for?" she angrily asked. Her question might be answered differently by different groups. Many academics would say that they are paid primarily to do research and add to the stature of their departments. Both the working class and women, however, more typically define work as that which benefits the community as well as the individual. In my teaching and my research I, like many working-class women, see myself as part of the community. And like many working-class women, I see myself as having a debt to pay back and a special understanding of the vulnerable (including students) who may need my help. When you've faced the prospect of being out in the streets, it's harder to walk past the people who are there. It's harder for us to lock ourselves in our studies and our libraries. And when we learn we must, as I have learned, we feel as much guilt as accomplishment. I have, I sometimes worry, "gotten ahead" because I have cut myself off from my family and friends. For the time being, I have closed off the possibility of any political or community involvement. I work for myself alone.

I have become this way because bitter experience has taught me the rules of academic survival. As I said earlier, I originally believed the hard work I put into teaching freshmen to write would count for a great deal. I was nominated for a teaching award. I felt optimistic. When I got my first job after receiving my Ph.D., it was a one-year appointment. Although in honesty the chair warned me that they might not be able to give me a tenure-track appointment, I was nonetheless hopeful. I taught business communications (they always needed someone to teach that course). I taught Western literature, a course that was not in my field and that required tremendous preparation. I joined the Composition Committee and helped devise questions for a proficiency exam that was essential to the department's writing program. When the chair told me they wouldn't be able to offer me a position for the following year, I was crushed. I felt used. As I analyze the situation, I realize I was viewed as a worker, someone like a domestic, brought in to perform tasks necessary for the family's maintenance, but never counted as part of the family. I had given extensive time to my students and to the department as a whole, and by doing so probably reinforced the department's assessment of me as one not suitable for a tenure-track appointment.

After leaving this university, I got another "worker" position (although this time I accepted it with full knowledge of my status) teaching composition and literature and administering the writing program at a major university. Before I arrived there, I had been warned by former faculty that because I was a non-tenure-track writing teacher, I would be looked down upon. Honestly, I did not find this to be the case. Most of the younger tenure-track faculty themselves had held similar positions. I never met many of the senior faculty, but those with whom I did interact were generally supportive. If this very large university was impersonal, it was also stimulating. Theorists and critics such as Jacques Derrida, Teresa de Lauretis, and Stanley Fish regularly came to speak. Their talks fueled many of my ideas, including some in this essay.

Yet I wondered (and wonder) about the university's priorities in setting aside large sums of money to bring in "superstar" speakers while many part-time lecturers are hired at subsistence-level salaries offering no security. The argument that could be made against bringing in such "stars" in some respects seems similar to arguments made against space exploration: we should spend our money bettering conditions at home rather than investigating new terrain. Such arguments always struck me as well-intentioned, but short sighted. The possible benefits of space exploration, of the potential discoveries, justify the expenditures. Likewise, a university must spend money on intellectual development, and all the faculty can benefit from hearing someone with a mind like Jacques Derrida's speak. But the discrepancy between what the superstars can demand and what the adjunct "workers" must endure nonetheless rankles. Perhaps it is disturbing because it underscores that academia is no ivory tower, as the cliché goes, but is a social institution complicit with the dominant society, a society that outrageously rewards superstars in many fields while ordinary people are exploited.

Readers may have sensed that I've moved away from my reaction to my own economic and professional insecurity. I've done so because my economic insecurity has been muted. Largely because of my husband's salary, I have been able to buy a Manhattan co-op, travel overseas, hire a maid—do many things someone making my salary would normally be unable to do. So a part of me feels I should not complain about academia at all. I am safe. Comparatively, so are many academics. There are people outside with real problems, people with no job prospects at all, people out in the streets with no homes. And perhaps I am complicit in their situation. Because people such as I can buy co-ops, housing for the working class is critically scarce. Yet if I were to refuse to buy a co-op, would that give one homeless person an apartment? I don't know. If Jacques Derrida were to refuse to speak in an institution that hired numerous part-time faculty, would that provide one adjunct with a full-time job? I don't know.

I, for one, am uncomfortable with the moral ambiguity of having owned property in a city filled with homeless. I've never had a desire to own property. On a gut level, the notion of sinking so much of one's savings (and borrowing so much) is unappealing. I like apartments; I was a happy renter. But the peculiarities of New York's housing made continued renting unfeasible. My husband and I, settled in a three-room, rent-stabilized apartment, desperately needed a fourth room for an office. We couldn't rent a four-room apartment for twice what we were paying. We'd get a tax break, we knew, if we bought a place. In short, economic realities pushed us into buying.

Universities too face economic realities. Professional organizations such as the Modern Language Association speak against the excessive use of part-time faculty. Many tenured and tenure-track faculty members I have known deplore the use of adjuncts as exploitative and unprofessional. To me, it often seems that if departments were forced to come up with the money to hire permanent faculty they would. But who are "they"? Department chairs, university deans, presidents, state legislators? Who is responsible? Sadly, I know that when I supervised adjuncts I regularly told them in December that I didn't know if we would hire them back the following semester. I would have liked to have treated my workers better—fairly. But I did not have the means. I thought it would do me or my workers little good to appeal to higher authorities. So I did not.

I don't know what the economic answers are, but just pondering them and related practical concerns is still troubling for me. As a working-class woman, I saw academia as a city on a hill. I gazed at it as the poor in E. L. Doctorow's *Ragtime* gazed into the ballrooms of the wealthy, trying to comprehend a world that would never be theirs. However tentatively, I have become a part of the academic world. I have achieved that dream and in the process of doing so have lost part of it. I am reminded of Bettelheim's analysis of the kibbutz mentality in *The Children of the Dream*. Kibbutz founders, Bettelheim believes, wanted Israel to be an ideal state and were indeed motivated to endure considerable hardship for the promise of this ideal state. Unfortunately, Bettelheim concludes, "the realities of the Middle East force Israel to be a garrison nation geared to defense, if not a war; a capitalist nation with many of the unpleasant features of a new nation trying to industrialize in a hurry." It may be a bit of a leap from the kibbutzim's vision of their nation and my vision of life in academe, but I believe the analogy holds. Now that the dream has been achieved, ugly political choices remain.

As a graduate student, I remained naively enraptured with the image of myself having a Ph.D. During the course of my advanced study someone told me I would never succeed in academia because I could not deal with the politics. Indeed, I was uninformed about how to play the academic game—how to work the conference circuit, network, hustle for jobs, promote your work. That ignorance has cost me years in temporary jobs. But I'm a good student. I observed what needed to be done and learned how to do it. I learned how to work long hours yet appear confident and relaxed the next day. I learned never to let my personal life interfere with my work. My learning has paid off. I published both poetry and criticism, got a number of interviews for tenure-track jobs, offers of tenure-track appointments, and now I actually look forward to the day when I will have tenure. As a student and a working-class survivor, I'm proud that I've been able (I think) to master academia's requisite skills. Yet I often feel tainted by the constant need to market myself and promote my work. Now I confront a political reality that seems antithetical to the epiphany of the nineteen-year-old girl who clutched her schoolbooks and envisioned getting a doctorate.

The vision had been replaced with concrete goals—a chance to do research and publish, to teach courses that interest me. I certainly feel privileged to have the opportunity my father never had—the chance to do the work I love. And I look forward to being a tenured, bona fide member of a department. As I said earlier, the word "tenure" evokes a sense of home for me, a sense I'm not altogether comfortable with. During a talk I heard last year, Teresa de Lauretis stated that women are often tempted to look at the feminist movement as a home, when perhaps they should be viewing it as a community. The latter construction, de Lauretis believed, would enable women to take more risks. Some of us in the audience, in later discussing her talk, worried that her analysis of home reflected a privileged position. Could, for example, the Chicana single mother, already at risk in our society, be faulted for viewing the women's movement as an alternative to her lost home? And, closer to our own "home," should those of us from the working class who have taken enormous risks in entering academia be criticized—or criticize ourselves—for trying to compensate for the security we have lost? We have abandoned the dreams our parents had for us—dreams of civil servants, homemakers, high school teachers, perhaps even of highly paid professionals. We inhabit a limbo where neither the working-class nor academics from the middle or upper classes understand us. Don't we need some security?

Yet as I write, my words seem to smack of nostalgia, a refusal to let go of a dream necessarily less ideal in being realized. Perhaps it is my construction of that dream, that home, which is creating problems for me. Perhaps it implies a stability that is too rigid to accommodate the complexities of class crossing. Perhaps de Lauretis is actually offering a newer, more viable construction of home, a construction we all need to consider. . . . Still, as one who is faced daily by homeless people and who once realistically feared the possibility of homelessness, I find her implicit criticism of home off-base. As an academic woman from a working-class background, I want to take the space I have achieved (however provisionally) and use it to build a supportive environment for myself and others. I am building community ties with efforts such as this anthology, but I must also take the space I inhabit and make it a home rather than a prison or a colony—a place where I am safe and where I can nurture rather than exploit.

To build a home that is flexible enough to facilitate growth, I try to acknowledge, even highlight, differences among working-class women academics and recognize the specific features of my own experience. Many of these, I believe, are historical; they are the result of the particular time in which I am living. If I had gotten my B.A. ten years earlier, I would have entered a different economic environment. Although growing up in a family that often verged on poverty certainly shaped my thinking, I believe my attitudes toward myself and many social institutions were solidified in my early adult years, years when I experienced severe financial hardship. The resultant disillusionment was, in many ways, typical of my generation. We saw many ideals tainted by economic and political realities, saw many yippies become yuppies and seemed, despite our population, powerless to influence the course of events. In this context, de Lauretis's call for community seems more on target, particularly for working-class women academics. We have never had a strong class and gender community. Some, such as I, are trying to build one now from the fragments of our academic and working-class experience. We are trying to forge a language that expresses our concerns out of the amalgam of whatever working-class dialect we grew up with (there are several), standard English, and academic discourse. In voicing our concerns, we will at least be recognizing our strained position in the academy and working toward a way of existing that is not complicit with the status quo either in the academy or in the larger society. I and others like me are trying to build. By the rivers of Babylon.

Bibliography

Aisenberg, Nadya, and Mona Harrington. *Women of Academe: Outsiders in the Sacred Grove.* Amherst: U of Massachusetts P, 1988.

Apetheker, Bettina. *Tapestries of Life.* Amherst: U of Massachusetts P, 1989. Apetheker encourages a separatist feminism, suggesting that women have a distinct way of seeing and interpreting the world and proposing that in order to avoid the marginality that is the result of the framework of traditional social theories, women must value their daily experiences and creations as the core of feminist work and thinking.

——. *Woman's Legacy: Essays on Race, Sex and Class.* Amherst: U of Massachusetts P, 1982.

Aronowitz, Stanley, and Henry Giroux. *Education under Siege.* South Hadley, MA: Bergin and Garvey, 1985. Without focusing specifically on issues of race, class, or gender, the authors of this book examine the delicate balance between conservative and liberal theories of education and discuss the merits and problems of each.

Barton, Len, and Stephen Walker, eds. *Education and Social Change.* London: Croon and Helm, 1985. While they do not address women's issues in particular, the essays in this volume examine the effects of current social changes on the educational system.

Belenky, Mary Field, Blythe Clinchy, Nancy Goldberger, and Jill Tarule. *Women's Ways of Knowing: The Development of Self, Voice and Mind.* New York: Basic, 1986. Through their interviews with 135 women who represent a variety of ages and social and ethnic backgrounds, the authors of this book describe five major perspectives (epistemological categories) from which women know and view the world.

Benstock, Shari, ed. *Feminist Issues in Literary Scholarship.* Bloomington: Indiana UP, 1987. This volume focuses on the basic split in academic feminist discourse between Woofian humanistic existentialism and sociophilosophical analysis. Leading feminist scholars explore the gap between these two situating poles of the field, but do not engage issues of class, race, or ethnicity.

Black, Naomi. *Social Feminism.* New York: Cornell UP, 1989. Black offers a new interpretation of feminism by perceiving two types of feminism: equity feminism, which incorporates women into existing male-dominated ideologies;

and social feminism, which emphasizes women's distinctive experience and values.

Bowles, Samuel. "Unequal Education and the Reproduction of the Social Division of Labor." *Review of Radical Political Economics* 3 (Fall 1971): 1–30. Through his examination of the history of education in America, Bowles argues that educational inequality, which is pervasive in the U.S. school system, is fundamentally linked to the class structure system upon which capitalism is founded.

Brodsky, Michelle, Mykela Loury, Abby Markowitz, Eden Torres, and Lauren Wilson. "Journeys in Our Lives: Learning Feminism." N.W.S.A. Conference. 1989. Tape #18.

Bunch, Charlotte, and Nancy Myron. *Class and Feminism*. Baltimore: Diana, 1974.

Clinchy, Blythe, Mary F. Belenky, Nancy Goldberger, and Jill Tarule. "Connected Education for Women." *Journal of Education* 3 (1985): 28–45. The authors of this article present an educational model which they deem appropriate for women in the academy.

Cohen, Yolande, ed. *Women and Counter Power*. New York: Black Rose, 1989. Although it does not focus on issues of class or the academy, this collection of crosscultural essays examines the position of women in society and politics and documents the emergence of feminine political theory, which develops strategies for the liberation of women.

Culley, Margo, and Catherine Portuges. *Gendered Subjects: The Dynamics of Feminist Teaching*. Boston: Routledge, 1985.

DuBois, Ellen C., Gail Kelly, Elizabeth Kennedy, Carolyn Korsmeyer, and Lillian Robinson. *Feminist Scholarship: Kindling in the Groves of Academe*. Chicago: U of Illinois P, 1985. In this volume, the authors do not focus on race or class, but examine the emergence and impact of feminist perspectives on a variety of academic disciplines, including history, literature, philosophy, and education.

Farnham, Christie, ed. *The Impact of Feminist Research in the Academy*. Bloomington: Indiana UP, 1987. Without focusing on issues of race or class, this collection of essays examines the impact of feminist scholarship on a variety of academic disciplines.

Flynn, Elizabeth, and Patrocinio Scheickart, eds. *Gender and Reading: Essays on Readers, Texts, and Contexts*. Baltimore: Johns Hopkins UP, 1986.

Freire, Paulo. *Pedagogy of the Oppressed*. Trans. Myra Bergman Ramos. New York: Seabury, 1978. In this ground-breaking book, Brazilian educator Freire proposed education as a tool for social and personal liberation, emphasizing dialogue, mutuality, cooperation, unity, organization, and cultural synthesis.

——. *The Politics of Education: Culture, Power and Liberation.* Trans. Donaldo Macedo. South Hadley, MA: Bergin and Garvey, 1985.

Giddens, Anthony. *The Class Structure of the Advanced Societies.* New York: Harper, 1973.

Giroux, Henry A. *Theory and Resistance in Education: A Pedagogy for the Opposition.* South Hadley, MA: Bergin and Garvey, 1983.

Grasso, Rena, Bonita Hampton, Lois Rita Hembold, Jan Lightfoot, Bernice Mennis, Karen Ruggiero, and Theresa Solis. "Pain, Survival, Triumph: Voices of Poor and Working-Class Women." N.W.S.A. National Conference. 1989. Tape #9.

Green, Laureen A. "Breaking the Barriers of Silence: An Interview with Audre Lorde." *Women of Power* 14 (1989): 39–41. In this interview, poet Audre Lorde talks about the challenges she has faced as a black lesbian woman in Western society and about her decision to act in the face of these challenges.

Guy-Sheftall, Beverly, Betty Schmitz, Susan Van Dyne, Emily Style, and Sara Coulter. "Engendering Knowledge: Feminist Transformation of the Curriculum." N.W.S.A. Conference. 1989. Tape #19.

Harding, Sandra. "The Instability of the Analytic Categories of Feminist Theory." *Signs* 11 (Summer 1986): 645–64.

Harstock, Nancy. "Rethinking Modernism: Minority vs. Majority Theories." *Cultural Critique* 7 (1987): 187–206.

Harstock, Nancy, Sonia Alvarez, Patricia Williams, Elaine Zimmerman, and Cheryl Schaffer. "Work, Race and Class: Making the Links in Theory and Practice." N.W.S.A. National Conference. 1989. Tape #2.

Hill Collins, Patricia, Sandra Harding, and Catharine Stimpson. "Critical Questions: Two Decades of Feminist Scholarship." N.W.S.A. National Conference. 1989. Tape #17.

hooks, bell. *Ain't I a Woman? Black Women and Feminism.* Boston: South End, 1981.

——. *Feminist Theory: From Margin to Center.* Boston: South End, 1984.

——. *Talking Back: Thinking Feminist, Thinking Black.* Boston: South End, 1989. In this collection of essays, Hooks talks about her own experience as a black female in the academy.

Howe, Florence. *Myths of Coeducation: Selected Essays, 1964–1983.* Bloomington: Indiana UP, 1984.

Jacoby, Russell. *The Last Intellectuals: American Culture in the Age of Academe.* New York: Basic, 1987.

Kornbluh, Joyce L., and Mary Frederickson. *Sisterhood and Solidarity: Workers Education for Women, 1914–1984.* Philadelphia: Temple UP, 1984.

Langland, Elizabeth, and Walter Grove, eds. *A Feminist Perspective in the Academy.* Chicago: U of Chicago P, 1981.

Lloyd-Jones, Richard, and Andrea A. Lunsford, eds. *The English Coalition Conference: Democracy through Language.* New York: MLA Publications, 1989. Without specifically addressing issues of race, class, or gender, this volume collects and distills the major conclusions of conference participants and suggests new directions for the future study of English.

Lunsford, Andrea, Helene Moglen, and James Slevin, eds. *The Future of Doctoral Studies in English.* New York: MLA Publications, 1989. This volume examines the initiation and development of graduate students within the university, without focusing specifically on issues of race, class or gender.

Martin, Jane Roland. *Reclaiming a Conversation: The Ideal of the Educated Women.* New Haven: Yale UP, 1985. In this book, Martin examines the evolving relationship between gender and educational theory, without focusing specifically on issues of race or class.

McClelland, Averil Evans. *The Education of Women in America: A Guide to Theory, Teaching and Research.* New York: Garland, 1990. This historical survey discusses the education of women in Colonial and Revolutionary times and concludes with material on feminist pedagogy, future research opportunities, and transforming curricula.

Moi, Toril. *Sexual/Textual Politics.* New York: Routledge, 1988.

Olsen, Tillie. *Silences.* New York: Delacorte, 1978. In documenting their history as writers, Olsen points out the relative silence of women as literary voices.

Patemand, Carol, and Elizabeth Gross, eds. *Feminist Challenges: Social and Political Theory.* Boston: Northeastern UP, 1986. In this volume, essays by Australian feminist scholars examine the theoretical and practical applications of feminist theory to a variety of academic disciplines.

Robinson, Lillian S. *Sex, Class and Culture.* Bloomington: Indiana UP, 1978.

Rosen, Bernard Carl. *Women, Work and Achievement: The Endless Revolution.* New York: St. Martin's, 1989. In this book, Rosen argues that industrialization has strengthened the position of women in the work force by stressing individuality and achievement, by broadening the quality and quantity of employment opportunities for women, by changing traditional sex roles, and by encouraging egalitarianism, which reduces sexual segregation in the workplace. This book does not specifically address issues of race, class, or sexual orientation.

Russ, Joanna. *How to Suppress Women's Writing.* Austin: U of Texas P, 1983.

Ryan, Jake, and Charles Sackrey. *Strangers in Paradise: Academics from the Working Class.* Boston: South End, 1984.

Shor, Ira, and Paulo Freire. *A Pedagogy for Liberation: Dialogues on Transforming Education.* South Hadley, MA: Bergin and Garvey, 1987.

Simeone, Angela. *Academic Women: Working Towards Equality.* South Hadley, MA: Bergin and Garvey, 1987.

Todd, Janet, ed. *Gender and Literary Voice.* New York: Holmes and Meier, 1980. Without focusing specifically on issues of race or class, the essays in this volume address the question of whether there is a distinctively feminine voice, style, and/or content in literature.

Wall, Cheryl A., ed. *Changing Our Own Words: Essays on Criticism, Theory, and Writing by Black Women.* New Brunswick: Rutgers UP, 1989. The essays in this volume are written by and about black women writers and address issues of race, class, gender, canon formation, and the perpetuation of literary traditions.

Welch, Sharon D. *Communities of Resistance and Solidarity.* Maryknoll, NY: Orbis, 1985. The author of this book, a feminist, white, middle-class American Christian theologian, discusses her dichotomous existence as both oppressor and oppressed and presents feminist theology of liberation.

Willis, Paul. *Learning to Labour: How Working Class Kids Get Working Class Jobs.* Westmead, England: Saxon, 1977.

Winthorn, Ann. "Dual Citizenship: Women of Color in Graduate School." *Women's Studies Quarterly* 14 (1986): 46–48. In this interview, six women of color discuss the barriers they encounter as they try to earn their degrees and explain that this discrimination influences their lives both within and outside the academy.

Contributors' Notes

PAM ANNAS teaches English and American literature, including a course in working-class literature, at the University of Massachusetts, Boston. Her publications include *A Disturbance of Mirrors: The Poetry of Sylvia Plath* and *Literature and Society: An Introduction to Poetry, Fiction, Drama, and Nonfiction* (with Robert Rosen).

PAT BELANOFF directs the writing program at SUNY, Stony Brook, where she teaches Old English in addition to undergraduate writing and literature courses. She has published *Nothing Begins with an N: New Investigations of Freewriting* (co-editor), *A Community of Writers* (co-author), *The Right Handbook* (co-author), *Portfolios: Process and Product* (co-editor), and articles in *PMLA, Journal of Basic Writing, Pre/Text,* and *College Composition and Communication.*

JACQUELINE BURNSIDE teaches sociology at Berea College. Her articles have appeared in *Appalachian Heritage* and *The Register of the Kentucky Historical Society.*

KATE ELLIS teaches English at Rutgers University, New Brunswick. She is author of *The Contested Castle: Gothic Novels and the Subversion of Domestic Ideology* and co-editor of *Caught Looking: Feminism, Censorship and Pornography* and is currently working on a novel about the sixties.

ELIZABETH A. FAY teaches courses in romanticism and feminist criticism at the University of Massachusetts, Boston. She is currently working on a book titled *Imminent Rhetoric: Gender, Discourse, and Intellectuality,* to be published by Bergin and Garvey.

CHERYL FISH teaches literature and writing courses at Hunter College and is working on a Ph.D. in English and American literature at The Graduate Center, CUNY. She has published review-essays and a collection of poems, *Wing Span.* Additionally, she is an editor of the journal *Poetry New York.*

PAMELA A. FOX, who teaches English and women's studies courses at Georgetown University, is a contributor to the forthcoming volume *British Political Novelists: Forgotten Women Writers, 1890–1939.*

SAUNDRA GARDNER is in the sociology department at the University of Maine. Her fields of interest include women's studies, feminist pedagogy, visual sociology, and the sociology of education. Recent articles have appeared in *Sociological Inquiry, Sociological Quarterly*, and *Sociology of Education*.

BELL HOOKS's publications include *Ain't I a Woman? Black Women and Feminism; Feminist Theory: From Margin to Center; Talking Back: Thinking Feminist, Thinking Black; Yearning: Race, Gender, and Cultural Politics*, and *Breaking Bread: Insurgent Black Intellectual Life* (with Cornell West). She teaches women's studies and theory at Oberlin College.

ELISABETH J. JOHNSON, who has recently retired after many years with the College of Public and Community Service at the University of Massachusetts, Boston, continues to teach part-time.

JOANNA KADI, an Arab-Canadian, working-class, lesbian feminist, has published several articles and short stories. She is currently editing an anthology of writings by Arab-Canadian and Arab-American feminists to be published by Kitchen Table: Women of Color Press.

DONNA LANGSTON teaches women's studies at Mankato State University. Her articles have appeared in a number of anthologies, including *Calling Home: Working-Class Women's Writings, Women in the Civil Rights Movement*, and *Changing Our Power*, of which she is co-editor.

VALERIE MINER is an associate professor of English at the University of Minnesota, Minneapolis. She is the author of *Trespassing and Other Stories* and of the novels *All Good Women, Movement, Blood Sisters, Winter's Edge*, and *Murder in the English Department*.

SHARON O'DAIR teaches English at the University of Alabama. Her essays have appeared in *Criticism, The Centennial Review*, and *Philosophy and Literature*.

LILLIAN S. ROBINSON is a visiting scholar at the Harry Ransom Humanities Research Center, University of Texas, Austin. She is author of *Sex, Class and Culture* and co-author of *Feminist Scholarship: Kindling in the Groves of Academe*. She is also a frequent contributor to *The Nation* and *The Women's Review of Books*.

HEPHZIBAH ROSKELLY teaches rhetoric and composition at the undergraduate and graduate level at the University of North Carolina, Greensboro, where she also works with the teacher education program. She has written *Farther Along: Dichotomies in Rhetoric and Composition* and *An Unquiet Pedagogy*.

PATRICIA CLARK SMITH teaches at the University of New Mexico. She has published articles on American literature and a book of poems, *Changing Your Story*.

SUZANNE SOWINSKA, an Arts and Humanities Fellow at the University of Washington, Seattle, is writing a dissertation titled "American Women Writers and the Radical Agenda: 1925–1940." She is a former contributor to and member of the editorial collective of the *New Women's Times* and the *New Women's Times Feminist Review.*

MICHELLE M. TOKARCZYK teaches literature and composition at Goucher College where she also directs the writing program. She has published criticism of contemporary American literature and a book of poetry, *The House I'm Running From.*

LAURA H. WEAVER has written numerous articles on theater and women's studies. Her work has appeared in *MELUS, Mississippi Folklore Register,* and *Children's Literature,* and in the anthologies *The Ethnic American Woman: Problems, Protests, Lifestyle* and *The Road Retaken: Women Reenter the Academy.*

ROSE ZIMBARDO, who teaches in the Department of Theater Arts at SUNY, Stony Brook, has published scholarship in the Restoration and eighteenth century, Shakespeare, the medieval period, and European drama. She has written *Wycherley's Drama, A Mirror to Nature: Transformations in Drama and Aesthetics, 1660–1732* and co-edited *Across the Curriculum: Thinking, Reading, Writing.*

Index